P9-DMH-550

MILE
MARKER
ZERO

ALSO BY WILLIAM McKEEN

OUTLAW JOURNALIST, *a biography*

HIGHWAY 61, *a memoir*

ROCK AND ROLL IS HERE TO STAY, *an anthology*

LITERARY JOURNALISM: A READER, *edited with Jean C. Chance*

TOM WOLFE, *a critical biography*

BOB DYLAN: A BIO-BIBLIOGRAPHY

HUNTER S. THOMPSON, *a critical biography*

THE BEATLES: A BIO-BIBLIOGRAPHY

MILE MARKER ZERO

·

The Moveable Feast
of Key West

William McKeen

Crown Publishers

New York

Copyright © 2011 by William McKeen

All rights reserved.

Published in the United States by Crown Publishers, an imprint of the Crown
Publishing Group, a division of Random House, Inc., New York.
www.crownpublishing.com

CROWN and the Crown colophon are registered trademarks of Random House, Inc.

Portions of chapter 13 ("The King of Gonzo") appeared in *Outlaw Journalist*
(W.W. Norton, 2008), in different form.

Library of Congress Cataloging-in-Publication Data

McKeen, William, 1954–
Mile marker zero: the moveable feast of Key West / William McKeen.—1st ed.
Includes bibliographical references.
1. Key West (Fla.)—Biography.   2. Key West (Fla.)—Intellectual life—20th
century.   3. Key West (Fla.)—Social life and customs—20th century.   4. Authors,
American—Homes and haunts—Florida—Key West   I. Title.
F319.K4M38 2011
975.9'41—dc22   2011005939

ISBN 978-0-307-59200-2
eISBN 978-0-307-59204-0

PRINTED IN THE UNITED STATES OF AMERICA

Jacket design by Laura Duffy
Jacket photographs: (sunset) © Nick Hanna/Alamy; (sign) Tony Hopewell/
Getty Images

10 9 8 7 6 5 4 3 2 1

FIRST EDITION

FOR TOM, *who willed this book*

FOR BEEF, *who helped make it possible*

FOR DINK, *who showed kindness to a stranger*

FOR MY FAMILY, *immediate and extended*

AND, OF COURSE, FOR NICOLE:

Here is a book about your hometown

Tom, we had an active night tonight. I spent a lot of time talking with Buffett down at Nicholson's house, and we both got very excited about the Key West years, the "missing years," the ones that you have so well documented. We're going to reconvene down there and go back over the stories, the photographs, and maybe do a little boating. Let's have "The Boys" back— Chatham, McGuane, whoever's alive. It's going to be good. We're going to have a little fun with this one.

HUNTER S. THOMPSON
Phone message for Tom Corcoran,
Christmas night, 2004

The open range, the open sea, the open sky, the open wounds of the heart, that's where writers shine.

THOMAS MCGUANE
Some Horses, 1999

I was in the face of a breaking wave in American culture. And I didn't understand it, or really know what it was, but I knew something was going on, and I knew I was in the middle of it.

THOMAS MCGUANE
Interview, 1999

CONTENTS

MILE
MARKER
ZERO

The Taco Man

The best laid schemes of mice and men go oft astray.
—ROBERT BURNS

The plane banked, dipping its wing to make the turn and begin the approach, and that's when Corcoran got his first good look at the island. Twice as long as wide, it was a bleached rock in the blue-and-emerald Caribbean. He saw neatly lined streets, an attempt to impose order on crushed shell and stone, but was struck by the relative absence of green. He hadn't been sure what to expect, but he had assumed there would be trees, lush vegetation, palms and bananas and coconuts. It was Florida; *it was the tropics*, for God's sake. Yet as the plane descended, he saw himself being swallowed by a flat, blazingly bright, overexposed world. He squinted as the plane came out of the blue and into the white.

This is it, he thought. *Couple months here and I'm done.*

He smiled, thinking about his post-college, post-Navy life. First . . . maybe graduate school, then maybe he'd settle down in elbow-patched glory as an English professor at some midwestern liberal-arts college, writing small but important novels, embraced by wife, dog, 2.5 children, and throngs of adoring students. It would be a good, if unexciting, life.

Tom Corcoran was lucky. He was in the last year of his Navy stretch, and so far had avoided Vietnam. The war had not been center stage in America when he'd enlisted back in 1963, but to those who saw their student draft deferments slipping away with each low grade, Vietnam took on a newer, bolder role. After two unremarkable years at Miami University of Ohio, Corcoran had decided to enlist, figuring he'd better beat the military at its own game. He could wait for the draft to take him and send him off in Army fatigues, or he could control his destiny. He wanted the Navy, the only logical choice for a boy from a Cleveland suburb. He also thought that if he was going to Vietnam, he might best serve his country from the relative safety of offshore. "If there was a war in the jungle," he said, "I liked the idea of fighting the war from a steel bulkhead instead of hiding behind a bunch of leaves."

He took a break from school in the summer of 1964, landing in Los Angeles, where he worked as a travel counselor by day and at night explored new frontiers of California bohemianism, soaking in the music and inebriants of the time. He figured this freedom was about to end, so he squeezed tight. He also figured his poor grades had sentenced him to the draft. So he skulked into the U.S. Navy Recruiting Office as if on the way to see the principal back at Shaker Heights High.

To his surprise, the officer behind the desk had some good news: *Give us your summers and you can still go off and finish school, College Boy.*

"What?" Corcoran asked.

"It's your lucky day, kid," the recruiter said. "All you got to do is give us your summers. When you're done with your degree, you're ours for two years. You even get to come in as an officer."

It was a revelation, a reprieve, and a second chance for Corcoran to chase his dream of becoming a writer.

And so Corcoran returned to Oxford, Ohio, for the fall semester in 1963. His grades went through the roof. He spent his summers in the service, and by the time he graduated, he had aced Officer Candidate School and entered the real world as an officer and a gentleman.

Corcoran became expert in guiding drone helicopters that flew by remote control and fired torpedoes at imagined Russian submarines. They had those drones in Vietnam now, with spy cameras mounted on the hoods, using them as small, low-flying, unmanned versions of U-2s. But despite Corcoran's skill—landing them easily on the pitching deck of the USS *John Willis*—he had still managed to avoid Vietnam.

So now it was late August 1968 and Corcoran was landing on six square miles of coral, on the downhill slide of his military career. Vietnam had already taken more than twenty thousand American lives. Martin Luther King, Jr. and Robert Kennedy had been assassinated that spring. That very month, student demonstrators and reporters had been beaten—some nearly to death—by officers of the law in a police riot at the Democratic National Convention in Chicago. The world had gone insane. But Corcoran was untouched. He had become so expert with his drones that he was loaned out to other ships to teach his magic to new sailors. He was looking at ten more months of that duty, and then freedom.

The Navy wanted to wring all it could out of him, so he was being sent to this bleached rock. Though he had studied English literature and business and hoped to become a writer, he was also left-brain strong, which made him a natural in the worlds of sonar and radar. He was reassigned from the *John Willis* for an eight-week program on anti-submarine warfare for officers. As he was a natural teacher, his commanding officers figured he would be a good ripple in the pond. *Give a man a fish; you have fed him for today. Teach a man to fish; and you have fed him for a lifetime.* Corcoran was a good investment.

Corcoran didn't care so much about the classes. It was merely eight more weeks eaten out of his indenture to the Navy. After that, maybe graduate school. He didn't really plan his life more than twenty-four hours in advance, and he was still flexible. Sometimes, he considered rediscovering his inner bohemian and getting back to California, and that hippie life he'd been reading about since he'd been wearing khakis. He'd don a new uniform of T-shirts and denim.

And then there was the decision about the women. He had yet to pick between the two girls he'd dated in college: Judy, the knockout who'd scored an ad-agency job in Boston right out of school, and Cornflakes, modeling in Manhattan. They called her Cornflakes because the spray of freckles across her nose gave her a wholesomeness that Kellogg's would kill to trademark. The body gave her something else, including a career as a fashion model.

Sixteen weeks, then a few months more on the *Willis,* and Corcoran was done. He'd worry about the women later. There were other women here, on this island, or so he'd been told. This was a plum assignment and the Navy ruled the little town. There had been a base here since 1823, and the locals were used to accommodating the officers and sailors, in all senses of the word.

He'd flown commercial all the way, but the last leg was on a sixteen-seat puddle jumper. He was the only military onboard. Most everyone else looked comfortable, despite the slight buffeting and the occasional sudden and unexplained drop. A tourist across the aisle blanched once, but Corcoran noticed that most of the passengers were blasé, probably locals coming back from a day trip to Miami.

As the plane descended, Corcoran saw the sun beginning its slow slide into the ocean. The airport was bordered by a canal on its left and Corcoran wondered if a poorly trained pilot ever overcorrected from the wide-banking turn and slid right into that open trench quarried out of the island's rock. But this pilot was on the mark. The landing gear dropped, the tires shrieked, the engines reversed—propelling the passengers forward—then the plane coasted, gloatingly, toward the terminal. As the pilot taxied up to the small, squat building, Corcoran gathered his belongings. The plane stopped at the gate, and he pulled himself out of his seat, towering over the other passengers in the aisle. Then they all marched, sheeplike, toward the open stairwell, down to the tarmac.

The blast of late-afternoon heat hit Corcoran's face as if it had been thrown at him.

Eight weeks. He could do that, even if it was in a furnace. Eight weeks is two months closer to freedom, to grad school or hippiedom, to long hair, to solving the Judy-or-Cornflakes dilemma.

Then again, there was that dream he had of being a writer and here he was, in this paradise with literary pedigree. And the Navy was paying him to be here. *Yeah, he could do it.* There were a lot worse things than being ordered to sixteen weeks in Key West.

Originally called Cayo Hueso ("island of bones") when it was a Spanish settlement, Key West's first white settlers found it littered with skeletons—from a battle or perhaps from a Calusa Indian burial ground. The name was anglicized into "Key West," presumably because the island is westernmost in the Florida Keys. Yet, for a brief period in its history, it was known as Thompson's Island, a name chosen by Commodore Matthew Perry to honor Smith Thompson, the sixth secretary of the U.S. Navy. Perry had sailed into the harbor and claimed the Rock for the United States in 1822. The following year, the Navy established a base there, and about twenty years after that the Federal Army built Fort Zachary Taylor on the western edge. It was the southernmost military presence on United States soil.

Within a few years, Secretary Thompson was forgotten and Key West returned to its earlier name. By the middle of the nineteenth century, it was one of the country's busiest ports. As the years passed, its proximity to Cuba, lax immigration laws, and a friendly climate made it one of the centers of the cigar industry, which led to a boom in shipping.

The island's literary history dates from that time. While the cigar workers diligently rolled tobacco, they listened to third-string actors read aloud. *The Three Musketeers* was a favorite. They loved Dumas, and Hugo. The cigar rollers, mostly Cuban, preferred Spanish writers, but the reading of Shakespeare brought a reverent hush to the rolling room. It was entertainment and education. It helped the cigar workers learn the language and learn to get along in the English-speaking town.

The island remained a strategic port but was relatively isolated until developer Henry Flagler brought the railroad down the Keys from the mainland in 1912. He connected this westernmost key to Miami and the rest of his East Coast Railway. At the end of the line, he built the massive Casa Marina Hotel, which rose like a mirage from the green Caribbean at the south end of the island, the only shore with much of a beach.

But a devastating hurricane in 1935 wiped out much of the railway and killed hundreds, including nearly four hundred veterans of the Great War who camped in the Keys, working on government construction projects. From the wreckage of the rail rose a new lifeline to the mainland. President Franklin Roosevelt ordered the construction of the Overseas Highway, a two-lane road piggybacking on the remaining track. It made for a long drive, but the trip to Key West was no longer the ordeal it had been in the days of island-hopping bridges and ferryboats. Soon it would be a destination for writers and artists hoping to work and play in this paradise.

Ernest Hemingway had come to town in the twenties. Poet Robert Frost was there around the same time, and made nearly annual visits. For most of two decades, Wallace Stevens would shuffle through the Casa Marina during his annual visits, reciting his poetry in his head. Tennessee Williams moved down in the forties, and before long, the streets were thick with writers and wannabe writers.

Forty years later, the writers and artists and musicians were still coming. Seven years after Hemingway's suicide, Tom Corcoran stood in front of The Old Island Inn, where Hemingway had first stayed, back in the twenties. Corcoran's home was the room up front, overlooking Simonton Street. Years later, he would learn that he bunked in the same room as the Big Guy.

Corcoran had lasted three days in Navy housing. There was a room shortage that summer and so the brass asked for volunteers to find apartments—the Navy would pay, of course—and ease the overcrowding in Bachelor Officer Quarters. Corcoran's hand shot up. *Sure*, he said, *I'll be glad to move off-base.*

"Suddenly," he recalled, "I was living in Key West. And I just kind of fell into the mode. Nobody said, 'You should get an apartment and buy a bicycle,' but I did."

And thus was his life derailed.

"I lived off-base but I didn't mingle much with the townies at first," Corcoran continued. Though he made a number of life-long friends, he also discovered that there was a significant percentage of loathsome vermin. "In those days, if you were in a group of eight or nine or ten junior officers, you'd find there were some who were weasels. The weasel ratio was very high. A weasel was a guy who didn't have a life and didn't care and didn't ever want one. No interest in anything, no sense of humor. There weren't a lot of guys you'd want to have a beer with."

Lonesome for the women in his life, he figured it was easiest for Judy to come visit; Cornflakes had high-demand photo shoots each week. So Judy came down for a month. They stayed in bed much of the time, but when they got up, they went to Captain Tony's and tossed back a few. Corcoran found himself favoring Judy in the Judy-Cornflakes war. Cornflakes was a glamorous model, and busting her out of that world of celebrity would be a tall order.

Soon, Judy had to return to Boston and Corcoran faced the last months of Navy life yawning before him. He found himself missing Judy, which struck him as extraordinary. He didn't think he was ready to settle down yet. He was still unsure what post-Navy life would be like. These eight weeks on the Rock were altering his trajectory.

Tom Corcoran was honorably discharged from the United States Navy at the end of September 1969. The world was still crazy. A half-million long-haired kids had a mud fest in a farmer's field near Woodstock in upstate New York, listening to three days of rock 'n' roll. A return to bohemian life seemed in order. Corcoran's release from active duty had come at his home base in Newport, Rhode Island, then he drifted back to Ohio to take stock and see old friends.

He hooked up with a college buddy named Jon Hilton. The two of them had met in 1964, working at the College Inn back in Oxford. Corcoran was just back from California and his Navy-recruiter revelation, dressed like a Beach Boy in huaraches, carrying a skateboard, and driving a beat-up 1948 Dodge sedan, decorated with Rat Fink decals. Hilton tended bar and Corcoran waited tables and took charge of the jukebox, stuffing it with house quarters when a gap between songs widened. "I had a pocketful of those things and I learned how to control a crowd," he said.

Music helped Corcoran and Hilton bond. Though they worked at the College Inn, Corcoran and Hilton hung out after work at Al and Larry's Bar, with a venerable rhythm-and-blues outfit called Maurice and the Rockets. "Maurice looked like a car thief, like a wolf in a cartoon," Corcoran recalled. "I don't know that I ever knew rock 'n' roll that was that pleasing ever again."

Corcoran and Hilton shared a common goal during their college days: to "get fucked up for the least amount of money we could spend." That was easy; at thirty-five cents a bottle, Budweiser was the premium beer. Schoenling on tap was a quarter.

They became close friends, but Hilton fell to the draft and Corcoran spun off into his Navy career.

Hilton had not escaped Vietnam, but he was back now and, like Corcoran, not sure what came next on his résumé. They met up back in Ohio in the fall of 1969, pooled their money, and drove to Florida in Hilton's Datsun 1600, ending up in Fort Lauderdale. They needed work, so they took construction jobs.

"By the time we got there, we were both broke and we dug ditches for beer money," Corcoran explained. They dug footers on a bridge site, lasted exactly one week by the watch, lined up at payday, and then turned their gaze south. "I got a paycheck and I said, 'Well, that's that career.'" Holding the money in front of Hilton's face, he said, "I know where I want to drink this beer."

They were caught in Captain Tony's gravitational pull, managing to arrive at the bar a few weeks before the owner's annual fishing vacation.

The little island had become the closest thing to home. Corcoran was a college graduate and a former Navy officer. But now, as he sat at the bar those afternoons, pissing away his money, he felt something else.

"Key West was peaceful, idyllic, tropical, and otherworldly," he recalled. It also was sanctuary. "I wanted to shut out the mainland, the shitty mess that the sixties had become. It was an alternative reality. And you could phone home from a pay booth and use American money."

He decided to stay.

That first night at Captain Tony's, a fellow sidled up at the bar and made conversation.

"Where you from?" he asked, nodding at Corcoran.

"Shaker Heights, Ohio."

"Oh yeah? What's your name?"

"Tom Corcoran."

The guy's eyebrows lifted. "You Marty Corcoran's brother?"

Small-world time. "Yep," Corcoran said. "Marty's my sister."

The guy's name was Mase Mason. Any brother of Marty's was a friend of his.

They sealed their new friendship with a few more beers—on Mason—and Corcoran and Hilton marveled at how quickly you could find pals in paradise.

"Where are you guys staying?" Mason asked, after a bit.

Corcoran shrugged.

"Well, you can have my place," Mason said, handing over the keys. "It's the Fogarty House, apartment two. I'm going shrimping. I'll be gone a couple weeks."

What great luck, Corcoran thought. He'd cleaned out his small savings account back home and sold his Navy uniform and sword, and he was coasting on the fumes in his wallet.

"Matter of fact," Mason mused over his beer, "you can have my girlfriend, too. Her name's Lee."

Mason went off shrimping, and although both Hilton and Corcoran liked Lee well enough, neither took up Mason's offer. Within a couple of weeks, when Mason came back, Corcoran and Hilton had moved to a small apartment on Simonton Street, within sight of The Old Island Inn, where Corcoran's Key West life had started . . . *where Hemingway's Key West life had started.*

Corcoran had made a couple of decisions. First, "I wanted to be the next Hemingway. I thought all I needed was a hammock and a nice tall frosty. I was in the right place." Second, it was Judy over Cornflake. Cornflake was being squired around Manhattan by *New York* magazine editor Clay Felker, attending parties with Tom Wolfe and Norman Mailer. She'd never go for the quiet life on the island. And that was part of the deal now. Corcoran knew that much.

As for Judy, those four weeks from the year before had grown in her memory. At work, she'd found herself imagining the island, wondering what a cold winter day in Boston felt like down in the tropics. She had hoped she'd get this call one day. She quit her job and moved to Key West with no promises.

Corcoran worked construction again, this time on the Navy base. It helped him pay the rent on this new house he got with Judy, over on Grinnell Street, near the Overseas Food Market.

Eventually they drifted away from Hilton and became an insular couple. They had nodding friends, and there was Captain Tony's, of course, but it was intense *make-love-until-our-strength-is-gone* time. They shut out most everyone else.

After a few weeks, Judy was pregnant. Corcoran was happy, but neither of them considered marriage. That was so Mainland.

As Corcoran would soon learn, living in Key West *was* different. The community was attracting a lot of other young people who were dissatisfied with the country and its status quo. Some came because they were disillusioned, heartbroken, or world-weary. Key West was a hideaway for others.

But there were also those who saw Key West as the place to experiment with their lives or their art. The lure of a no-holds-barred society on a rock in the blue water of the Caribbean was intoxicating, and so an extraordinary group of young people began the journey down Highway 1. When Tom Corcoran made the decision to stay in Key West, he had no idea that a decade later, he would still be there, having befriended and collaborated with some of the greatest artists of his generation.

A postcard afternoon, *one of those first weeks in 1970, still inhaling the aroma of the sixties. . . .*

Tom Corcoran sits on a barstool in Captain Tony's. This is where Hemingway used to drink. It's the original Sloppy Joe's. That place across Duval that calls itself Sloppy's . . . sure, it markets itself as Papa's favorite bar, but the locals know Captain Tony's has the history.

Corcoran is sitting there, drinking his beer, when a hippie rides up on a three-wheeled bicycle. He's a white guy but they call him Afro because of the mushroom cloud of hair that encircles his head. Corcoran gets off the stool, walks outside, and checks out Afro's bike. In the basket are taco shells, sauce, a bottle of soda, a handful of napkins. He's seen Afro riding around on the thing, not sure what the deal was.

Afro's just looking at him.

"I want your job," Corcoran says suddenly.

Afro shakes his huge, hairy head. *No way.* He's the Taco Man; he is *The Shit* on those languid afternoons in Key West when people get the munchies.

Corcoran doesn't want to let go of this fantasy, no matter how small or fleeting. "If you ever get tired of your job," he says, "I want it."

"Sure, man," Afro responds. Then he gets on the bike and pedals away.

"*Tacos!* Right here, get your tacos!" They come from a place a couple of blocks away, a place called Pancho's.

Two days later, same time of day, same barstool: Corcoran's sitting there, putting a beer in intensive care when he hears this horrible clattering noise.

He turns around and sees Afro riding the three-wheeled bike into Captain Tony's, right through the front door.

He gets off the bike and starts to walk away, nodding at Corcoran. "It's all yours, man."

2

Island of Bones

This spring they dug up the parking lot behind some
clip joint on lower Duval and found an Indian grave,
the huge skull of a Calusa seagoing Indian staring up
through four inches of blacktop at the whores,
junkies and Southern lawyers.
—Thomas McGuane, *PANAMA*

The ground is full of bones, millions of crushed, bleached-out bone fragments, mixed in with dirt and sand.

It's not clear to whom the bones belonged. Perhaps they are all that remains of the Calusa, an ancient civilization on the southwest coast of Florida around twelve thousand years ago. The Calusa were by all accounts fierce, and though most of the tribe lived on mainland Florida, some historians believe strains of Calusa DNA inhabit those fine bone crystals in the sand underneath tourist flip-flops. But it could be that the first human dwellers in the Keys were explorers from the Tequesta tribe, which lived on the opposite side of the mainland from the Calusa, on the site of modern-day Miami. The Matecumbe Indians in the Upper Keys slid through Gulf waters in canoes made from hollowed-out cypress logs, living off fish and whatever small game they could catch on the islands. They may have ventured to the end of the archipelago, to Key West and the Dry Tortugas.

Whatever the identity of the inhabitants, it's clear that some form of human lived on Key West as early as 3000 BC.

When the Spaniards arrived in the early seventeenth century, not all of the skeletons had been crushed to powder by human feet. Piles of bones formed prehistoric landfills and even hale and hearty explorers were taken aback.

Westerners called it the Isle of Bones, hence the name Cayo Hueso on the first Spanish maps of the region. In addition to the new name, the Spaniards brought disease, which did what warring tribes of Calusa, Tequesta, Matecumbe, and visiting Seminole could not do: rid the Keys of Indians. Along with brave and noble explorers, ships from the Old World brought early ancestors of Euro Trash who raped the Indian women, filling them with the seeds of New World epidemics and beginning the process of genocide. To speed along the extinction of the civilization, the new arrivals also killed some and gave others the alcohol used to commit slow suicide.

By 1763, Spain was tired of Florida and decided to hand it off to England, in exchange for Cuba. The Brits didn't do much with the Keys, and after staying out of Florida for twenty years, the Spaniards returned in 1783 and reclaimed the peninsula. It stayed Spanish for another four decades until an impatient American traveler docked on what the English speakers then called Bone Key.

It was 1819 and New Jersey businessman John Whitehead was on his way from New York to Mobile, Alabama. The captain of his schooner anchored at a small deserted island. Whitehead looked askance at the rock and scrub rising out of the blue-green water. The captain planned to trap a few turtles for soup. There were also deer on the island and the fishing was good.

Whitehead was annoyed. He was always on his way *somewhere*, and here he was—*nowhere*. But as he watched the turtles and flamingos on the shore, he began to see possibilities. There was a natural harbor, probably one of the reasons the captain had stopped. Whitehead studied the topography. The island was thick with mangroves, but those could be cut through. He knew it wasn't far from Nassau. He also knew that Cuba was nearby, and the captain assured him that Mobile was just across the Gulf of Mexico.

As an investor, Whitehead knew the *location-location-location* mantra of the real estate tycoon. He figured Bone Key was ideally suited as a way station for New York ships sailing to New Orleans and other Gulf ports. It was a good landfall for travelers from Havana. As the captain pulled anchor for the rest of the trip to Mobile, Whitehead was at his ear, asking questions. By the time he got off the boat in Alabama, Whitehead had made a grand plan. He would turn Bone Key into a major port.

Spain still owned Florida, but Whitehead and other businessmen were ready to pounce when the inevitable sale to the United States occurred. Three years later, Whitehead was in the audience at Pensacola, the Florida Territory's capital and the town closest to Mobile, when General Andrew Jackson supervised the ceremony that reassigned Florida's nearly sixty thousand square miles to the United States.

Since Whitehead's visit to the island, he had taken a partner. John Simonton had disposable-money connections that Whitehead lacked. He was buddies with Andrew Jackson, the Indian fighter then six years away from the White House. Simonton bought into Whitehead's island dream and they set to work to acquire Bone Key.

Years of dispute never really settled the question of the island's ownership. At one point, as Simonton and Whitehead sought to develop the town, three parties claimed ownership. Key West was, in that sense, an early time-share. But Simonton and Whitehead were nothing if not tenacious, and they eventually began erecting their dream village when their official status could still best be described as squatters.

One of their first orders of business was to find a new name. Visitors might be spooked by the constant reference to the decayed corpses and piles of bones, so in 1821 they took the Spanish name Cayo Hueso and morphed it into "Key West." It wasn't much of a stretch in terms of language, and it did make geographic sense, in a way, since the island was westernmost in the Florida Keys.

Simonton brought in livestock, allowing them to root through the island's interior and clear out the pesky vegetation. When he saw that some ships passed by the tiny village and its harbor—so small, it looked from the decks like a squatter colony of fishermen—he began to make overtures to the Navy, trying to lure them down by boasting of the great strategic advantage a base in Key West would offer. As the mangroves were cleared and a small grid of streets laid, Simonton continued to spread the word about Key West, this new city growing from the shimmering tropical waters. Smith Thompson, secretary of the United States Navy, was dubious, so he sent his number one man, Lieutenant Matthew Perry, on a voyage south to see if the island was everything Simonton claimed.

A month after Simonton and Whitehead began their adventure in the mangroves, Perry arrived on the USS *Shark* and was quickly impressed by the magnificent harbor. It was hard not to be overwhelmed by what Whitehead and Simonton were doing. Perry looked around the island, admiring the wildlife and the construction in progress. All of this, and it was a jewel in an iridescent sea. Not bad, Perry thought, as he prepared to write a glowing report to Secretary Thompson.

Perry told Thompson the port had a tremendous strategic advantage should the nation be attacked by enemy navies. Satisfied that something important was happening for which he wanted some credit, the lieutenant planted an American flag, claiming Key West as part of America. He then told the handful of inhabitants that he was changing the name. It was going to be Thompson's Island, named after his boss. It was a wise move, since he wanted to be Commodore Perry someday.

Perry kept the island in the hands of Simonton and Whitehead. In gratitude, they waited until Perry had sailed north, then changed the name back to Key West.

The Caribbean, despite its serene appearance, is tough to navigate in storms. In the nineteenth century, ships often ran aground on the hard coral and the cargo had to be removed. This wasn't a case of good Samaritans helping stranded motorists. Whoever salvaged the wrecks either kept or sold some of what they found. Shipwrecks were big business for the Bahamas and for Cuba. America wanted a cut of the action and Simonton and Whitehead hoped Key West would become the port of choice for wreckers.

They knew it wouldn't be easy to realize their vision. With the title to the island cleared, they faced other obstacles. Though Key West was scrubby and unpopulated, it was in the middle of what had become a one-stop mayhem center for pirates.

Before there was a theme-park ride and a movie franchise, there were genuine pirates of the Caribbean, and few of them were as charming as actor Johnny Depp.

The real Blackbeard—historians believe his name was Edward Teach—shared little other than a controversial wardrobe and poor hygiene with the character Depp played in the *Pirates of the Caribbean* films.

Blackbeard was wild-looking, with his beard twisted into Rasta-like ringlets. He strung lengths of hemp in his hair that he had soaked in saltpeter before setting it on fire. The hemp smoldered, giving his huge hairy head a smoky aura that made him even more terrifying to his victims of plunder. He carried six guns strapped to his body and regularly consumed a drink that packed a wallop. Adventurous souls today might sprinkle Tabasco sauce in their Bloody Marys and call themselves weekend warriors of drink. Such would be wimp style to Blackbeard, who salted his rum with gunpowder.

Once Blackbeard set up ship in the waters around Key West, a tradition of lawlessness began that carried through well into the twentieth century.

The waters were also thick with privateers—opportunistic free-enterprise pirates who sailed for a sponsor country, contracted to share the booty retrieved with the nation under whose flag they sailed.

Pirate news was the tabloid stuff of the day. Generations had grown up with stories of these rogues of the high seas. Pirates had used Key West as a convenient dock and hiding place while on the run.

A century after Blackbeard, when Simonton and Whitehead were getting serious about platting streets and civilizing the island, the pirates were annoyed, and, as they were wont to do, caused some mischief. One lurid newspaper article told of pirates who'd seized a vessel near the Cuban harbor of Matanzas, relieved the passengers of their entrails, and then used the stretched-out guts to hang the passengers from the masts as they slowly died.

Here was another good reason for the Navy to build a base cheek by jowl with the new settlement, Simonton argued. The new owner thought Florida needed to discourage piracy and privateering and leave the salvaging of wrecked ships to the new entrepreneurs.

So in 1822, President James Monroe approved the creation of the West Indies Squadron of the United States Navy, charging it with wiping out piracy in the Caribbean. But the pirates used small, sleek vessels, tucked into lagoons bound by thick mangroves, easily camouflaged from the bulky, somewhat clumsy frigates as they cruised the coasts. The squadron commander, James Biddle, had only modest success against the outlaws, and after a year of futility, the Navy recalled Biddle and replaced him with the bad ass of the ocean sea, David Porter.

Porter used different tactics than Biddle, whose modus operandi was always to wait for an attack. Porter, on the other hand, went after the pirates. He chased them, found them, fought them, tried them, and executed them. Within a year, he could brag that the waters around Florida were virtually pirate-free. With each pirate death, however, came stories of buried treasure, often told on the gallows, as the rogues tried to delay their executions. The stories brought an influx of treasure hunters, those gullible and willing enough to try to find chests of gold doubloons buried "near the second tree from the highest point of high tide on the sixth of March"—or some such tale.

Stories of Porter's good deeds stretched all the way up the coast, to New York and Boston. Coupled with his name was the name of Key West, the newly proclaimed pirate-free zone. It was safe, and with bad-ass David Porter on the watch, it was likely to remain that way. Builders and merchants and land speculators started making their way down. Soon there were shops, bars, hotels, homes. The hammering and yammering continued. All kinds of sharpies hit town. The pirates might be gone, but piracy continued in the form of free enterprise, as wreckers rescued cargo from the ships that ran aground on the rocks and kept much of the booty as payment.

The United States government had no qualms about wreckers, and in fact thought it was a grand idea to have them in Key West. The wreckers from the Bahamas and Cuba had done quite well. The settlement on the island allowed America to establish a foothold and cash in on the trade.

Things were going smoothly, but Porter was pissed. He'd been ordered to stay there, but he hated the place. He liked women, yet was surrounded by men. He didn't like mosquitoes. He liked plays, he liked dancing, he liked the high life, but all he saw around him were lowlifes. He was constantly in a bad mood, so he took advantage of the chronic confusion over ownership of the island and declared martial law. Whitehead had been bragging about the town's strategic advantage, so now Porter suggested it was a military installation and nothing more.

He confiscated a lot of private property and building materials, using the lumber to construct more-hospitable quarters and offices for the Navy garrison. He told his men to gather the livestock of the Key Westers, slaughter it, and grill it for dinner.

Porter was well on his way to Hitler status when the island was hit with yellow fever. The Navy got hit especially hard, and finally sick of the place, Porter left for Washington. A new naval contingent was on its way down when Porter went AWOL, the Navy secretary having been alarmed by Porter's messages about sickness and the moral turpitude of the citizens. Captain John Rodgers had been a friend of Porter's, but he found the stories of Key West's near collapse to be mere exaggerations. He realized what a great strategic role the island could play, especially since most everything that needed to get to the American West was best served by sea. Goods were shipped from Boston or New York, down the coast, through the Straits of Florida, into the Gulf of Mexico, and up the old Mississippi. Hot or not, skeeters or not, women or not, Rodgers decided Key West must be reinforced.

Rodgers was Jekyll to Porter's Hyde and the town quickly recovered from its naval dictator. By 1828, with Porter safely gone, the settlement began to take off. His brother's tales of the fortune to be made in paradise lured William Whitehead from New Jersey.

Unlike his brother, William wasn't a businessman but an artist and a dreamer. His plats of Key West are notable not only for the geometry of the street layouts but also for the quality of the execution. As larger buildings were constructed, William would sit and sketch the finished structure. Then he would use that building for his vantage. After a warehouse was built, William climbed to the roof and looked out to the harbor, sketching the closest thing to an aerial view of the city that the century would see.

Within ten years of first laying eyes on the rock, John Whitehead could look out over the land now and see five hundred residents . . . Key Westers . . . "Conchs," as they came to be called, after the weird, spongy, and ultimately tasty critters found inside the huge shells dancing in the waters offshore. The residents found all sorts of uses for the pink sea creature—filleting it, grilling it like steak . . . chopping it up into something like slaw . . . and soon its name became local slang for residents. They were Conchs (pronounced *Conks*) and they were a world unto themselves.

Though Key West was part of the Florida Territory, the Conchs didn't do much business with the capital city of Pensacola. Instead, Key Westers looked to Havana, ninety miles south. Stuck like a dart out in the Caribbean, inaccessible except by ship, Key West developed its own culture, as much Latin as Anglo, with a geographical isolation that led to a spiritual and cultural isolation as well.

The geography brought more military, and when the town was two decades old, the United States Army began construction of Fort Zachary Taylor on the island's far western point, a military defense that would be needed if there were war with Spain. Though the settlement was still heavily male—construction workers, Navy, Army—women began to arrive and the town took on a semblance of normality, with fine two-story houses nestled among the palm trees. But just as the community took on the appearance of home, nature intervened with a devastating hurricane in 1849 that destroyed all but a handful of buildings. For the first of what would become many times, the city began to reinvent itself.

Only eight buildings survived. Docks were picked up and scattered like toothpicks around the harbor. *It was insane, wasn't it? Building* *a town on this little rock skipped like a stone over the Caribbean? Were they crazy?* Maybe it was time to end this experiment and take everything back to the mainland.

Apparently they *were* crazy, because Key West was rebuilt. Privateering and wrecking bolstered the economy in the early days, but in the middle of the nineteenth century, Key West became known for sponging. Greek divers plucked the prolific sponges from the clear waters around the island, and at one time, 90 percent of all the sponges sold in the country came from Key West.

During the Civil War the town held a strategic advantage, thanks to Fort Zachary Taylor. Most everyone at the fort was an engineer, engaged in finishing construction. Nevertheless, the fort girded for an attack by the Confederate townsfolk. Though there was a lot of hostility and some businesses and homes flew the Stars and Bars, Fort Taylor remained in Union hands.

In the years after the Civil War, an influx of Cuban immigrants changed the culture again. Though cigar making had been around nearly as long as the town, that business boomed after the war. By the 1870s, there were twenty-nine cigar-making firms, which employed more than two thousand workers, and the town produced sixty-two million stogies a year. A little over a decade later, there were sixty-four cigar factories and nearly ten thousand workers.

By the last decade of the century, a hundred million cigars were being produced annually in Key West. But tensions began to fester between the workers and the factory owners. When workers struck, the owners shipped in new workers from Cuba, and the town sheriff had to step in and guarantee order. Within the decade, the business died and factories moved up the coast.

Again the city had to reinvent itself, and showed a remarkable ability to do so. By the turn of the twentieth century, Key West was Florida's most populous city and yet also its most isolated, approachable only by water.

That it was able to recover so quickly is largely due to Henry Flagler. A former partner in the Standard Oil Company with John D. Rockefeller, Flagler decided to take his robber baron earnings and head south. He saw Florida's Atlantic Coast as the American Riviera and established his first beachhead in St. Augustine. There he built the massive Hotel Ponce de León and a private estate.

But St. Augustine, not far from the Georgia line, could still get cold on occasion. So he headed farther south, and began constructing railroad lines to follow his path.

He built another huge resort hotel, the Ormand, near Daytona Beach in Central Florida. But still: it got cold sometimes, and so he headed farther south, and so did the rails.

At Palm Beach, he built The Breakers, his most ostentatious hotel, and finally thought he could settle. But one uncharacteristically cold winter had him move sixty miles south, to Miami. The railroad followed.

Eventually, he set his sights on Key West. The city was 128 miles from the mainland as the crow flew, but people couldn't travel on crows. Laying the rails would be the greatest challenge engineers had yet faced. Still, Flagler saw Key West as the pot of gold at the end of the rainbow.

He gathered his engineers and builders and began connecting the dots over the water. His Florida East Coast Railway brought tourists from Boston and New York and Philadelphia, dropping them off at the string of resorts he'd sprinkled down the coast. He took the rails down to the jewel of Key West.

What became the Florida Overseas Railroad was, for its time, the Eighth Wonder of the World. It took seven years and four thousand men to build it, and not even three hurricanes could quell Flagler's enthusiasm. He was on the first train when it pulled into Key West in 1912, where, of course, he had built a magnificent luxury hotel, the Casa Marina. The railway was one of the most important

engineering feats of his time and Flagler had left parts of his legacy all the way down the coast. The Key West arrival was the high point of his life.

Within a year, he was dead.

Pirates of swash and buckle were mostly gone by the end of the nineteenth century, but the buccaneer legacy remained in the blood of the Conchs. Wreckers and privateers gave way to new generations of smugglers. By the time Ernest Hemingway arrived in the twenties, Prohibition was in full force and the well-schooled smugglers knew how to get booze past the feds. It's a story Hemingway would tell in the one novel set in his adopted hometown, *To Have and Have Not.*

By the time Tom Corcoran moved to the island in 1970 and started selling tacos, the contraband of choice was marijuana. Key West and those mangrove-choked islands up the road were the prime entry point for the weed that was changing the face of the nation.

The town's lawless past defined its history. Through prehistoric Indian wars, ownership disputes, pirate raids, and Prohibition-era rum-running, the community was built on a foundation of vice, and that was as much a part of its charm as it was its legacy.

3

The Template

*In the first place, the Gulf Stream and the other great
ocean currents are the last wild country there is left.*
—ERNEST HEMINGWAY, "ON THE BLUE WATER"

Tom Corcoran lay in bed and took stock: college grad, five years in
the Navy, bright guy, your basic up-and-comer . . . and here he was
selling tacos from a three-wheeled bike.

He'd look over at Judy, sleeping peacefully, her belly methodically
rising. There was someone in there and he or she was going to need
food. Someday that someone would need clothes and want to go to
school and head off to college to learn to become ungrateful. Then he
or she would toss it all away and sell tacos. *Justice, poetic.*

Corcoran was not terribly troubled by dark thoughts, which he
generally confined to the bedroom ceiling. In daylight, with Judy
awake, he was lighthearted when the role demanded it. If he had wor-
ries, he hid them behind his brilliant disguise.

Lying awake in bed, Corcoran would reason himself through to
optimism. He had gone through school, reading, studying literature,

writing short stories. Some of his classmates, such as P.J. O'Rourke, were already getting published. If they were making it, why couldn't he? The rule was: Live life first, so you have something to write about. So here he was, *living*.

Awake, listening to Judy's soft breathing, he'd conclude that this turn of events might be fiscal disaster on the mainland but spiritual and artistic salvation on the island. Key West was crawling with writers. The dude who wrote *Midnight Cowboy*, he lived here. That McGuane kid who wrote *The Sporting Club*; him too. Tennessee Williams still ambled around town. This was king-hell turf if you wanted to be in the lit trade. After all, this was where the biggest and baddest of them all, Ernest "Papa" Hemingway, had worked and played three or four decades back.

Young writers came streaming down U.S. 1, their Volkswagen Beetles crammed with tie-dyed shirts and decaying Modern Library editions of the big guns. And every duffel bag had a mottled Scribner paperback of *For Whom the Bell Tolls* . . . or *A Farewell to Arms* . . . or, hunted down for the trip to Key West, *To Have and Have Not*.

Tom McGuane, Jim Harrison, Phil Caputo . . . eventually every young male writer of that generation came south, needing to deal with Hemingway's ghost. They came to Key West, many of them, to take part in the literary cock-measuring contest with Papa. He'd been gone thirty years by the time McGuane arrived, and it had been nearly ten years since Hemingway had put a gun in his mouth at his last home, up in Idaho.

Some wanted to be *like* him. Some wanted to take measure *against* him. But there was no denying that Hemingway's presence was still so large, and his shadow so long, that if you were a writer with aspirations of being a literary he-man, a stint in Key West was on the itinerary. Hemingway was the template. Hunting and fishing, drinking and brawling . . . all the manly pursuits were de rigueur.

There's a reason for all this, Corcoran thought.

Ernest Hemingway had spent most of his adult life on the Finca Vigia, his estate on a hill outside Havana. But getting to Cuba was hard in the seventies, and possibly dangerous. Under Fidel Castro, it had become too risky even for Papa.

No, if you were a writer and you wanted to challenge Hemingway on his own turf, you had to come to Key West, where he remained, even in death. The owners of his old home on Whitehead Street had opened it to the public just three years after the suicide, and made good money taking people on tours through the living room and lush backyard. Sloppy Joe's, where he once drank, was beginning to market itself with his image, the Yousuf Karsh portrait of Papa near the end, gazing at the horizon of some other world. Tourists descending on Key West got drunk on Hemingway musk. The Key West Island Bookstore could barely keep his work in stock.

Ernest Hemingway spent a decade and change in Key West, from April 1928 until he sailed his boat to Cuba in April 1939. During the Key West years, he wrote much of his most significant work, including *A Farewell to Arms*, *For Whom the Bell Tolls*, *Green Hills of Africa*, *Death in the Afternoon*, and some of his finest short stories. He spent nearly the entirety of his second marriage there, and two of his three sons were born there. But on that day in April 1928 when he came down the gangplank of the Peninsular & Occidental steamship from Havana, staying in the little town for longer than an afternoon was the furthest thing from his mind.

After World War I, Hemingway had settled into expatriate life in Paris and begun his writing career. Though a mere journalist, he was the confident braggart of the expat gang, memorably dubbed the

Lost Generation by Gertrude Stein. Hemingway was just another member of the club, not one of the officers. Other American writers living and writing in Paris were more successful, including F. Scott Fitzgerald, Ezra Pound, and John Dos Passos. Stein and Pound had published a significant number of books before the Paris days, and of the younger writers, both Fitzgerald and Dos Passos beat Hemingway into print by a half decade. In that company, Hemingway learned his craft, developing what would become one of the most influential and certainly most imitated styles in the century's literature. Recalling that time a quarter century later, he wrote, "If you are lucky enough to have lived in Paris as a young man, then wherever you go for the rest of your life, it stays with you, for Paris is a moveable feast."

Though nearly the same age, living in the same city, and traveling in the same circles, Hemingway had never met F. Scott Fitzgerald. Fitzgerald became a campus favorite with *This Side of Paradise* in 1920. Five years later, he had published *The Beautiful and Damned* and *The Great Gatsby* when he finally crossed paths with Hemingway in a Paris bar. Fitzgerald was already familiar with Hemingway's writing, mostly his articles for the *Toronto Star*, and had told Maxwell Perkins, his editor at Charles Scribner's Sons, to sign Hemingway to a book contract. He had lavishly praised Hemingway to Perkins, saying his was the most exciting American literary voice of the twentieth century.

Aside from the articles in the *Star*, Hemingway hadn't had much success and was envious of Fitzgerald and somewhat suspicious of the accolades he was sending his way over champagne. Sincere or sarcastic? He couldn't tell. (He also couldn't tell when Fitzgerald was merely drunk and bored; Hemingway once mistook his new friend's inebriation for a stroke.)

With a small Parisian press, Hemingway had published what was essentially a pamphlet, *Three Stories and Ten Poems*, in 1923. Again with a small publisher in Paris, he had another story collection the following year, *in our time*. This was picked up by eccentric American publisher Horace Liveright and became Hemingway's first American book. The young author felt confident enough to capitalize the title for readers back home and *In Our Time* appeared in America in 1925 on the Boni and Liveright imprint. By this time, Max Perkins was being hectored regularly by Fitzgerald, and so to make his young author happy, he signed Hemingway to a Scribner's contract, publishing two novels in 1926, *The Torrents of Spring* (a slight work, both a parody of and tribute to Sherwood Anderson) and *The Sun Also Rises*.

So this was Hemingway as the twenties roared to their conclusion. He'd married and had a son, but by 1927 he had fallen in love with a writer for the Paris edition of *Vogue*. Pauline Pfeiffer wasn't French. She was from Piggott, Arkansas, by way of the University of Missouri School of Journalism. She was living the life of a fashion writer in Paris when she ran into the freight train named Ernest Hemingway. The now-marginalized first wife, Hadley, watched as Pauline became her husband's inamorata. Problem was, Hadley liked Pauline. She said she would agree to a divorce if her husband and Pauline still loved each other after spending three months apart. They did, and after his first divorce was resolved, Pauline Pfeiffer became the second Mrs. Hemingway, on May 10, 1927.

Around that time Hemingway became restless, complaining more often about Paris, about French manners, about the bitter cold that came with the rain. He confessed all this in letters to friends, and one of them, John Dos Passos, wrote back, ecstatic about one of his recent stops. *Go to Key West*, he advised. *It's the best place for Ole Hem to dry out his bones.* So Hemingway decided to move his feast across the Atlantic.

As Hemingway looked at Key West from the deck of the steamship, he saw nothing remarkable. It was April 6, 1928, and he was wearing tweeds and a necktie. The sultry air of the island was stifling at first and Key West made a rotten impression. They planned a short stay. Pauline, by then pregnant, intended to give birth in the bosom of her family, and the bosom was located in Piggott, Arkansas. The young Mrs. Hemingway's benevolent uncle, Gus Pfeiffer, had ordered a Ford for them and it was to be waiting for the couple on arrival in Key West. The plan was to get off the boat, take delivery of the car, go for a quick spin around the island, then head north.

When the Hemingways finally got through customs, there was no sign of the Model T. Carrying their luggage, the young couple walked the six blocks to the Trevor & Morris Company, the local Ford dealership. After trudging through tropical heat, they learned that ferry transport had delayed the arrival of the Model T. *Would they like to stay upstairs?* Hemingway looked up at the showroom's ceiling. *We have rooms up there*, the Ford dealer said, nodding toward the roof. *Would you like to rent one?* Hemingway shrugged, and they took a room on the second floor, with a balcony overlooking the street, offering a great view of the harbor a few blocks away.

Slight and pregnant, Pauline was eager to lie down and she immediately settled into the mattress, splayed under the ceiling fan. Her restless husband decided to take a stroll. He walked down the stairs, nodded at the Ford salesmen as he passed the showroom, then stepped out onto Simonton Street. Hands clasped behind his back, he began ambling toward what he assumed was the central part of town.

After the cold Paris damp, this tropical air with its oppressive humidity was uncomfortable, and he began removing the vestiges of that other world—the tie, then the thick wool coat. He wondered if Dos was insane. *"Just what Ole Hem needed."* Not bloody likely. But as he walked, he took note of the flowers and the small but well-maintained yards of the homes. And the houses, too, were different: frame, with gingerbread and elaborate porch carvings. Here fish swirled along a porch roof. And here, atop the stairs up from the lane, were real gingerbread men—carved and painted white, of course—welcoming visitors to the porch. Most of this was made, as Hemingway would soon learn, in the woodworking shop of Francisco Camellon, who used a horse-pulled lathe to make his elaborate cuttings. That first afternoon, however, Hemingway wasn't as concerned with the construction as he was with admiring the care and precision of the final product.

As he strolled, he began to fall in love with the town's charm, which in part was due to the intimate details that made the small moments of life so delightful. Dos Passos had said the place was "faintly New England," but with tropical air. Some of the houses could have been uprooted in Nantucket and towed south by a barge. Others looked like remnants of the Spanish past. The mixture and the diversity intrigued him.

Back at his room, his wife and his work awaited. His valise contained his latest work in progress, his big novel of the Great War. For now, it was a penciled bundle of a hundred yellow sheets from a legal pad. He'd conceived the novel in Paris after the war, but needed to live more before he could write it down. But the writing had been difficult in Paris. As he walked the charming streets of Key West, he opened his mind to the possibility of staying—just for a short while—to see if he could make some progress on the novel. So far, his books had not brought much money, and though he appreciated the car and other financial aid from Uncle Gus, self-respect demanded not only that he produce something that he was proud of but also something that made money.

That afternoon, the love affair began. It didn't take long for the little village to intoxicate Hemingway with its fishing and its splendid isolation. He returned to the room, refreshed, and told Pauline that maybe a stay here would do Ole Hem some good after all. *We'll still get to Arkansas in plenty of time*, he assured his bride. She smiled, happy to see him so invigorated. He went to the bureau, picked up his valise, withdrew his manuscript, and set to work, thankful that he wasn't motoring up the Keys toward the mainland. The delay was a blessing.

Days passed and he explored more of the island. There were several suitable bars and no shortage of entertainment. In the morning, when he preferred to write, the island was quiet. It was another world, far removed from Paris and its forced and sometimes false sociability, the walled neighborhoods, and the perpetual rot of that which is antiquated. Key West was a small, lush, subtropical paradise.

They had been in town only a few days when Hemingway checked the post office for forwarded mail. He found a note saying that his parents were upstate, looking over some land they had bought near St. Petersburg. His father had sent the note to Paris and it had been shipped to Key West. Hemingway hadn't told his parents he was returning to the States. Suddenly he wished the car had arrived, so they could start their trip to Pauline's home in Arkansas, now with a stop in St. Pete to surprise the old man. Instead he sent a telegram, urging his parents to visit him in Key West and meet their new daughter-in-law.

Afterward, he amused himself by fishing off the pier. It was around noon and a ship was arriving. He glanced up, but went back to the task at hand, wondering if the ship's wake would drive more fish toward his hook or frighten them away. Then he heard the whistle—not a ship's whistle, but a deliberate call. It was the way his father used to signal him. He looked up at the deck of the steamship and saw his father waving to him.

His parents had taken a weekend cruise south from St. Petersburg and visited Havana. Now they were docking at Key West on the way back. As soon as his parents came down the gangplank, father and son embraced. Clarence Hemingway was delighted to see Ernest, whom he had assumed was still in Paris.

Dr. Hemingway's appearance was also a surprise to his son. The once vigorous man was frail, so shrunken that his shirt appeared to belong to a much larger man. He was weakened by diabetes, heart disease, and stress, and his once brown-auburn hair was now varying subtle shades of white. Financially, he was also stretched thin. Hemingway read worry on his father's face. Maybe it wasn't a good time for Florida land speculation. Still, seeing his beloved son lifted Dr. Hemingway's spirits and his eyes shone.

The same could not be said for Grace Hemingway. Relations between mother and son were frigid, and would remain so until she died. In contrast to her husband, she was husky; her face was so red and raw it looked boiled, plastered with a forced smile.

Hemingway convinced his parents to spend some time, even if just the afternoon. He quickly ushered them to the Trevor and Morris Apartments, eager for them to meet Pauline. Dr. Hemingway took to her immediately, offering to pray for her and for the health of the baby. She was as charmed by the father as she had been by his son.

Grace Hemingway and her new daughter-in-law circled warily for a bit, but when the sniffing period ended, they seemed pleased with each other. Mother and son, however, still observed a wall of tension and regret. Though they agreed to delay their departure for an afternoon, Dr. and Mrs. Hemingway could not be persuaded to make a longer stay. Hemingway squired them to a local restaurant for a six-course meal (fifty cents per plate), featuring chicken and yellow rice, garbanzos and turtle steak, and showed them a bit of the island. It was warmer than the elder Hemingways were used to, but the doctor kept on his tweed suit jacket and didn't loosen his bow tie. Ernest was jaunty in his shirtsleeves, sweater vest, and loafers, babbling with excitement as he showed off the town. His mother scoffed at the slow pace and the laziness reflected in the populace.

At the end of the afternoon, Hemingway put his parents on the train. They would be in Miami by late evening, and by then he would have written a few more pages of what would become *A Farewell to Arms*.

He never saw his father again.

A week later, the car arrived, but by then Hemingway had made friends and was in no hurry to leave. While fishing up the Keys, he had been mistaken for a gangster because of a curving purple scar above his right eye, an injury from the war. George Brooks was near the pier when he spotted the ruffian, and his interest in him was professional. Brooks was a prosecutor, and so he approached the stranger and asked him to state his business. Soon he learned that Hemingway was recovering from a decade in Paris and was struggling to write a book. Brooks saw there was no threat and immediately began to think of Key Westers who might be good friends for the new man.

Through Brooks, Hemingway met Charles Thompson and Eddie Saunders, both of whom became lifelong friends.

Thompson owned a hardware store and Brooks sent Hemingway there, telling him that fishing was best when it wasn't solitary. Thompson, whom Hemingway called Karl, was at first put off by the scruffiness and the scar but was soon won over by Hemingway's ebullient personality and enthusiasm for fishing. The day after Hemingway walked into Thompson Hardware and introduced himself, they were out on the water, tarpon fishing in Thompson's outboard.

Saunders, known as "Captain Bra," was an expert captain, an émigré from Green Turtle Key in the Bahamas, and, at forty-two, a dozen years older than the young writer. Soon, Hemingway's pier fishing gave way to overnight trips in the Marquesas with his new friends. Key West became more attractive with every catch.

Pauline felt otherwise. After her position as a fashion writer for *Vogue* in Paris, Key West seemed like a significant step down. The little village had its charms, and she wanted to please her husband and give him the room for his work and play, both so important for him. Still, pregnant and stifling hot in the clammy humidity, she didn't share his attraction to the place. She felt it was just another hick town that happened to be on an island in the blue water.

She knew something about hick towns, being from Piggott, Arkansas. In her letters home, however, she swallowed her frustration and was instead rhapsodic about life in Key West. She had been serious about returning to the Arkansas family bosom for the birth, but now, with the buddies and the fishing and the drinking, she wondered if she'd ever get her husband out of there. *Life here is wonderful*, she wrote to her father, Paul. *You really must come visit.* She hoped to lure her father down to Florida, mostly so that he would take her back north, away from the oppressive tropics.

The plan worked and Paul Pfeiffer announced that he was coming for a visit. Upon his arrival, there was an initial chill between Pfeiffer and his new son-in-law. A devout Catholic and wealthy businessman, Pfeiffer had a bouquet of reasons to dislike Hemingway. First, and most damningly, he had divorced his first wife to marry Pauline. That was an obstacle the size of Everest. Then came the new husband's certain life of poverty. *Who could make a living from writing? What kind of fool would try?* He saw the marriage as a pauper's sentence for his daughter.

Pauline negotiated a truce between the two and they agreed that fishing together might be a good idea. Soon, Pfeiffer began warming. *Oh, dear*, Pauline thought. Her plan was going horribly awry. Now her father was here in this steambath of a one-horse town and he was *liking* it.

The couple had been a month in the Trevor and Morris Apartments. Pfeiffer was down the street at the Colonial Hotel. Initially, the plan was for Pauline to take the train north and have Ernest and her father drive up in the Ford that had finally arrived. Hemingway cringed at the idea.

Christ, he told friends, *the bastard hates me. Why would I want to spend all that time in a car with him?* He tried to jovially manipulate Pauline. *Honey, why not take your father with you? I don't mind driving up alone.*

But fishing accelerated the thaw, and before long, Paul Pfeiffer was in no hurry to leave. He met Charles Thompson and Bra Saunders. Fish were caught. Rum was tossed back. After Piggott, Key West was paradise to Pfeiffer. Soon, Hemingway began to think about assembling a "mob" along the lines of his gaggle of friends in Paris. Pfeiffer, he decided, could be a charter member.

Hemingway began summoning friends to Key West, just as Pauline was preparing to put herself on the train for the north and motherhood. While Hemingway ignored his pregnant bride, he wrote letters, nearly begging his pals to come. "Christ, this is a fine country," he wrote, having fallen in love again with America.

Hemingway wanted to make sure his old friends got to know his new friends, particularly Thompson and Saunders. And so they came: Dos Passos. The painter Henry Strater (Hemingway called him Mike, of course). Bill Smith. Despite the fact that his mother had just died, another friend, Waldo Peirce, made the trip.

Oh God, would it never end, Pauline thought. Even her father was drunk on Hemingway's charisma. *You go ahead, honey. Mother will take care of you. I'll stay here and fish with Ernie.*

"Ernie." Or was it "The Old Master" today? Hemingway tossed nicknames around, bestowing them on his friends and on himself. Not yet thirty, he had already taken to calling himself The Old Master. He was going to be a literary legend, by God, and he needed to make sure everyone knew it.

He'd be there in time for the birth, he assured her. But first, he had this fishing trip planned for the Dry Tortugas. . . .

———

Drowning in the tsunami of testosterone, Pauline Hemingway boarded the Florida East Coast Railway and began her journey to Arkansas, to give birth. Her father stayed with her husband and his assembled Mob. The drinking and brawling and fishing continued. In New York, in the literary world, Hemingway would have been riding the crest of his new celebrity. In Key West, no one cared who he was, unless he was buying the next round (which he often did with Paul Pfeiffer's money). "People don't stare at me on the streets," he said.

For a couple of weeks, Hemingway enjoyed being part of this mixed crowd, in the town he called "the St. Tropez of the Poor." Some members of the Mob were writers and artists, who'd come from exotic places. The others were the locals, the Conchs, unpretentious everyday souls who owned hardware stores and were guides for the tourist fishermen. They all got along. Thompson called those assembled "as grand a group of men as ever came together." Most of them stayed at the dollar-a-day Overseas Hotel and drank religiously at the speakeasy of Hemingway's friend and charter boat captain Josie Russell. (Hemingway dubbed him "Sloppy Joe.") He loved showing off the small riches of his newly discovered hometown to the out-of-town friends, and for two weeks, they closed down most of the bars and caught a sizable number of fish.

As the nights grew longer, Hemingway was aware that the macho idyll was near its end. His out-of-town friends had lives to which they needed to return, and Hemingway realized, with some resignation, that he had an important date in Arkansas. So he and his father-in-law took the new Ford on a cross-country road test.

He made it to Piggott to be with the still-pregnant Pauline, after a long and debilitating trip. Pauline felt alone and miserable, owing in large part to the suffocating Arkansas humidity. It was worse than in Key West, because there was no lilting breeze off the Atlantic. Not long after arriving in Arkansas, seeing that the child was not yet born, Ernest took off for Kansas City to see old friends. Pauline was infuriated, but her husband returned before the big day.

Patrick Hemingway was born on June 27, 1928, by cesarean section and in the swelter of summer. Impatient with the ceremonies of birth, Hemingway admired his spawn and loved his young wife, but soon longed for life outside Arkansas. He thought of hunting out west, of the gang back in Paris, and, frequently, of the blue water of the Gulf Stream.

He worked best as a man in motion. Most of his early books were written on the road, in hotel rooms, in borrowed lodgings, edited on trains. He worked in Paris, in Spain, in Key West, in Piggott, and then out in Montana.

But it was Key West that felt the most like home. After his few weeks there in 1928, and the planting and fertilizing of new friendships, he realized that he wanted to return. Before leaving, he had asked Thompson to keep his eyes open for a good house he could rent when he came back in 1929.

Thompson found something in time for the Hemingways' return the next year. That year, not pregnant, Pauline was happier and began making her own circle of friends. Hemingway again assembled his Mob. Key West had full hold on his heart now, and so Pauline did not object when Hemingway asked Thompson to look for "something permanent." They were often on the road—hunting out in Montana, visiting family in Illinois or Arkansas, sometimes in New York to oversee the world of publishing and the machinery of celebrity.

The something permanent turned out to be a mansion on Whitehead Street that had been built in 1851. With help from Uncle Gus, they bought the massive house for eight thousand dollars in 1931. It needed some repairs, and a lot of out-of-work Conchs who'd been living on occasional day labor during the dark days of the Depression were happy to do Mrs. Hemingway's bidding. By the time Pauline considered the house suitable for habitation, another son had been born. Gregory was also a cesarean birth, and Pauline was advised not to again attempt conception.

And so the family settled, as much as it ever settled, into the largest house in Key West. Hemingway was nearing his full-celebrity status. Hollywood made movies of his novels. He published stories in major magazines and was soon to begin making regular contributions about Key West life to *Esquire*, the new monthly founded by Arnold Gingrich. To earn enough money to buy the thirty-eight-foot yacht he named *Pilar*, Hemingway banged out *To Have and Have Not*.

In Piggott, Hemingway had met Otto Bruce. As it happened, Bruce had married a Key West girl and brought her back to his home. It was a good conversation starter when they met. As their friendship bloomed, Hemingway sought to lure Bruce—by then nicknamed Toby—back to Key West. Eventually, Toby gave in and the Bruces moved down, with the understanding that Toby would help the author with the machinations of day-to-day life, to navigate the full-time job of Being Ernest Hemingway.

Hemingway was a living legend, already Papa long before his hair lost its color and his face earned its creases. His house, soon to be enclosed as a fortress by a brick wall (built by Toby Bruce) because of his fame and leering fans, was in prime island real estate, across the street from the lighthouse. Hemingway gave off a different sort of light. Instead of warning sea captains of dangers along the shore, his was more like a flame that drew people toward him and toward the island.

4

A Different Society

Why did I write? Because I found life unsatisfactory.
—Tennessee Williams

Maybe it was once a child's bicycle, before alterations turned it into a taco stand on wheels. Perhaps it had been a Schwinn, or a Huffy, something with streamers on which a proud father had pushed his nervous six-year-old down the street for a maiden ride. But now it was a three-wheeled bicycle made for commerce—built for cargo, not speed.

Whatever alterations it had had, they had been made in the small metal shop on the USS *Bushnell*, a sub tender ported at the U.S. Naval Air Station on the westernmost point of the island. Charley Jackson, a chief petty officer on the *Bushnell*, moonlighted onshore with Pancho's, a little Mexican place he owned on the corner of Duval and Amelia. He was Central Pennsylvania beefrock, right out of high school and into the Navy, so for him it was three hoots and a blast that college boy Tom Corcoran, *an ex-looey J-G no less,* worked for *him,* bicycling through the tourist streets, selling tacos and advertising Pancho's. To Corcoran, who was riding around town with a cooler full of meat and doing bicycle stunts for the girls, the joke was on Jackson. Who was getting the better end of this deal?

That first night, Corcoran had looked over the bike, with its oversized basket and the few tools of the trade left by Afro: squeezy bottles for hot sauce, a roll of paper towels for napkins, a few cups for sodas. "The bike had a bright aluminum box behind the seat," Corcoran recalled. "It was maybe thirty inches wide and thirty-six inches front to back. Up top, I had a Styrofoam cooler with the grated cheese, chopped lettuce, and hot sauces. Down low, there was a metal pot full of the premixed taco meat. A small gas torch on the lowest possible setting kept it warm."

Despite carrying a mini-kitchen, Corcoran turned into hell on wheels. He rode through the Duval Street neighborhoods late afternoons and evenings, dispensing tacos for tourists and a dedicated group of local customers. Judy, pregnant and often miserable, waited in their small apartment, trying to keep cool in front of the Holmes rotating table fan. Other expectant fathers headed out the door every morning in neckties to a stifling office, but Corcoran's office on wheels was locked in the yard. He'd ride over to Pancho's and pick up his supplies. The shells, made fresh daily, were bundled in plastic sleeves. He'd fill the metal pot with enough meat for 150 tacos. Everything else was preserved in the Styrofoam.

Fifty cents apiece or three for a dollar. He split 50–50 with Pancho's. Corcoran was Taco Tom to the locals, serving food, jokes, wisdom. He'd toss back a beer or two as he was winding down at night, and start stunts in the middle of Duval. He could pull back, pop a wheelie, and ride around in circles on two thin tires. On top of the taco money, he'd get tips for his tricks. "Things were slow in 1970," he said. "I'd do anything for a laugh."

For the time and place, the money was good. "A two hundred dollar paycheck every week was handsome," he said. Plus, when he'd get home at one in the morning, he and his pregnant girlfriend could feast on taco-meat sloppy joes for free.

He was a college graduate, coming off four years as a naval officer. From that to selling tacos was an odd career trajectory, a disappointment to the *why-did-you-go-to-college-in-the-first-place* family back in Shaker Heights. But Corcoran wasn't concerned with how his life was playing back in Ohio. He was in Key West and was making enough to support his girlfriend and whatever was in her belly. It was paradise, with enough hungry tourists to keep him in business.

Taco Tom quickly became another fixture, an adopted local, and it wasn't just the visiting Canadians in the knee socks who gave him business. He became the vendor of choice on those muggy nights when the first half-dozen beers kicked in and the munchies hit.

It was there, on Duval Street with sunset approaching, that Corcoran met him. He heard him first, with that *huh-huh-huh* laugh that he never swallowed, that turned into a form of breathing, the aural equivalent of his riverboat-gambler smile. Writer Rex Reed likened his voice to what a swamp alligator would sound like. "His tongue seems coated with rum and molasses as it darts in and out of his mouth," Reed wrote, "licking at his moustache like a pink lizard. His voice wavers unsteadily like old gray cigar smoke in a room with no ventilation, rising to a mad cackle, like a wounded macaw."

Corcoran beheld the spectacle: this man-of-some-years approaching the taco cart ("My, my, my," he drawled, "what *have* we here?"), in the company of a bunch of . . . well, more of a *gaggle*, Corcoran thought . . . tanned and buffed young men. He smiled and looked over the tacos on display, fingers agile and mobile ("His hands flutter like dying birds," Reed said). Entry into the old man's group must require pedigree as a fashion model, Corcoran thought, as he looked over the man's companions. The young men were teeming with testosterone and sculpted pectorals, looking bored and haughty. "He had an entourage that looked like the Olympic swimming team," Corcoran said of the first time he saw Tennessee Williams.

As a boy, Williams would lie in bed and close his eyes, shutting out the world. He imagined a real father, a sister who was whole, a nurturing mother, and a normal family.

He had a father, of course, but on the road as much as he was, selling those damn shoes, he might as well have been dead and gone. When he was home and drinking, the boy often wished that the old man *was* dead. But for his grandparents and those few friends who came to see him, life would have been unendurable.

When Tommy Williams opened his eyes, it was nearly so. Conflicted as he was in his feelings toward his mother, Edwina, he felt the greatest love for his sister, Rose. She gave him purpose; he was her protector. Her schizophrenia was diagnosed at an early age and treated as a mortal embarrassment by their mother. Father was absent, so it was not an issue for him. Tom was diagnosed with diphtheria at seven and so both of the Williams children were shut-ins, under the unvarnished influence of Mother Edwina.

They lived in the grandparents' large house in Clarksdale, Mississippi, a quiet town in the northern part of the state, with grand wraparound-porch homes for the wealthy white population and narrow shotgun shacks for the blacks. It would be home to a number of musicians and entertainers and the supposed site where blues singer Robert Johnson sold his soul to the devil at a midnight-darkened crossroads.

Bedridden, young Tommy closed his eyes and imagined a different life, and eventually several different lives. "I took to solitary amusements," he said, "and I developed a very fine, very deep imaginative life." Edwina encouraged her son's flights of fancy. An imagination, she told him, was a wonderful means of escape.

When he was thirteen, his mother gave him a typewriter to write down the stories he imagined. He loved her for it, but in his stories, she often appeared as a hectoring, demanding shrew.

By adolescence, he was recovered from diphtheria and the family moved to St. Louis, where he continued writing stories. He went off to college at the University of Missouri, but his father disapproved of his son's ambition, and so the boy was summoned home after freshman year to learn the shoe trade. He hated it, and so he did other work too.

He ticked off the far points of his curriculum vitae: "I was a manual laborer. I was a clerical worker. I waited on tables. I was a telephone operator in a hotel and I liked that because I became addicted to listening in. I have never heard more peculiar conversations since. When I went to California, I worked on a pigeon ranch. Later, I came to Florida to work as a teletype operator in Jacksonville."

Eventually, he convinced his father to let him attend Washington College in St. Louis, and he showed enough promise to be admitted to the prestigious writing program upriver, at the University of Iowa. There his thick accent earned him a nickname from classmates. They could tell he was from the South, but they got the state wrong. They called him "Tennessee."

"It's better than being called Mississippi," Tennessee Williams said when he told the story. At other times, thick with honeyfuggle, he claimed the name was because his family had helped create the state. He was known for telling the same story with endless variations. When it came to his name, the conclusion was always the same: *I liked the sound of it.*

By the time he became a regular customer of Taco Tom, Tennessee Williams was a quarter-century deep into celebrity. He had taken the story of his family—his wounded sister, his embarrassed and domi-neering mother—and told it several times. His success began with its telling in *The Glass Menagerie* in 1945. In 1947, his *Streetcar Named Desire* and its star, Marlon Brando, revolutionized both play-writing and acting on stage, and there were traces of Mother Edwina in Blanche DuBois. The story was again told as *Suddenly, Last Summer*. Rose, his damaged sister, was institutionalized in 1937 and later underwent a prefrontal lobotomy. Williams finished college the next year and began his wandering.

Throughout his life, Williams found several homes: Clarksdale in his youth, St. Louis in his adolescence, and New Orleans and New York in his struggling days as a young writer.

But Key West was always his safe place, his refuge, from the time of his first visit, in 1941. One of Williams's early plays, *Battle of Angels*, had been an epic disaster in its debut on the Boston stage and Williams thought a Southern climate would make for a more hospi-table place to lick his wounds. He traveled a lot during these years—in Louisiana, New Mexico, California, Massachusetts, Georgia, and New York—but Key West became his holy land, his divine umbilical cord.

He hoped to rewrite *Battle of Angels* (and did, eventually bring-ing it back fifteen years later as *Orpheus Descending*) and also stay fit by swimming daily. "Key West was the southernmost point in America," he said. "I figured I'd be able to swim there."

When he first came to Key West, he took a room at the Tradewinds, an old mansion at the corner of Duval and Caroline streets. He lived in a small cabin, built out of mahogany, behind the main house—the slave quarters, he called it—and he liked being near the raucous partying that was already a part of Duval Street life. As Williams recalled the neighborhood, "It was the center of the action for the pub-crawlers and the night people, Navy officers, singers, entertain-ers, artists, and writers, and some members of the town's social set."

The town was not even a decade removed from the time of

Hemingway stalking the streets, and he was living in Cuba when Williams moved in. (Williams tried to meet Hemingway once in Havana, but the face-to-face never came off because Hemingway missed the telegram that Williams was on the way.) Hemingway had pub-crawled with his Mob. Williams soon developed his own army with whom he socialized. The townies might call them Tennessee's Mob, but he hated that characterization. He might occasionally go out with friends—mostly writers, such as Gore Vidal, Christopher Isherwood, and Carson McCullers—but more often than not, they sat in the front parlor of the Tradewinds and listened to the tinkling from the piano bar.

After a few visits, he found a suitable cottage. Out back, next to the small pool (with the mosaic of a rose tattoo he had stenciled on the bottom), there was a small building he called "the Madhouse," to which he retreated each morning to write. Key West offered him the perfect balance of work and pleasure. "In New York, I get up much later," he told an interviewer. "In Florida, I begin work around daybreak and work until I get tired." He had only one goal: "The one I set for myself every morning—that I will be able to go on working, because that is my great joy."

Being Tennessee Williams, America's greatest dramatist, required that he leave the sanctuary of the squat home in Key West from time to time. He'd go to Rome, to visit the woman he considered his dearest friend, the actress Anna Magnani. Often, theater business took him to New York. "I can't stand living in Manhattan," he said, "but at the same time, I know I need the psychiatric treatment, and the medical treatment I receive" in the city.

When director Daniel Mann was scouting locations in 1955 for a film version of Williams's play *The Rose Tattoo*, he chose Key West. The action took place in a Gulf Coast town in Mississippi, but Mann decided that Key West had more amenities than Biloxi or Pascagoula, and certainly more reliable good weather for shooting.

When Williams wrote the play for the Broadway stage in 1951, he had imagined the central role, that of Serafina Delle Rose, for Magnani. But Magnani's English was not considered good enough for the elocutionary requirements of the theater. Maureen Stapleton, a twenty-five-year-old from upstate New York, was given the role and spoke in an Italian accent. Stapleton became one of America's most admired performers, but when the time came to make the film, Williams insisted that Magnani—in his view, the world's greatest living actress—be given the role. In his *Memoirs*, Williams wrote of Magnani: "She was as unconventional a woman as I have known in or out of my professional world, and if you understand me at all, you must know that in this statement I am making my personal estimate of her honesty, which I feel was complete." Williams insisted that if the film was to be made with his endorsement, she would be in it.

Deal, Mann said. While looking through the streets of Key West for the ideal home for Magnani's character, Serafina, the location scout found the perfect exterior on Duncan Street, and secured filming rights from the owner. But the scout told Mann and his producer, Hal Wallis, that they would need to intrude on the property next door in order to construct Serafina's goat pen. The scout worried that the owner of that second house might object.

Of course Williams and his longtime lover, Frank Merlo, did not object to the studied dilapidation being constructed in his yard. In fact, they asked both Magnani and the film's male star, Burt Lancaster, to use their house for their on-location dressing rooms.

Williams considered the stage version of *The Rose Tattoo* a relative failure, so he allowed the film company to turn over his script for adaptation to Hal Kanter, a journeyman television writer (eventually, he would produce the popular *All in the Family* series) who had recently begun trying his hand at screenplays.

It was the first major film to be shot in Key West. Although Hemingway set his novel *To Have and Have Not* there, when it came time to make the film, director Howard Hawks bowed to pressure and changed the locale to Martinique. The federal government objected to showing scenes of smuggling between Key West and Cuba. That wasn't all that was changed for the film. Hemingway had bet Hawks that his book was unfilmable. In a way, the author won the bet because Hawks and his screenwriters (including William Faulkner) decided to ignore Hemingway's plot and write about events that *might* have happened earlier in the lives of the main characters, played by Humphrey Bogart and the nineteen-year-old actress who would become his wife, Lauren Bacall.

So the movie stars did not come to Key West. Burbank, California, filled in for Martinique.

In one scene of *The Rose Tattoo*, Magnani rushes through the Mardi Gras Club, in search of her no-good man. Look carefully at the men at the bar and you will see both Tennessee Williams and Frank Merlo.

Though he considered the work a failure (and perhaps so by the standards of the man who had written *The Glass Menagerie* and *A Streetcar Named Desire*), the film was highly regarded, and Magnani, his great friend, won the Best Actress Academy Award, beating Katharine Hepburn, Jennifer Jones, and Susan Hayward.

As the years passed, Williams assumed the literary-celebrity role that Hemingway left behind when he departed for Havana. Williams loved his Key West routines. He'd rendezvous with a neighbor, a young writer named James Leo Herlihy, for a morning walk that ended at the beach, where they took a ritual swim.

His longtime companion, Merlo, died young, and a parade of visitors spent the night in the Williams guest room. Whenever Truman Capote came to town, Williams would round up some of the local Cuban boys as eye candy. "It was a little weird," said Danilo Cisneros, one of those boys. Young, athletic, and beautiful, Cisneros just stood around in the living room, drinking a rum punch and being ogled. "They didn't want anything of us," Cisneros explained. "They just liked to look."

It was that time, the early seventies, that Tennessee Williams often surrounded himself with the "Olympic swimming team" that Tom Corcoran saw when he served the great dramatist the first of his tacos.

Tennessee Williams was a magnet for the young writers who hit town. When Herlihy came to Key West, he was just stepping into his mid-twenties and had published some short stories in "small, but important" literary reviews. He peppered Williams with questions and learned what he could about the construction of drama and narrative, eventually publishing the novels *All Fall Down* and *Midnight Cowboy*.

Herlihy was not the only apprentice. When he was in town, Williams was nearly ubiquitous, one of the most accessible of the literary giants of his time. Young writers hung on his every word. His extravagant homosexuality provided a model of behavior for the young gay men who began to descend on the laissez-faire island village.

Those young men benefited from some of Tennessee's struggles.

In the sixties, a local family opened the Bone Island equivalent of a sophisticated nightclub, a place called Raphael's. Williams came in with members of his entourage and tossed around money and laughed his swamp-alligator laugh, having a great old time. As he was leaving, though, the owner, the local Grace Kelly, came over and placed her hand on his forearm. "I hope you enjoyed yourself," she said, "but we would rather you not come back." He tried not to break his smile, but his brow furrowed. "Don't get me wrong," she went on, "but we don't want this place to get a reputation as a homosexual hangout." Still, frozen smile on his face. "You understand," she continued, "we're just getting started." Somehow, he managed to hold the smile. "Of course," he said. "Good luck with the place," and he stepped outside, into the balmy night.

The local Grace Kelly was part of the Old Guard, though in a town with so much transient history, "old" was a relative term. By the end of the sixties, attitudes were changing.

It's as if God had picked up the country at California and shook it, so that all of the loose pieces ended up in that reservoir tip at the country's southeast edge. You could go no further to that edge than to land in Key West. As the sixties disciples, rejects, and failed philosophers headed down U.S. 1, they discovered a different society on the island. By then, it didn't matter if you were homosexual, heterosexual, or undecided. Those gay men and women who began the trek to Key West found a community much more accepting than Tennessee Williams had. That it was so accepting was in part because of the forced smiles and awkward situations and freeze-outs that Tennessee Williams had endured, often with enormous grace.

It began to change in the late sixties, and by the early seventies, Key West was a different town. In that time, in that place, nobody cared who you fucked.

┌─────────┐
│   │
│   5   │
│   │
└─────────┘

McGuane

It was kind of a free-fire zone, where you could figure
out what you wanted to do. You were in a sympathetic
culture to be an artist. It was a real chance to find out
a lot in a short time in a small space.
—THOMAS MCGUANE

One night, Corcoran is slinging the taco meat on Duval. He'd gotten to know Tennessee Williams and James Leo Herlihy and some of the other literary lights. Selling tacos was a great way to meet people, and since he wanted to be a writer, working as a street vendor did more than put food on the table and in Judy's pregnant belly. It was a way to meet writers, to ask questions, to learn about the craft. It was a way to study what he knew would be the subject matter of the books he planned to write: human behavior.

So here's this guy walking toward him, a real brick of a guy, looking at him cockeyed.

"Hey, what're you doing?" the guy yells at Corcoran, big rabbit-teeth smile. There's a pause for him to gander at the meat wagon on wheels.

"Sellin' tacos."

"Yup," Corcoran says.

"I can see that," the guy says. "I mean, what are you *really* doing? Are you a writer?"

Corcoran says yes, he wants to be a writer.

He looks up suddenly and Corcoran sees he's got a glass eye, which he seems to be holding in with a squint. "What's your name?"

"Tom. Tom Corcoran."

"I'm Jim, by the way. Jim Harrison." Turns out, the Harrison guy is a writer.

The next night: It's busy and Corcoran can't even catch a piss break.

"Hey, Tom!"

It's Harrison coming toward him, with this tall guy with the kind of scraggly hair that you rarely see outside of California.

"How you doing?" Harrison asks.

"All right," Corcoran says. "Been swamped tonight."

"This is my buddy Tom," Harrison says, thumbing the big tall guy.

"How you doin'?" Corcoran asks, then immediately turns away, taking care of a weaving girl standing a little too close. "Two or three?"

"Two. No, wait. *Three.* Yeah, three."

Corcoran looks up again and catches the big man's eye. He can see right away he's been stung, his eyes smarting. But then someone else wants Taco Tom's attention. Next time he glances toward Harrison, he sees that he's backed away with the big guy, that other Tom, and he sees the eyes are still wounded.

Christ, the big man's face seems to say, *I've been reviewed in the* New York Times. *They're calling me the Hemingway of my generation. And now I'm dismissed . . . by a fucking taco seller.*

And that was the beginning of a lifelong friendship between

Tom Corcoran and Thomas McGuane, the most revered writer of his generation.

Tom McGuane was no monk. He was a hippie, tall and lank-haired, stoned and inscrutable, conversant with all of the major inebriants of his generation. He loved being with close friends, loved to fish, loved to have a good time. He seemed like the perfect candidate to be a Key West Writer, but he was so goddam serious.

Jim Harrison was serious too, but he knew how to relax, open a bottle of wine, invite some friends over, throw a few things in a saucepan, have some more wine, and invite some more friends over. Harrison carried a gleam in that good eye, and squeezed *pleasure* with intensity. Working, he was a literary packhorse, but when that part of his day was done, when the clock hit 5:00, not 4:59 but 5:00, he set aside the world of letters and began to live the rich and full life his work so well celebrated.

McGuane suffered the affliction of always knowing exactly what he wanted to do. He was single-minded to the extreme. From the time he hit double digits, before he had any idea of *what it was* he wanted to write, he knew he wanted to be a writer. "I thought writers were extremely romantic," he recalled. As a kid, he embraced some of the usual boys' books with handsome hairy-chested heroes. Thor Heyerdahl's *Kon-Tiki*, with its rousing story of crossing the Pacific on a raft, made a strong early impression. Because he devoured adventure books, he assumed all writers lived such wide-open Cinemascope lives. Soon he moved on to Jack London, and then began working his way through Thoreau and Tolstoy. He took up literature with vigor, feasting on the great American writers, then the English, then the Russian. He loved Turgenev, Gogol, and Chekhov—Chekhov was his solace. "His writing leads from perception to perception," McGuane said later in life, as a mature writer. "There is nothing in his writing that is bad for a writer, in terms of influence."

McGuane and Harrison were friends by virtue of their roles in the literary trade. Both were from Michigan and had met at Michigan State. Both loved the Manly Arts of Hunting and Fishing and Drinking and Fucking. But though you could joke around with Jim, McGuane was just *too serious*.

So Harrison goaded him. *"Tom! Come on, Tom! Let's go over to Duval, eat some tacos, drink a couple beers, take a few bites out of the crowd, and see what's going on."*

Harrison wanted to save McGuane from the clutches of academia. If you wrote small-but-important novels and didn't sell them to Hollywood, then you probably had to get a day job as a teacher, usually some English professor gig, looking out on rows of moony adolescent girls, shooting their goo-goo eyes up at a handsome devil like McGuane. Sure, McGuane could have gone that way, but what would have fed his libido would have ruined his art.

The problem with being an academic writer and a teacher was that it made you sedentary. Instead of being in the world, you watched it from the ivory tower window.

"I like images of the natural world that seem to rise naturally, rather than some MFA from Iowa, or Compton State Junior College of the Creative Arts," Harrison said. The graduate degree in creative writing was, in his view, meaningless. "It's a pyramid scheme, see? You can have MFAs if you can then have MFAs that will teach more MFAs. And they keep publishing in these little, little magazines, and they keep track of that."

Instead of indulging in academia's reverse snobbery, Harrison asked himself—and McGuane—the big question: *What's* wrong *with going for the big one?*

What was wrong with going for all of the literary gusto, of trying to hook the big fish and reel it in? These academics and MFAs and

Ph.D.s, all they seemed to want to do was write their smug little novels for their smug little friends, experiments in fictions—yes, they added the s when they were particularly pretentious—that showed an utter contempt for people other than themselves. They had no interest in a life outside their own, and reveled in a world of limited standards of human acceptability.

"I told a rather snotty younger novelist that he was going to have trouble eventually because he won't talk to people," Harrison said. "I think it's very helpful to talk to everyone. You don't know what's going to happen. I think academic writers have that problem of insufficient exposure because they're stuck in one place for at least nine months of the year."

So McGuane avoided becoming stuck in one place. But if it wasn't to go fishing, it took a lot of effort to get him out of his new house on Ann Street, cheek by jowl with the temptations of the Duval Street bars. It was a house of many assembled parts. The front-porch columns came from Lexington, Kentucky, where they had adorned the porch of the artist Henry Faulkner. Key Wester John Hopkins, then renovating his Ann Street house, admired the columns during a Kentucky visit and Faulkner said, *You want 'em?* And so they were sent to Key West. When one stepped off that overly regal porch, a walkway led to the street—and the walkway was made of bricks from the original Duval Street.

Just a block from Duval, the island's one-stop alcohol-and-party center, McGuane lived within sniffing distance of rotting puke in the gutters. Yet he managed—for a while, at least—to avoid those temptations. All eyes were on him. He was a Writer, after all. The Hemingway of his generation; that's what the critics were saying. And here he was, in Papa's old hometown.

If he wasn't writing or making love to his wife or playing with his son, he didn't have much of an interest in anything beyond fishing and literature. He and Becky stayed home in the evening and sat together reading after little Tom was in bed. They were secure in their island cocoon.

So Harrison made it his mission to reintroduce Tom McGuane to life, in all of its majesty and folly.

Thomas Francis McGuane III was born on December 11, 1939, in Wyandotte, Michigan, before the town was fully swallowed by the urban sprawl of Detroit. Eventually, after becoming successful, the McGuane family moved a bit farther southeast, away from the industrializing Detroit, to the more bucolic town of Grosse Isle. There the family settled into a century-old house on a bluff that looked across the river to Canada. The house had been a stop for the Underground Railroad.

Tom McGuane's father—Tom the Second—owned Tom McGuane, Inc., a successful automobile-parts manufacturing company in Detroit, but he was not native. Both Tom the Second and Alice Torphy McGuane were from Massachusetts. He came from Ayer, a small town nestled in the Nashoba Valley, thirty-five miles northeast of Boston, where his father worked on the railroad. "He came up hard and he grew up during the Depression," McGuane said of his father. The elder McGuane ended up winning an athletic scholarship to Harvard, but rather than reveling in this invitation to the table, it soured him even more. McGuane said his father "went to Harvard as a simple poor Irish kid," and "it left him socially embittered because he was despised by the Gentleman C types at Harvard, the legacies and air-head Brahmins." Tom the Second rowed on the school's crew, pushing back his anger with each oar stroke. "He had a bitter beef with the cards he'd been dealt but also had a huge capacity for work," McGuane said. "He was an alcoholic all his life and never missed a day's work." He met his future wife, Alice Torphy, while she was home for the summer from Regis College. She was staying with her family in Fall River, a coastal town south of Boston. She studied English, and one of the things that attracted her to Tom the Second, aside from his rugged good looks, was his knowledge of books. They shared a devotion to reading.

After marriage, with some of Alice's family's money, Tom the Second established the auto-parts business, requiring a move to Michigan, the center of that industry, and away from their shared love of Massachusetts. They never felt that Michigan was home, no matter how long they lived there. They were strangers in a strange land, Catholics in a bastion of Protestantism. McGuane went to "a crappy little parochial grade school," which he despised. He had few friends (there were only eight students in his grade) and even the playground didn't offer any pleasures. "I never had the nerve to go on the monkey bars or swing," he recalled. "I was just totally afraid of other children. As a young kid, I was a terrible student. I remember that I was so uninterested in reading that my parents tried to bribe me to read books."

The McGuanes didn't want to abdicate their eastern sensibilities and interests, even though they lived in the wild west of Detroit. They held on to the things they loved about their culture, and they read the authors the middle class of their generation read: Ernest Hemingway, F. Scott Fitzgerald, Thomas Wolfe, and so forth. The McGuanes loved language and literature and passed that love on to their three children, particularly their eldest son. "I grew up in a household with lots of books," McGuane said, "and there was a family magic about the printed word." Words were savored at the family table. "I like language that makes me crazy, that's like tidal movement," McGuane added. "My passion is language and human perception, not necessarily in the form of stories."

Using language was a spectator sport in the household. McGuane early on recognized the power of words used well, and what force he could wield with this skill. It helped him deal with his fear of his schoolmates. He began to escape the grips of fear "by becoming known as a sort of wit, as being a funny person. People began to like me for that." It was a defense mechanism that avoided conflict. "You know how all young boys want to be tough guys," he said. "Well, I was a tough guy because I said a lot of outrageous, unrepliable things." Soon he found that language was his weapon of choice, when he discovered that he had "the ability to talk your way out of things."

He also learned, from his mother, the power of brevity, which served him well. (His novels would rarely run past 220 pages.) If the eldest son was telling a story and went on too long ("as I tended to do"), his exasperated mother would give him her get-to-the-point look.

"What do you think of cottage cheese?" she would ask.

As young McGuane began his reply, his mother would leave the room in the middle of his sentence.

The point of storytelling, he thus learned, was to tell the story efficiently, with no wasted words.

Other than literature, fishing drove the engine of McGuane's young life. "I conducted a mixed-bag sporting life," McGuane wrote of his early childhood, "catching perch and rock bass on worms, some pike on Daredevils, some bass on a silver spoon." McGuane was always fishing or practicing his cast in the living room, holding his bamboo rod by its Portuguese cork grip.

In the summers, as soon as the last school bell rung for the year, Alice McGuane packed the children off to Fall River, where family awaited. Tom the Second stood in the driveway, saying good-bye to his wife and children: Tom, his sister Marian, and baby boy Joseph.

During those summers, nestled in the bosom of his mother's family, McGuane developed a sense of where he came from, from a family of "heavy-duty Irish." As a young child, he fell in love with the family's ritual storytelling and came to love the art of narrative and the music of language.

"My mother had four or five brothers who were always fantastic storytellers," he said. "My maternal grandmother's house was kind of a through-the-looking-glass place for me; it was just full of people who really valued wise-cracks and uncanny stories—that was the structure of life in that house, and the really unforgivable sin was to go on too long."

Each year, the golden summer ended and Alice McGuane and her children went back to Michigan.

The family was comfortable, but not comforted. Tom the Second "was a very, very hard-working person driven by a lot of things, probably anger as much as anything, and without any vision of a good life, peace, or happiness," McGuane said of his father. "But he left me for a long time with the impression that anger should be your motivation in life. You got up in the morning and you said, 'I'm going to kick somebody's ass today.' "

Tom the Second spent long hours away from home and family. Still with the scholarship chip on his shoulder, he worked harder than anyone else, so that he could finally earn what those Harvard classmates had been given. "My father hated people with money," McGuane remembered, "yet he became one of those people." For years, Tom McGuane battled the assumption that he had grown up a rich kid. His family attained a level of comfort, but it was something the children got to see happen as they grew up.

Years later, McGuane wrote: "I remember when I was twelve, my mother told me that she thought we were now middle class. . . . [I] remember thinking from the look on her face that she thought it was a real achievement."

As McGuane lurched toward his teenage years, there was a good deal of tension between father and son, and the only common ground was on the water. "We had good times together only when fish were present," McGuane said. "When I was a little boy, my father and I were very close, and as I got older and he got more obsessed with his business and became more of an alcoholic, he kind of drifted away from me."

He began high school in Grosse Isle but was held back—*failed,* they avoided saying—in ninth grade, primarily because of discipline and behavior problems. That was the last straw for Tom the Second, and so at the urging of the Grosse Isle principal, Young McGuane was sent to board at Cranbrook Kingswood School in Bloomfield Hills, about thirty-five miles north, on the other side of Detroit.

McGuane embraced certain parts of boarding-school life. He worked his way from junior varsity to varsity on the soccer team. He joined the premed club and wrote humor and advice columns for the school paper, *The Crane.* It was the mid-fifties and the crew-cut nation was awash in conformity under the benevolent governance of that bald guy in the White House. McGuane was different.

"I was not very good about authority," McGuane said of his adolescence. "I was in trouble and in jail when I was young, and I couldn't imagine working for anybody." Writing was his way of not having a boss. By the time he was sixteen, he decided it was time to get past the fantasy of being a writer and actually become one. He began his long apprenticeship in front of the yellow legal pad.

His instructors were not impressed. "I was considered a bad student," he said. "I didn't get much encouragement from teachers."

In 1957, after finishing his junior year at Cranbrook, he decided to spend the summer in Wyoming. Cranbrook was coed, and McGuane, good-looking brute that he was, had attained a girlfriend whose father owned a ranch out West. They could spend the summer together, they decided, if McGuane signed on as a farmhand.

He fell in love with the country, if not with the girl, and began to feel he would end up there. "That was a decisive moment in my life," he recalled. "I knew that I was going to move to the West as soon as I was out of school, and that's pretty much what I did." The ranch was in Sunlight Basin, just east of Yellowstone, on Clarks Fork, which cuts through the mountains, flowing at first southeast, then turning north-east into Montana, where McGuane would eventually make his home.

Back in Michigan at Cranbrook that fall, he felt hunger pangs for his new life in the West, but he managed to graduate in mid-June 1958, spending that summer in Massachusetts again before starting college in the fall. At the University of Michigan, he couldn't even muster a single grade-point for his average. His grades were so low, they could only aspire to the level of failure. After a semester, he left the land of the ugly football helmets and landed at Olivet College, a private church-affiliated school that was in midstate, not far from Kalamazoo and Battle Creek. Removed from the hard-drinking dis-tractions of Ann Arbor, the quintessential college town, McGuane did somewhat better. But only somewhat.

The summer after his disastrous freshman year, he was at Har-vard, taking part in the school's open-admissions program, and studying with Gerald Chapman, the revered creative writing teacher. Chapman recognized McGuane's talent, but feared the young man. "He was so intense it was frightening," Chapman said years later.

McGuane made another run at Ann Arbor in the fall of 1959, but when that again didn't work, he started the new decade back at Olivet. The academic ping-pong ended that fall, when he landed at Michigan State University in East Lansing. There, he found a place where he could flourish.

Up in the north country, Michigan State had a below-the-salt reputation, and consequently had an academic inferiority complex. The University of Michigan (*Big Blue!*) was where the best and the brightest were supposed to go. But McGuane and Jim Harrison were proud products of the school downstate.

"It turned out that the people did relatively well," Harrison said of his Michigan State friends. "I used to get teased by people from the University of Michigan: 'How come you went to the cow col-lege?' I'd say, 'So did McGuane and Richard Ford.' "

McGuane ended up graduating with honors and being admitted to Yale University's School of Drama in 1962.

But he had made a couple of acquaintances at East Lansing, the sort of people who altered the trajectory of another person's life. The first was Portia Crockett, an ethereal beauty and a direct descendant of David Crockett, hero of the Alamo and one-term congressman from Tennessee. The other was Jim Harrison, a poet of enormous talent and literary energy. McGuane married Portia, known as Becky, and began a lifelong friendship with Harrison after reading his first book of poetry. "He wrote me a letter," Harrison said. "We trout-fished and we corresponded ever since."

Define the perfect "writer's wife," and keep in mind it was the mid-sixties. Friends often described Becky McGuane as beautiful, inspirational, nurturing, and quiet, able to hold things together for her obsessed and über-talented husband. If she was the perfect lover, mother, and muse, then that was a good thing, because Tom McGuane was a man on the move and he needed someone who could keep things up and keep them together.

After Michigan State came Yale. At that point, McGuane saw himself as the second coming of Eugene O'Neill, seeking to learn the craft to become a great playwright. Later, when he began writing for film, he was grateful for his course work at Yale. At the time, the fatuity of the show-biz elements drove him to write novels. With a novel, he was the sole proprietor of the characters, the plot, and the themes.

The magnificent Yale library, though, was alone worth his indenture in New Haven. This was when he immersed himself in world literature and became a full-blown bibliophile.

McGuane wrote his first novel, *Fire Season*, during his first year at Yale. He convinced novelist William Styron, then finishing *The*

Confessions of Nat Turner, to champion it during the elder novelist's visit to campus. Styron told McGuane to send the manuscript to his editor at Random House and to drop his name. Editor Robert Loomis rejected the book, but he sent McGuane a letter that made him feel more elated than rejected. To McGuane, the exercise and the commitment were what mattered. And all of the time spent on *Fire Season* was not lost. (Revised, it would eventually become his second published novel, under the name *The Bushwhacked Piano*.)

Tom and Becky traveled to Ireland for the summer of 1964. On their return, he finished his master of fine arts degree and produced his first play. He then took his wife off to Spain and Italy, following a Hemingway trail. He pursued the manly arts and, in Spain, added bullfighting to his literary he-man repertoire. He didn't drink at all. He worked diligently on his manuscripts—more novels—and the young writers he got to know in Europe were stunned by his control and his virtuosity.

That level of restraint would not last.

The friendship with Harrison began as a rivalry at Michigan State, where they had circled each other warily. But after the publication of Harrison's first book of poems, *Plain Song*, in 1965, they began corresponding. The openness of the letters was the foundation of their close friendship. Each wrote three or four letters to the other during an average week. The geographic distance was no barrier. After the barrage of letters began volleying across the Atlantic, McGuane realized he had found the most important friend of his life, a friend with whom he could share his passion for writing. "Whenever we are around each other," McGuane said, "we leave with a new enthusiasm to write. I rely on my conversations with Harrison 'to restore the original luster.'" As Harrison said, "We talk about literature as if it were vital, as if it were a substitute for religion."

McGuane returned to the United States in 1966 and was awarded a prestigious Wallace Stegner Fellowship at Stanford. He had sub-

mitted *Fire Season* with his admission application, and was deemed
to have promise. So with his now-pregnant wife, he moved to California. There he was, near the zip code of the vaunted Summer of
Love, but rather than hanging at the corner of Haight and Ashbury,
he stayed cloistered in Stanford, writing. And writing, and writing.

The Stegner Fellowships were a sign to young writers that they
were On the Way Up. To McGuane, the experience was more of
a shoulder shrug. Stegner was a fine novelist and historian of the
West, but McGuane found him an uninspiring, profoundly mediocre
teacher. But it was Stegner money that bought McGuane time and
a modest income to support his growing family. As unimpressed as
he was by Stegner, he was even more underwhelmed by his fellow
students. In his opinion, they were ignorant of great literature, and
more interested in war protest than fulfilling their promise as artists.
As always, McGuane was the most serious guy in the room. He was
actually writing—another novel, and another. Most of them were
going into the wastebasket, where he felt they belonged (so he said
later), but he was writing.

By the end of his Stegner year, he still did not have the elusive
publishing contract. He'd been playing touch-and-go with an editor
at Dial Press about *Fire Season*, and it looked good for an eventual
publication. But then the editor in chief of the publishing house—
E.L. Doctorow, later to become famous as the author of *Ragtime*—
pulled the rug from under the deal. McGuane wasn't told why, but
after a long courtship, the marriage was called off. By this time,
McGuane was best described as brokenhearted. He looked at the
manuscript that had been nurtured and loved and coddled, and he
could no longer stand it.

There was nothing else he could do. *Nothing.* All he knew how
to do was write, so he went back to it. He concocted an odd, knotty
story about two friends doing a destructive manhood dance in northern Michigan, alternately destroying each other and the century-old

sporting club to which they belonged. One of the men was the son of an auto-parts magnate, and both of them were immersed in the manly arts of hunting and fishing. But McGuane's life was only the jumping-off point for the narrative. He used himself "to sort of lift the edge off of the material so that I can enter." A month and a half after the Doctorow smackdown, he had a new novel. He sent it to Harrison first, and awaited his friend's judgment.

He was always impatient and couldn't stand waiting, so he took off on a ramble. He ended up on a beach in Mexico, alone, curled in a sleeping bag by the fire. He was roused one morning by a police officer, summoning him to the local telegraph office. There he got the news: Harrison not only liked the book, he also had sent it to Simon & Schuster, and the company was offering McGuane a contract to publish *The Sporting Club*.

It was 1968. The book advance wasn't much, but sale of the movie rights allowed Tom and Becky McGuane to make a couple of major purchases: a small ranch in Montana's Paradise Valley and a home in Key West.

"I first came to Key West as a boy with my father to go fishing," McGuane recalled, noting that his father would say during these visits, " 'What the hell is everyone doing here anyway? Why aren't they up north working?' He thought the whole world was falling apart, to see all these young people driving down here to be part of the sweaty pile."

But it was something else that brought McGuane back. "When I decided to come back . . . it was because I associated the island with writers, readers, and writing." There was a lot to love about the island—the climate, the magnificent waters for fishing, the exotic tropical atmosphere, and, of course, the ghost of Ernest Hemingway ambling down the streets. When *The Sporting Club* appeared, the big-time book critics compared McGuane to the old man, one of them even calling him the Hemingway for the Love Generation. So McGuane figured he might as well come to the island and deal with the shadow.

The rest of the country was becoming one polyester world of sameness. Golden arches rimmed the western deserts. Interstate highways ironed out differences between states, blanding the country so thoroughly that Georgia looked like Wisconsin and Tennessee looked like Oregon. But for the horizon, it was all the same. There was great movement toward the center, and that made more room on the fringes.

Key West was the end of the road, the last outpost for an American original, a place closer to a foreign capital than to the largest city in its state. It was, in 1970, a blend of locals, the old-line Conchs, and those resolute hippies who'd come south searching for a place to test-drive the dreams articulated in the sixties. Here they'd try to unfold the blueprint they'd drawn up for the peace-love-and-understanding society that hadn't gone over up on the mainland. The hard hats and the love-it-or-leave-it types hated all of that hippie blather, and they especially despised all of the antiwar sentiment and the mistreatment of the troops coming back from Vietnam. So things were at a stalemate up on the mainland. But here in the Keys . . . *this* was the place to give those Utopian pipe dreams some air. Let's see what happens. Even the old Conchs shoulder-shrugged. If Key West had a motto, it was "Hell, We'll Do Anything Once."

It was this laissez-faire, along with the fishing and the literary atmosphere, that drew McGuane to Key West like a siren. "I thought for a long time of living in the West Indies," McGuane said, but "I didn't want to get out of touch with the culture that I was raised on, and which I had something to say about."

This was where his art could flourish, McGuane thought, and where he wanted to raise his family.

"It was a great place," he recalled, "but none of us had a pot to piss in basically. You could do your work and the other people around town were trying to write something. There was no pressure on us from the outer world to do anything."

6

The Boys

Always do sober what you said you'd do drunk. That will teach you to keep your mouth shut.
—Ernest Hemingway

The people of Key West are proprietary about sunset. They regard it as municipal property, and if the town fathers could figure out how to do it, they'd slap a tax on it.

But they could also argue for a patent on morning. Nobody does daybreak like Key West. Smell Cuban bread baking. At Five Brothers Grocery, get a whiff of the *sofrito* they put on the stove as soon as they unlock the doors. Brown, creased old *señors* gather at the coffee stand on Flagler, drinking fragrant, rip-your-head-off espresso and arguing about the politics on that island ninety miles away. The gringos wait for their *café con leche* and cheese bread, eavesdropping on the old men, trying to pick out words from the gutteral Spanish. A Buick Riviera comes to a dead stop in the middle of Flagler to let a rooster cross the street, and a woman in a flowered straw hat waves as she bicycles her Beach Cruiser past the boys from City Electric as they sip coffee from plastic cups and contemplate getting into their truck to start their rounds.

It's worth setting an alarm—or staying up all night—to enjoy this gentle, sun-drenched spectacle: the scent of seaweed, mingling with frangipani and gardenias; the sea and its cacophony of fragrances; the good-natured incoherence as people wait for their first *café con leche* to take the edge off the too-bright morning.

There isn't a change of seasons, but there is a change of smells on the island during that time the rest of the country calls fall-to-winter. Key West luxuriates as it awakens, stretching like a cat arching after a nap, basking in the mingled scents of sea, flowers, and cooking.

McGuane began a routine of spending half his year at his ranch near Livingston, Montana, and the rest of his time in Key West, which he soon grew to love. "It's a southern town without the burden of southern history," he said. "I like the fecund smell that the island has. I love to be out on the ocean . . . and the ocean is one of the last frontiers where we can live in a civilized way next to that great wilderness."

Jim Harrison came to visit, and to drink and fish. He read McGuane's new work, the seven-thousandth rewrite of *Fire Season*, and pronounced it ready to be loosed upon the world as the follow-up to *The Sporting Club*. Soon the big man had another Simon & Schuster contract and another sale to the movie industry.

McGuane had no bigger fan than his champion, Harrison, and he in turn played a major part in jump-starting Harrison's career as a novelist.

Harrison was a poet. He had gone an unusual route, bringing out his first collection of poetry, *Plain Song*, without serving the long apprenticeship of publishing a poem here and another poem there, usually in some microscopic literary review from a liberal-arts college, gradually earning his way up to a collection. Harrison started at the top of the poetry heap. An editor at the prestigious independent publishing company W.W. Norton saw a Harrison poem and asked if he had enough for a book. *Sure,* he lied, then began writing like hell.

But when Harrison had an accident, McGuane suggested his friend put his recuperating time to good use.

"I wrote *Wolf,* my first novel, partly because of Tom," Harrison said. "I'd fallen off a cliff grouse hunting. I was in traction for five weeks in a hospital and Tom says, 'While you're laid up, why don't you write a novel?' We'd been talking about it. I scored the novel musically first. I just made a structure of ups and downs . . . flats . . . I scored it like a symphony. So Tom said, 'Why don't you write it?' So I did."

Harrison had been subsisting on grants and English-department paychecks, but the grant money ran out and he had to rely on the largesse of his brother, who was a respected university librarian back east. He sent him the only copy of his *Wolf* manuscript, hoping he would be able to make photocopies for distribution to editors.

Though he was in a forced isolation when he wrote *Wolf,* Harrison was a man out and about in the world—from where his stories, his characters, and his lyricism came. Harrison feared that McGuane's voluntary isolation not only was bad for him as a writer, distancing himself from the non-sedentary lives on which writers feed, but also created a psychological seclusion, a moat that separated Tom and Becky McGuane—and now their new son, Thomas IV—from the rest of the world.

So Harrison took him out of the house for the short walk to Duval, introduced him to Taco Tom, and showed him around, bringing him out like a blinking mole. It was to be a long, slow process, getting this literary Boo Radley out into the world. For every baby step into the lives of the Conch bourgeois, McGuane took two steps back toward solitude, to the edge of artistic loneliness and isolation.

When painter Russell Chatham came for his annual time in residence at Chez McGuane, he was startled by McGuane's work ethic. "He would never go out to a bar with Jim and I," Chatham said. "Tom wasn't drinking and so he never left the house, so Jim and I would just strike out."

Chatham was a serious fisherman in his native California and in the trout streams of his adopted Montana. He was still learning when it came to fishing the flats, but there was no doubt that he was good.

Guy de la Valdene was also a serious and superb fisherman. He was an honest-to-God French count who'd been introduced to McGuane by fishing guide Woody Sexton a couple of years before, when the McGuanes had rented a place on Summerland Key. Valdene was learning the flats from Sexton, serving an apprenticeship under the talented guide. Sexton realized that because of Valdene's literary interests, he would get along with the young writer.

And that's how these friendships were formed: *Russ, this is Guy. Guy, this is Jim. Jim, this is Russ.*

McGuane was the hub who brought these spokes together around the turn of the seventies. Valdene (his first name is pronounced like de Maupassant's) had such a fine income that he could afford to be nearly a full-time sportsman, yet he was also gifted as a writer.

Within the group, there were several levels of connection. Chatham and Harrison loved to carouse together. Valdene often joined, but only during the period when he was divorced. Harrison was not as serious about fishing as Chatham, and when it came to fishing seriousness, Chatham couldn't hold a candle to McGuane and Valdene.

"I was kind of the rich sporting friend," Valdene said. "All I did was fish."

Valdene first began going to the Keys with his wife and small children. His early days with Chatham, Harrison, and McGuane were G-rated. When he got to know McGuane, he fell in love with Becky McGuane's homemade chicken-salad sandwiches, which she'd pack in the skiff's cooler. But for the locale, it wasn't much different from an Andy-and-Opie fishing expedition, except that Valdene and McGuane were more serious and single-minded than the typical day-tripper on the water.

"Guy would pull a skiff for thirty miles, looking for fish," McGuane marveled. He put himself with Valdene as the most serious sportsman of the group. Harrison would fish, but after a few hours in the motherloving sun, he and Chatham would begin agitating about the bars and the women ashore.

"It was just kind of unwritten that Tom wasn't going out with us," Chatham said. "I mean, we weren't misbehaving that bad at that time. We just wanted to go out and have some drinks. And just be out. It wasn't like we had some great program going. We weren't getting laid or anything like that."

Valdene remembered hearing someone describe Chatham, Harrison, and himself as "bad influences" on McGuane. "We were portrayed as these three fellows who came down and partied and kept him away from his serious work," Valdene recalled. "In Key West, it was very tempting to do whatever you wanted to do."

Corcoran learned a lot during his stint as Taco Tom, soaking up the salt-of-the-earth stuff he felt that writers needed in order to remove the academic stench from their writing and restore a connection to everyday experience. Pushing tacos also helped him make some good connections—first Tennessee Williams and now this odd couple, Harrison and McGuane.

"What I really wanted to do, of course, was write," Corcoran said. "I thought all I needed was a hammock and a rum drink and a portable typewriter. I actually did write an alleged novel, which wound up very bad and I threw it away."

McGuane, meanwhile, was fresh off selling his first two books to Hollywood. The show-biz hipsters now saw him as the next big thing, the long-haired, drug-generation Hemingway for the hippie demographic. The summer before, a couple of stoners with a hand-held camera had filmed a glorified biker movie that redrew the rules in Hollywood. Now everyone was looking for the next *Easy Rider.* So McGuane came to mind: *He has long hair, right? Shit, he looks like he just walked off the* Easy Rider *set. And he writes books? Damn, he's our boy. Sign him up to write screenplays.*

And so, like the mortal drudge he was when it came to work, Tom McGuane began researching and writing for the movies.

Before long, he had his new friend, Tom Corcoran, watching his every move, learning to write screenplays at the elbow of Quick-Study Boy.

Corcoran lasted ten weeks as Taco Tom. He trained understudies who took over the taco bike for Pancho's. In the meantime, Corcoran went to work tending bar at the Old Anchor Inn, one of the legendarily sleazy bars in a town with no shortage of such things.

"People slept in their cars behind the bar," Corcoran recalled. "The restrooms often flooded; you walked on bricks to keep your shoes dry. Men in clothes swiped from clotheslines gambled tens and twenties at the pool table. The picket fence lining the sidewalk was erected to appease the city; there had been too many complaints of saloon patrons falling out the front door."

The health department was not vigilant then. "Dogs would sleep on the bar," recalled Dink Bruce, one of the town's local celebrities.

In those days before Key West was a part-time playground for the very rich, the Old Anchor Inn was the great equalizer for the town's residents, both "the natty and the ratty." It was the sort of place where an out-of-work actor might recite the soliloquy from *Hamlet* while balancing a mug of beer on his forehead.

Bud and Dorothy MacArthur kept the Old Anchor Inn running, bringing in $6.99 cheapo charcoal grills from Sears and cooking burgers and weenies by the back door, sometimes spilling the indoor picnic out into the vacant lot behind the bar. Friendships formed like amoebae: this couple brought in two more couples, who brought in three singles and five more couples, and before long the place was filled.

For locals, who knew it as the Snake Pit, the Old Anchor Inn was a haven for people who pounded their drinks. It wasn't the sort of place that really bothered with the visiting proles from Ohio. Once, a guy with a wooden leg unscrewed it, filled up the hollow append-age with beer, and passed it around the bar. This was no place for the faint of heart.

Corcoran was a natural bartender. He was good slinging the booze and the bullshit, and he knew how to rock a jukebox. He had passed this skill on to Judy, now three months pregnant and tending bar for Captain Tony. She became expert at squeezing the life out of that jukebox as well. They'd work into the wee hours, meet for the walk home, and fall into bed every night just before dawn, stinking of cig-arettes and rotting beer.

But Corcoran lasted only six weeks at the Old Anchor Inn. He was man enough to withstand the frenzy of the crowd and the occasional errant spew of puke. In fact, it was his cool in these situations that got him another job offer. Talent such as his would not go unrecognized in a small town with a big bar scene.

A guy named Vic Latham came in one day, had a couple of drinks, and had an alcohol-inspired epiphany.

"Corcoran," he said, "why'n't you come work with me?"

Latham managed the Chart Room, the bar attached to the Pier House Resort. He had ties to New Orleans, so he was a pure profes-sional when it came to booze and saloons. He wanted to turn the Chart Room into something special and had a vision of tag-teaming Corcoran with an out-of-work shrimper, a raconteur named Phillips

Clark who'd been hanging around the bars, making some noise. Clark was already on board.

Latham, Corcoran, and Clark: They became the Holy Trinity of good times in Key West, starting that spring in 1970. Corcoran's pals from the taco days started showing up there to drink, listen to the music, and hang out, watching the tourists. Here was this funky little bar, mostly locals leaning over the mugs of beer, and it was right in the middle of a fancy-ass tourist resort, the Pier House. Three of the Chart Room's walls were windows, looking out on the pier and the bay, so tourists stumbling by might look in at some of America's finest writers and artists, as if preserved under glass. Sometimes, those fine writers and artists were looking out at the Pier House crowd, checking out the women brave enough to go topless on the resort's sundeck.

Harrison loved the Chart Room, and even got reluctant Tom McGuane to come drink a beer there on occasion. When their other friends were visiting—Valdene, the nobleman and sportsman, and Chatham, the gifted artist friend from Montana—the Chart Room was their bar of choice.

Harrison's plan to draw out McGuane was working. At the Chart Room, McGuane dipped his toes in the waters of sociability. Valdene said McGuane was "definitely the fulcrum" for the gang being assembled. "Jim and Tom had gone to Michigan State together," he remembered, "and then Tom met Russell Chatham in California. Tom was Jim's friend, and became my friend, and Chatham's friend, and the three of us came down basically to visit him. I always had a boat, and Tom had a boat, and we would not necessarily always fish together, but we kind of worked the fishing out."

Harrison said McGuane's "obsession with the sporting life . . . caused a dozen lasting friendships for a dozen friends in Key West and Montana." As men are wont to do, Harrison expressed his fondness for his friends—Chatham, in this case—with insults.

"Chatham is a pig," Harrison wrote in a tribute to the great artist, "a glutton, an alcoholic, occasional dope fiend, a cook of the highest caliber, a faultless wine expert; he looks like a geek, is terribly out of shape, often lazy and irascible, runs from trouble . . . the most outrageous sex maniac I've ever known, a manic-depressive, a lousy husband and provider, a lout, an incredible angler, a financial wimp and swindler, a kind, generous, curiously noble, and implausibly faithful friend."

Somehow, into this mix fell Valdene, the family man. He'd bring his wife and children down, but they wearied of the daily fishing on the flats and soon went home. Valdene would stay. "We fished," he said, "but we also partied."

Valdene's life story reads like an adventure novel, beginning with his French father's escape from war-torn France in a purloined Nazi submarine. The family landed, quite rich, in Palm Beach at war's end, when Valdene was born. He had a European-boarding-school education, accented by summers fishing and guiding in the Bahamas. He was a true gentleman of leisure when he was introduced to Tom McGuane on Summerland Key one afternoon. McGuane had written his first major piece for *Sports Illustrated*, called "The Longest Silence." Valdene had done a question-and-answer for *Field and Stream* about sailfishing with a fly rod. They exchanged compliments, and McGuane sent Valdene a note: "By the way, would you like to come fish in Montana in October?"

Their friendship grew from there. When McGuane got the Ann Street house in Key West in 1970, Valdene became a regular visitor. "I would start coming down for tarpon," Valdene recalled, "and we started fishing together."

It was through one of these McGuane-led fishing trips that Harrison formed his artistic bond with Chatham. Chatham was nearly the same age, had been born in San Francisco, and had been raised in a number of towns in northern California. By the time he made his first visit to Key West, he was a successful painter—"successful," of course, being a relative term in the world of painting. He'd done his time sleeping in his van, but he had been having one-man shows since he was twenty. Now, in his early thirties, he was making his Key West debut.

"In those days, it was a much smaller scene," Chatham recalled. "We were told in no uncertain terms not to go over to the shrimp docks at night." Still a roughened seaport town with a complement of sailors, there could be trouble—for the unholy trinity of homosexuals, drug addicts, and hippies. With his extravagantly long hair, McGuane was a likely target. Chatham, too, had wavy and flowing blond locks that were controversial among certain sailors and local rednecks.

So they clustered together, fished during the day, drank at the Chart Room all evening. They all cooked. Harrison was the most elaborate chef; he could spend three days preparing a meal, but he bowed and scraped before Chatham. "He's perhaps the greatest cook I know," Harrison said.

Life was good. If the goal was an artistic utopia, they were off to a good start.

They would spend the day fishing, then "The Boys"—as they were known—came into the Chart Room for a late-afternoon happy hour, to discuss their catches and their misses and drink the heat out, and keep the conversation at hurricane force until early evening.

"Because Harrison was more of a night owl than Tom, he'd be around in the evenings after dinner," Corcoran said. "He'd sit at the bar, regale folks with tales. It was only a five-minute walk back to Ann Street. Harrison was more of a bar guy than the others anyway. He enjoyed company and conversation."

The owner of the place was Walter Perry, who posted these rules and ordered the Chart Room's brain trust—Latham, Corcoran, and Clark—to follow them:

- Our drinks will cost 25 cents more than any other place in town.
- Do not serve a drink you'd be ashamed to serve in your own living room.
- Locals get every fourth drink free.
- Local politicians get every third drink free.

"Within two years' time, we made the Chart Room *the* institution in Key West," Corcoran recalled. The posted bar rules, naturally, drew all the local pols and muckety-mucks, so public policy was debated and (often) made at the tables.

Music was vital, and Corcoran took charge of the Chart Room's. He was dealt a pretty poor hand, a rotten house-brand turntable and only three albums.

Corcoran's tech savvy kicked in. He got a cheap car cassette player and wired it to play through the turntable, and he began making tapes for the Chart Room. They were mixes—different artists, different styles, different moods. Corcoran was the Arturo Toscanini of mix tapes. He knew how to pull the strings of his audience.

Pretty soon, people were coming for the music almost as much as for the beer.

"The Chart Room was a trip," said Murphy, everyone's favorite underage hippie-chick regular. "It had all the Bubbas who ran local government. There were lawyers, boat captains, writers, hippies, and bums. The Bubba System worked overtime there. You put that mix together, with all those people sitting around and drinking and telling lies, and that's the place that virtually ran Key West."

In a town full of bars, the Chart Room stood out. But there were several other popular hangouts. "The bar scene *was* the scene," Murphy recalled. "There was Howie's, a piano bar. All the hot Navy pilots hung out there. Sloppy Joe's was for the tourists and the old-timers. Captain Tony's?" Her brow furrowed. "That was sort of a mixed bag. The Anchor Inn?" She laughed, shaking her head. "That place scared the tourists away. Then there was Louie's Backyard. Even back then, in the early seventies, it was kind of upscale. That didn't mean people weren't snorting coke by the back bar. Back then, they partied pretty hard."

Later, when she was drinking age, Murphy did some time as a barmaid, working at Sloppy Joe's and at the Half Shell Raw Bar, an open-air saloon and restaurant on the docks at Schooner Wharf.

"One of my regulars was J.P. Donleavy," she recalled of her time at Sloppy's. The author of *The Ginger Man* didn't advertise his notoriety and Murphy didn't realize who he was until nearly the end of her tenure slinging drinks. "He kept to himself. He always ordered the same drink—Belz Scotch—and used cash; no credit cards. Once you'd get him going, though, he was talkative. But he always came in alone and left alone."

But it was the Chart Room that regularly attracted the locals in the power structure as well as the hottest writing and artistic talent.

Corcoran became fast friends with Phil Clark, his fellow Chart Room bartender. "We looked at Phil as some kind of wild Caribbean adventurer," Corcoran said. "He'd spent a lot of time in the Virgin Islands with characters of dubious repute, and Phil had already been busted for trying to fly some pot in from Jamaica. He had been a bartender in New York, claimed to have dated [model and actress] Lauren Hutton before she was famous, lived with the Mamas and Papas on the beach in St. Thomas, hung out with gunrunners and professional gamblers. Phil had plenty of tales to tell, and occasionally one of his old cohorts would breeze through Key West, and would fit the mold of modern-day pirate."

The one thing on which everyone agreed was that McGuane was
the eye of this particular storm. Still serious about his writing, he
wouldn't renounce his spartan work regimen, but he did begin to
see socializing not as an evil but perhaps as something energizing
that could provide him fuel for his writing. Everything, of course,
remained secondary to his writing.

To those who had thought him a drudge, McGuane could in his
defense argue that his work ethic was paying off. When Hollywood
bought the rights to the rewritten *Fire Season*—now known as *The
Bushwhacked Piano*—he sold the Ann Street place and purchased his
second home in Key West. This house on Von Phister Street was in a
tonier neighborhood, just a mile across the island, but another world
from the drunken debauchery and temptations of Duval Street. The
new place was near the Casa Marina, Henry Flagler's enormous resort hotel at the end of the continent. The neighborhood was quiet,
home to the clerisy of Key West, a better place for his wife and young
son, with a guesthouse out back he could use as a writer's studio. It
was as close to a cloistered suburban life as the crowded little island
could allow. Here he was in paradise, but because of his seclusion,
he might as well have been in Winnipeg. His guesthouse had all the
amenities—a bathroom and a small kitchen, swirling, burnt-orange
Cuban tiles throughout—that fought off all of the excuses to leave
and avoid The Work until that day's pages had been written and
stacked neatly on the table. The guesthouse was his rectory, where he
worshipped Quality Lit and hoped to add to the canon of American
letters. As monk or galley slave, he labored away in the little hut for
most of the day. A bookworm, he called himself. A man of letters.
That was his life. *The next Hemingway.*

7

Nowhere to Hide

*Little islands are all large prisons: one cannot look at the sea
without wishing for the wings of a swallow.*
—RICHARD BURTON

Despite his occasional test drive of life as a Key West nightlife figure, McGuane continued to see himself as a Serious Writer, and to act like one. He still put in his time in front of the legal pad every day, even though he didn't spend as many hours as he used to laboring in the guesthouse. He liked to hunt and fish, but his work always came first. Now that he was on the party circuit, it was difficult—but still, work came first.

His dedication to his craft became part of his public image. Whenever a book reviewer or a magazine essayist searched for a name of a writer who had such seriousness of purpose, it was usually McGuane's name that got pulled from the ether.

Even his old man had to admit that McGuane had something. Bookish man that he was, lifelong reader, sideline participant in literature,

Tom the Second might have felt twinges of envy as he regarded his son's career. *The Sporting Club* was no compulsive page-turner. And good for that. Tom the Second recognized literature, and literary aspirations, when he saw them. So he didn't care if *The Andromeda Strain* outsold *The Sporting Club*. That wasn't the point. The critics liked the book. It earned fine reviews, as one of those small-but-important novels. And McGuane's editor was raving about *The Bushwhacked Piano*, which—in its rewritten form—featured Key West as a character.

So how much success did McGuane need in order to impress his old man? He was a Writer—something his father probably always wanted to be. He was respected, and a film of his work was going to be shown on the big screen. He had earned enough money to have a ranch in Montana and a nice home down here in paradise, the mecca for American writers.

"When my father drank," McGuane recalled, "he would get very nasty about my work. He would ask me, 'Who do you think you are, Ernest Hemingway?' and I would answer, 'Ah, no, I'm a little better than *that*.' Well, then, he'd really go through the ceiling."

Just as Hemingway had his Mob and Williams had his entourage, McGuane began to assemble his gang—Harrison, when he visited; Chatham, the painter; and Valdene, the aristocrat. "I'll tell you what I am," Valdene said. "I'm a rich guy that writes a book every ten years to try to justify his existence. McGuane and Jim Harrison are real serious writers." He also said, "You don't say you are a writer in the same breath with Tom."

McGuane had that talent of assembling people, fertilizing friendships, and watching them grow. Even though they were all part-time residents of Key West, they couldn't avoid becoming involved in the town's tangled political and social structures. They had a notion that the idyllic society they all had dreamed of as the idealistic children of the sixties could actually happen on the two-by-four island. They wanted to see if they could make it so.

―――――――

Key West might have been paradise, but it wasn't without trouble. The little town was the American melting pot, but the ingredients didn't always blend. There was a constant tension between the Cuban population and the ruling Caucasian class. After the 1959 revolution, a lot of Cubans had escaped Castro and landed in the section of Miami known as Little Havana. In the early sixties, many Key West Cubans headed north. But tensions between blacks and whites began boiling. Cubans who came to the States and succeeded, buying into the power structure, became some of the Bubbas in the Bubba system. Since they'd fled communism, they were inherently conservative and looked at blacks as professional victims.

Key West High School was integrated, but that didn't mean everyone got along.

As the seventies began, it was another minority that was causing consternation. Hemingway's high profile drew the literary he-man types, while the vocal and visible presence of Tennessee Williams started drawing more homosexuals. The *Key West Citizen* bemoaned not only the influx of gays, but also the proliferation of drug and narcotics users and a scraggly bunch of young folks known as hippies. Apparently, the editor of the *Citizen* had a rigid standard of human acceptability. "At least three prominent homosexuals have given 'aid and comfort' to suspected drug users," the newspaper editorialized, noting that it was odd since "homosexuals generally tend to stick with their own group."

By virtue of that grouping in the *Citizen*, the Chart Room was a one-stop center for the degenerates ruining the island, in the minds of the locals. A lot of the local powers that be drank there, but so did pot smugglers, writers, and other ne'er-do-wells.

Hippies seemed to cause the cops the greatest consternation. The homosexuals were not liked, but they were tolerated because they were generally richer and boosted the local economy. "It was a redneck town from before," Corcoran recalled. "But the gay guys had some clout. So they'd say to the cops, in defense of the young hippies, 'Hey, we employ these people, so don't hassle them.' A lot of these gay businessmen were very successful up north, but they cashed out and came south because they were tired of being in the closet. No one was in the closet in Key West. There was a lot of tolerance. After all, there was nowhere to hide. There were no secrets on the island."

Tom Corcoran, Dink Bruce, and other denizens of the Chart Room had the feeling they were in the middle of something—at the very least they were in a great place at a great time—and so they wanted to preserve the moment in words and pictures. *Solares Hill* was the vehicle.

Most of Key West is barely above sea level, but the highest point of land, at eighteen feet, is called Solares Hill. At that elevation it barely has the right to be called a hill. But it is the highest point of all the Keys, and is next to the Key West Cemetery. A local entrepreneur borrowed the hill's name for his new publication.

Solares Hill was an underground magazine, a counterculture alternative to the *Key West Citizen.* Like a lot of small-town newspapers, the *Citizen* was understaffed and looked at the world as a series of meetings to be covered. There was not enough staff to cover the town's real life.

For a small give-away paper, *Solares Hill* packed a strong punch. Tom McGuane published his fishing essay, "The Longest Silence," in July 1971. It had appeared earlier in *Sports Illustrated,* but McGuane wanted to participate in the homegrown publication. James Leo Herlihy, one of the reigning literary stars on the island, due to the success of *Midnight Cowboy,* gave *Solares Hill* a long and thoughtful interview.

Balancing the heavy-duty contributors was a photo feature called "Current and Groovy."

But the publication seemed intent on being the voice of reform (at least reconsideration) of the status quo and middle-class values. *Solares Hill* covered the community as being more than a series of meetings with the city commission, the beautification committee, and the noise-abatement task force.

When Padron's Grocery on Whitehead Street—a business that catered mostly to blacks—was firebombed in 1971, *Solares Hill* interviewed a roundtable of black residents to discuss their fears. The black teacher interviewed requested anonymity and conveyed the greatest anxiety around the table. There had been an *it-can't-happen-here* feeling in the town. This was a *live-and-let-live* place, right?

And there were no other major racial incidents. But the mainland, with all of its violence and the boiling Liberty City ghetto in Miami, was just up the road.

Bill Huckel was founder and owner of *Solares Hill*, and was, in Corcoran's words, "just a good-natured hippie," driven by public service and missionary zeal to publish the paper.

Huckel was a hero to that hippie-artsy community in Key West. "Bill Huckel put a lot of people to work and got a lot of creativity going," Murphy remembered.

Huckel was part of the Chart Room crowd, and so one day he approached Corcoran about doing something for the paper.

"I hear you're a writer," Huckel said.

Corcoran nodded.

"I want you to write something about the Chart Room, about all the news you pick up from all of the city types."

Corcoran refused, calling the idea nonsensical. He saw nothing but a shitstorm if he wrote down what he overheard. But Huckel was persistent. He wouldn't give up pestering Corcoran every time he came into the bar.

Finally, Corcoran gave in—but on his terms. He began writing a column called "Mock Turtle Soup," using "Lyle Johnston" as the byline. The pen name was a throwback to college days. He shared the name with Miami of Ohio classmates Geoffrey Norman and David Standish, who worked for *Playboy* and used "Lyle Johnston" when they wanted to moonlight for a competing magazine.

The "Mock Turtle Soup" columns named names. Corcoran used a lot of what he overheard at the Chart Room, but nothing really damaging. He avoided hard-hitting or controversial stuff, keeping it light and breezy.

Though Corcoran thought his "Mock Turtle" columns were innocuous, he didn't realize the sensitivity of Key West's powers that be.

He was behind the bar one afternoon when he looked up and saw a heavy-duty trio at one of the Chart Room tables. That was not unusual. What struck him was that they were all staring at him: city manager Ron Stack, Sheriff Bobby Brown, and city attorney Manny James.

Corcoran was a little unnerved. He took a piss break and when he squeezed back in behind the bar, he glanced at the table: still, the stares. Finally, the three of them got up and ambled over.

"We had a tip that marijuana is being stored in this bar," Stock said.

"Naw," Corcoran shrugged. But he knew better. Phil Clark kept his product warehoused in a Chart Room air-conditioning duct. "Where'd you hear that?"

Stack yammered on and Corcoran glanced down at one of the bar towels. He saw a marijuana leaf sticking out from the folded towel. *Shit*, he thought. *They rolled that up in the towel while I was pissing.*

The door opened and a uniformed cop came in. *This is really going to go down*, Corcoran thought. Then he remembered: The best defense is a good offense.

He unrolled the towel. "This?" He screwed up his face in disgust.

"This is from a plant, not a baggie. Here . . ."—and then he tossed the leaf into an ashtray, pulled out a match, and quickly lit the evidence. "Look at this!"

He held the burning ashtray in front of Stack, Brown, and James. "That's not marijuana; that's some plant's leaves that fell off." He shoved it under the nose of the sheriff. "Bobby, does that smell like pot?"

The sheriff nodded no.

The three of them watched the "evidence" go up in smoke.

The uniform laughed. There were bad guys and there were look-away guys on the Key West police force. This guy was a look-away. He was still chuckling when he hit the exit.

"Tom." Stack's brow furrowed and he looked Corcoran in the eyes. "We weren't after you. We're after . . . *Lyle Johnston.* Have you seen him around?"

"I heard he died yesterday," Corcoran said.

"Is he still dead?" Stack asked.

"Oh, yes," Corcoran said. "I also heard he would stay that way."

From the time of the pirates—and probably before—Key West had brought out the animal in people, turning men and women into crazed, sweaty creatures. Maybe it was the times or maybe it was the heat, but Key West was ground zero for lust and greed and most of the other deadly sins.

In the twentieth century, the sixties is seen as the decade of free, robust, and wide-open sex. But the so-called sexual revolution took a half decade to get started. By the seventies, things were in full flower.

A knock on the door to borrow a cup of sugar might bring an unexpected result.

Or a woman might walk into the Green Parrot near closing time and point at the bartender. "You! Let's go to your apartment."

"Actually," the bartender says, "I don't have an apartment. It's a house."

The woman scowls. "You want to fuck or not?"

"The house it is," he says.

There was stand-up fucking behind the shelves in Key West Island Books, screwing on the grass in Bay View Park, fucking against the sea wall, blowjobs on the park bench by the courthouse, blowjobs in the front row of the Strand, cunnilingus by the Pier House pool, finger fucking on the Afterdeck at Louie's Backyard. The girls lavished their bodies on the world and men followed in their wake, panting nearly, so horny they would copulate with a wallet.

Lust made people crazy.

Occasionally there'd be howls and snorts of outrage and some self-appointed moral crusader would go all Elmer Gantry about the depravity, but the townspeople shrugged it off. Deep within the town's marrow was that *live-and-let-live* island attitude that's found in greater quantities in Key West than in any other place on Earth.

The seventies were the last gasp of prolific, wanton love. Within the decade, news came that sex could kill you, that there was something out there that penicillin could not cure. As one writer said of the era, that was when the fun stopped.

Lust was a legacy of island life.

Back in Montana, which is where McGuane had established the northern branch of his Key West gang, Russell Chatham was a serious artist, painting massive landscapes that managed to reflect the exacting beauty and astonishing light of Paradise Valley. But when he hit the streets in Key West, usually on a fishing-and-drinking pilgrimage to McGuane's with Jim Harrison, Chatham was a churning urn of sexual funk.

During the first of the annual residences in Key West, Chatham and Harrison bunked at McGuane's house, staying out all night and coming in when McGuane was rising for his day of fishing and writing. The vacations were exhausting because of the nonstop partying-and-angling schedule that Chatham in particular maintained.

Chatham and Harrison were dedicated artists, which meant they were poor. They had to have some scheme to make the Keys trips possible.

"Jim bullshitted *Sports Illustrated* into giving him an assignment," Chatham recalled. "I kind of got in on that thing too. The first three or four stories I ever wrote I sold to *Field and Stream* and a half a dozen others to little magazines—*Saltwater Sportsman* and stuff—but the first story I ever submitted to *Sports Illustrated,* they bought. I was at the fuckin' top of the heap the first time out. The way it worked was if you gave them an idea and they okayed the idea, then you were on an expense account. You went where you were going to go and you did what you were going to do and they paid all the expenses. And if you turned the story in and they didn't like it, they rejected it. But they still paid your expenses. How could you fuckin' lose?"

The freelance assignments were more important, however, for underwriting playtime for The Boys.

It was a simple plan. "You could fly to Key West for a few hundred bucks," Chatham said, "and once we were there, Guy paid for the house and for the food and everything. He'd rent a house with a swimming pool. Fuck, it was luxurious. We had to have some place for the girls to get naked."

And disrobing was the first step in the objective. In terms of getting women naked, the Picasso of the form was Dink Bruce.

Everyone in town knew Dink Bruce. His father, Toby, had been a great pal of Ernest Hemingway's, so McGuane and other writers sought out Dink for stories of his childhood and what Uncle Ernest was like in private life.

Bruce recalled that when he was assigned in high school to write a paper on the "true meaning" of *The Old Man and the Sea*, he went home and asked a visiting houseguest for help.

"Well, Dink," Hemingway began. "I took the *Pilar* out to go fishing. And I knew this man in Cuba who went fishing and lost his big catch to the sharks. That's what it's about."

Bruce delivered his report to his teacher, who told him he obviously knew nothing about Hemingway and his work.

On the surface a quiet and unassuming man, Bruce was nonetheless masterful at getting women to take off their clothes in his presence. The secret was his boat.

"I just tell women if they want to ride on my boat, clothing is not allowed," he said.

Bruce seemed to cross paths with every celebrity who came through Key West. He didn't seek them out; they found him. In Key West, Dink Bruce was royalty.

One celebrity who befriended Bruce was Pulitzer Prize–winning editorial cartoonist Jeff MacNelly, who paid tribute to Bruce's gift with a painting. It showed Dink Bruce, hand steady on the tiller as he cruises the flats, surrounded with exotic and fantastically large-breasted naked women. MacNelly gave Bruce the original, but there are prints all over town, including one over the urinal at the Key West Yacht Club.

Chatham also seemed to have a Vulcan mind meld when it came to women and getting them unclothed.

"The locale suggests promiscuity," Chatham said of Key West. "It's almost like it's an unwritten flashing sign: *If you're here, be prepared to get undressed.* There was shit that went down that you couldn't get away with any other place in America."

Jim Harrison's publisher was Seymour Lawrence, who had been so successful as an editor that he had his own imprint—Seymour Lawrence/Delacorte Press. Sam Lawrence (as he was known to friends) was the model of a respected and successful book publisher, until he hit the streets of Key West with Chatham, who once called himself "one of the greatest pussyhounds of all time."

"Sam was a straight guy—when he got there," Chatham said. "Then we went out to dinner and there was this girl there and she was a fuckin' knockout. We were all looking at her, thinking, 'What's the deal here?' We got done with dinner and Sam had his eye on her. At that time the gay scene had really ratcheted up. It was an outrageous scene those guys had.

"So we ended up in some bar that was a gay bar and there were hundreds of people—noise and lights and shit. This girl looked like a regular, normal girl. She wasn't dressed up like a hooker with lots of makeup. I'm standing there, at the bar, looking at her, and I put my arms around her, put my hands on her ass. She got this funny, weird look in her eyes. I picked her up and sat her up on the bar. I leaned her back, so her head's over by the bartender. People just crowded in on us. I pulled up her dress and she doesn't have any underwear on, and I start eating her pussy. All this while the bartenders are feeding her drinks. And I'm thinking, 'This is what I came here for.' "

The crowd at the bar cheered Chatham's performance with the girl, but then it was time to leave.

"We went over to Buffett's house afterwards," Chatham said, "and Sam thought she was his girlfriend and I said, 'I don't think she's your girlfriend, Sam.' He actually offered her a lot of money to marry him."

Later during that stay, Chatham and Valdene got the girl to come over to their house.

Once inside, she said, "I'm going to fuck both of you guys."

Music to the ears.

They moved toward the bedroom, but before the essential parts were exposed, the girl startled Chatham and Valdene.

"I want you to stretch me," she said.

Chatham didn't understand at first. "What do you mean—
stretch you?"

She outlined the procedure with the precision of a personal
trainer. "One of you guys get hold of my feet and the other one get
hold of my hands and pull as hard as you can."

"Why?" Chatham asked.

"Just because that's what I want you to do."

By this time, Valdene was laughing uncontrollably.

Chatham said, "What we would rather do is fuck you."

She said, "Oh, that's fine too. If you stretch me, that's okay."

And it was.

It was the tropics, Chatham said. That's what made him crazy
with lust. If it weren't for the fishing and the friends, he'd rather
be back in Montana, no matter what the weather there. He was the
dedicated artist in Montana, the loving father of a number of fine
children with former wives. He was social *and* socially conscious—
back in Montana.

But in Key West, he was a man in passion, riding a mad horse.

8

The Failure

The music business is a cruel and shallow money trench,
a long plastic hallway where thieves and pimps run free,
and good men die like dogs. There's also a negative side.
—HUNTER S. THOMPSON

We call her Murphy. She had a first name, a regular girl's first name, and a musical, somewhat common Hispanic surname. But everyone just called her Murphy, her mother's maiden name.

In the counterculture ethos of the time, there were certain types of female hippies. There was that willowy, ethereal, long-hair-parted-straight-down-the-middle girl, channeling Judy Collins and Joni Mitchell, eyes wide and unblinking, like a wren, kind of mysterious and aloof.

And there was that other type—also beautiful, but with an Afro hair explosion, glasses the size of cantaloupes, big beautiful eyes, and a toothy, inviting smile, talking a mile a minute. This type was game for anything—road trip, concert, party . . . you name it.

Murphy was that second type, and everybody loved her.

She was from Miami, but ever since the first time she came to Key West as a teenager, she considered it her home. She was what they called a "Freshwater Conch." She didn't set eyes on the place until she was seventeen, but by the time she was in her early twenties, nobody in the town who knew Murphy could remember a time when she hadn't been around.

Her mother had come to Key West first, liked it, then brought the kids down. This was 1967. Murphy was the oldest, so once the family got settled into Fogarty Cottage, Mom told Murphy she could go off on her own, have some fun, and do whatever she wanted to do. She even gave her a handful of mad money, a reward for all the help with the little ones.

So Murphy, underage but not advertising it, went out on the town, walked into some bars, and met some people. Through those people, she met others. They liked Murphy—who didn't?—and so she became a kind of mascot for the bohemian group of mostly writers and musicians. "I loved it," she said, "but eventually I had to go home."

Back home, high school life couldn't compete with Key West. Luckily, in thanks for being so responsible with the brothers and sisters, Mom gave Murphy a lot of license. Key West was an easy bus trip away during the school year. Summers were wide open, and she spent every moment she could in Key West.

All the aspiring writers and musicians and actors on the island eventually got to know Murphy. And she got to know so many more interesting people than she would ever meet in Miami.

Miami in the late sixties was still the province of retired vacationers from the Midwest and Canada. This was Miami before cocaine and Cubans and coolness. This was your grandfather's Miami.

Miami had a small bohemian scene, but nothing like what Murphy'd seen in Key West. A lot of artist types were Provincetown people. Since the days of Eugene O'Neill, Ray Stannard Baker, and

John Reed, Provincetown, Massachusetts, had been the summertime home for bohemian writing culture. It also became an oasis for homosexuals, who liked the laid-back attitude of the town. But it got cold in the winter, and Provincetown moved south. Tennessee Williams had made the Key West–Provincetown run for years, and others followed suit.

Where there are writers, there are soon songwriters and actors and artists. A lot of the Conchs were conservative folk by nature, and normally they didn't cotton to weird artist types or homosexuals. But that feeling ran up against the island's laissez-faire attitude. One of the nicest things about the people of Key West was that they generally believed in leaving other people alone. "People who live on islands are more tolerant," lifelong resident Dink Bruce explained.

The townsfolk were a diverse lot, but they all genuinely shared the virtue of forebearance. The community was a little bit of everything, with mixtures of Cubans, Bahamians, transplants, and locals with their accents at once gutteral and lilting. As one writer said, it was "an artist's colony, homosexual colony, hippie colony, Cuban colony. . . . If you like to screw sheep and you bring a sheep in the front door, no Key Wester will say a word. Try to sneak a sheep through the back door, and you're in big trouble. It is not that the people care what you do; it's that they have to know about it."

Key West was the reservoir tip at the eastern edge of the country and people came floating down from Provincetown, from Ohio, from way up north, even from Miami.

Somewhere along the way, Murphy met Jerry Jeff Walker.

Jerry Jeff Walker was the perfect name for a country-folk bar singer, made up after he read the job description for sixties singer-songwriter. His real name was Ronald Clyde Crosby and he was from upstate New York. But when he decided to become a sensitive singer-songwriter, his name wasn't filling the halls, so he came up with "Jerry Jeff Walker." Soon, things began to turn around.

Jailed for drunkenness in New Orleans, he shared a cell with an old tap dancer he soon immortalized in his song "Mr. Bojangles," which he recorded for Atco, a revered independent rock and soul label. It was a modest hit. Recorded two years later by the Nitty Gritty Dirt Band, the song sold a million copies. Then it was fair game for every singer on Earth to have a whack at it, and most of them did, from Neil Diamond to Bob Dylan to Sammy Davis Jr.

So in 1970, Walker was living the life, and one night that life took him to South Florida. Florida was a good, warm-weather place to gig. And on a swing through Key West, Jerry Jeff Walker met Murphy.

"He had just recorded a live album in Coconut Grove," she recalled, "and he moved to Summerland Key. He'd just broken up with his wife."

Summerland was just thirty miles up U.S. 1, easy driving distance from Key West, even with a snootful. Walker met Murphy, and before long they were together.

"I got in trouble," Murphy said, "and I had to go home and have a baby."

Walker settled with Murphy and now the baby boy, Justin, in Coconut Grove, to be near Miami's one real folk club, the Flick, which was a regular gig for Walker. He still traveled the folk circuit, sometimes taking Murphy with him (Mom or friends watched the baby), but Coconut Grove became home.

Nashville was an inevitable stop for a folk or country musician in that era. It was still the Old Nashville, with wavy toupees and Nudie suits and the Grand Ole Opry at the Ryman Auditorium. Folk singers and younger country performers were looked down upon as grubby hippies, though that was beginning to change. Bob Dylan, the furry-headed symbol of American Youth, had been recording in Nashville for half a decade. Some of the studio musicians, the "Nashville Cats," as they were known, began growing their hair. Though things were changing, Nashville was still seen by younger musicians as an inevitability.

Walker was visiting Nashville, kissing rings and paying dues, when his music-publishing rep said he wanted to take him out on the town, to wine and dine. The rep brought along another one of his clients, a young kid who seemed to have the worst luck in the world.

Walker and the kid hit it off. The kid looked up to Walker—by God, he'd had a hit song—and they spent most of the night drinking and talking, losing the publishing rep somewhere along the way. Walker saw that the kid got back to his home, a somewhat primitive little cabin on the west end of Nashville. Walker told the kid to look him up sometime, "whenever you're in the mood to come to Coconut Grove."

The kid went inside the cabin, trying like hell to not wake his wife, because it was nearly dawn and that would just be Reason No. 4,032 for her to leave him. Instead, he stood there in the laundry room of his rickety cabin, looking down at his matched avocado-hued washer and dryer, and wondered what in the hell he had done to deserve this life. He'd finished college and tried his hand as a journalist, writing for *Billboard* magazine. But he wanted to be a performer, he wanted to be like Jerry Jeff Walker, and live in a place with a name like Coconut Grove, instead of here in Nashville with the avocado appliances and a woman in the next room who hated the air he fucking breathed.

Face it, he thought. *You're a failure.*

And that's when Jimmy Buffett decided to change his life.

James William Buffett was born in Pascagoula, Mississippi, on Christmas Day in 1946. He grew up in Mobile, Alabama, attended Catholic school, and served as an altar boy. He went to Pearl River Community College before transferring to Auburn University and finally graduating from the University of Southern Mississippi, where he earned a degree in journalism. But he had something other than newspaper work on his mind.

"I started out wanting to be a Serious Southern Writer," he wrote. "My mother had made me a reader and stressed the legacy of my family's Mississippi roots. William Faulkner, Walker Percy, Eudora Welty, and Flannery O'Connor were household names—Mississippians who had made people take notice." (He was off a bit on O'Connor's geography—she was born in Savannah, Georgia.) Raised with a reverence for these great southern writers, like McGuane, he grew up with an appreciation for the power of language used well.

He began playing guitar while in college at Auburn University and performed at coffeehouses. He played for change on New Orleans street corners. "I was a shy, awkward kid from Mobile, kind of a wallflower. My roommate had a guitar, and even though he knew only three chords, he always seemed to be the center of attention with women. I said, 'Teach me those chords.' So I learned the guitar and started hanging around folk clubs, watching the bands . . . and the women—all the time, women—were hanging around the band. I thought, 'This is the job for me.' "

He headed for Nashville, the closest music mecca. "The only reason I went to Nashville was because I didn't have the money to buy enough gas to get to L.A.," he said. Because of his background in journalism, he was able to get a job with *Billboard*, the bible of the music industry. Though the magazine was headquartered in Los Angeles, it had significant bureaus in New York and Nashville. Buffett turned out to be a pretty good reporter, and in his short career he broke one major story: the breakup of the celebrated bluegrass duo Flatt and Scruggs.

He lucked out, getting a foot in the door not long after his arrival. His career as a recording artist seemed off to a good start when he secured a deal with Barnaby Records, an independent label owned by smooth-voiced and well-sweatered singer Andy Williams. The label rose from the demise of Cadence Records, which had been successful as the first home of the Everly Brothers in rock 'n' roll's golden era. Williams took the assets of Cadence and established Barnaby with the reissued recordings by the Everlys, then in vogue with the late sixties rock 'n' roll revival. Barnaby began looking for new talent and scored with novelty singer Ray Stevens's serious ballads "Mr. Businessman" and "Everything Is Beautiful." Williams signed his then-wife, French chanteuse Claudine Longet, to a contract. Buffett was another result of the label's search for new talent.

He signed with Barnaby in 1970 and was pitched by the company as a country-and-western entertainer. It was the middle of rock 'n' roll's first real exploration of its country-music roots. Four years before, Bob Dylan, then the most important player in popular music, had begun recording country-tinged albums in Nashville. Dylan's former backing band emerged from his shadow and, known simply as The Band, had recorded two influential albums that drew on the roots of country music. The Byrds switched directions, played country music, and soon spawned the full-tilt country band the Flying Burrito Brothers. Good Old Boys were springing up everywhere as cosmic cowboys and Times Square shitkickers.

So it made sense for Barnaby Records to position its newest artist as the latest Nashville longhair. With his drooping desperado mustache, Buffett looked the part. The music-industry geniuses at Barnaby agreed that he was perfectly cast.

Buffett disagreed. "They assume if you come from Alabama, you listen to country music," he said. "I didn't really like it much. All my early influences were out of New Orleans. . . . So it was a gumbo type of musical experience. I'd listen to the radio from New Orleans—Benny Spellman, Irma Thomas, and great old black New Orleans artists."

But country was hot, Buffett was white, and it was Nashville. Barnaby teamed him with novice producer Travis Turk—who would follow another path to a long and successful career as a voice actor—to create the album *Down to Earth*. Buffett wrote all of the songs (two in collaboration), but they were not standard country fare. The lead track, a song called "The Christian?" was an indictment of hypocrisy. Johnny Cash could get away with songs like that, but not an unknown kid from Alabama. The cover showed Buffett looking out the window of a car, half buried in the mud by the Cumberland River. He looked miserable.

The album went nowhere. It sold 324 copies on its release. Three singles were issued, but they all died on the vine. "The Christian?" upset some of the country-music disc jockeys and they made it clear they weren't interested in hearing any more from Jimmy Buffett. Still, Buffett supported the album by playing the usual gigs on college campuses and at coffeehouses and folk-music clubs. "It was a bad time," he recalled. "Yelling at the college kids to shut up so I could hear myself play." He'd wished to be successful overnight, but he didn't really expect it. So he stayed on the circuit and he and Turk began moving toward making another album.

The second effort, *High Cumberland Jubilee,* was recorded in 1971 but not released. Barnaby Records claimed the master tapes had been lost, but there was grumbling from Buffett that "lost master tapes" really meant "your first album stiffed and we want to bury you."

One of the girls who had liked Buffett's guitar playing was Margie Washichek, and they had married in 1969, moments before his expected stardom. Now it was 1971, the *High Cumberland* tapes were lost, and Jimmy Buffett was in the laundry room of his cabin and Margie was sleeping a couple of rooms away, dreaming about how unhappy she was in her marriage. And that was when Jimmy Buffett had his Jerry Jeff Walker epiphany.

Buffett had been playing the usual assortment of clubs throughout the South but had never gotten the most-desired booking on the circuit: the Flick, in Miami. Everyone wanted to play the Flick, mostly because of the weather. Artists lined up asshole-to-belly-button for a chance at a January or February booking there. But it was a significant venue, weather aside. It regularly drew Joni Mitchell, Fred Neil, John Sebastian, and other established artists.

Buffett was popular with the club owners in St. Augustine, Florida, and Athens, Georgia, and the other stops on his never-ending tour. He asked all of them to call Warren Dirken and put in the good word for Jimmy Buffett. Dirken was the persnickety owner of the Flick and he didn't return a lot of phone calls. But finally, owing to Buffett's persistence, Dirken gave in and offered to put him on the bill.

Buffett called Walker immediately. "Sure, man," Walker said, confirming that the offer was still good for a free place to stay in Coconut Grove.

"I was flat broke at the time," Buffett recalled, "and left the Mercedes with Margie. I had bought it as a status symbol and then couldn't afford to fill it up with gas. It was the only thing of any value that we had, and she deserved it for putting up with my rather shallow and immature attempt at being a husband."

During his *Billboard* days, the magazine had given Buffett a company Diner's Club card. It was long since expired, but Buffett held it up to the cute girl at the TWA ticket counter at Nashville International Airport. His thumb covered the card's expiration date as she typed the numbers into the system for a one-way ticket to Miami. His charming grin hit her in the face full blast, and it worked. On a rainy and miserably cold day in late October 1971, Buffett got on the 727 headed south.

Jerry Jeff Walker was waiting for him at Miami International. After the backslaps and *how-are-you*'s, Walker drove him to Coconut Grove in his candy-apple red 1947 Packard sedan, whose front vanity plate read "Flying Lady."

To Buffett, Miami was paradise. He'd left behind cold drizzle, a failed marriage, and a career going nowhere. Here, at least there was sunshine, good weather, and Jerry Jeff, who seemed incapable of unhappiness. At home, Buffett met Murphy and the baby and got settled into his room at the back of the house. That afternoon, he sat in a lawn chair and beheld the beauty of tropical Florida.

"I was sitting under a cluster of royal palms with a breeze coming off of Biscayne Bay," he recalled. "I was barefoot, in shorts and a T-shirt, eating lobster salad and drinking ice-cold beer, laughing and listening to Murphy's stories of Key West."

Buffett showed up at the Flick the next day, surprised to find it in a nondescript strip mall. It was well before the place opened. He brought his guitar, planning to introduce himself to owner Warren Dirken and check out the setup for that night's show.

Dirken was unimpressed with the scruffy kid. He was arguing with a produce seller and made Buffett cool his heels. Finally, he told Buffett he was two weeks early for his booking. *Are you sure?* Buffett asked. Dirken glared. "Bullett, you open in two weeks. See you then." Buffett knew this was the right day, but swallowed the correction. No reason to piss off the owner of the most coveted gig on the circuit. *OK, Mr. Dirken,* he said. *See you in two weeks.*

So he slunk back to Casa Jerry Jeff and told his sad story. The host shrugged. "Asshole club owners," was all he said. Buffett was wondering what he would do with himself for the next two weeks. He didn't want to outstay his welcome.

It was the irrepressible Murphy who had the *aha* moment that altered the trajectory of Jimmy Buffett's life and the course of American popular music.

"Hell, Jerry Jeff," she said, "let's go to Key West."

In the interlude before the road trip, Buffett served as an assistant mechanic for Walker's Flying Lady. Walker took the car into Hank & Bill's Garage and Buffett earned his keep by helping to install a new fuel pump and a new carburetor. They had to order a brake drum and it didn't arrive for a week, but finally they were ready for the trip down U.S. 1. With Jerry Jeff driving, Murphy riding shotgun, and Buffett and baby Justin in back, they set off on a trip that would include a stop at all of the major bars in the Keys. Sprawled across the backseat with Justin, Buffett let the little boy strum his guitar.

"This was Kerouac stuff, and I loved it," Buffett said. He recalled his first trip to Key West as a "tropical Fellini movie."

Off of Card Sound Road—the route through Key Largo used by residents, not tourists—they stopped at Alabama Jack's, an open-air seafood place barely a stone's throw from the blacktop. Mosquito repellent required. Crab cakes, shrimp, cold beer, nattering with the locals, who were, by all accounts, crazier than shit. It beat the hell out of Nashville.

Then the trip continued as they merged back on Highway 1. They crossed the bulging bridge at Jewfish Creek and rolled into Islamorada. Buffett had made it that far once before, during a college spring-break trip. South of Lower Matecumbe Key, on toward Marathon—all of that was virgin territory.

The water was a mixture of emerald and blue and the sun made it shimmer. Buffett couldn't take his eyes off of it. The sky was huge, with nothing to block it. The world was a thousand shades of blue and green.

It's a 155-mile drive from Coconut Grove to Key West, and even with two-lane traffic on U.S. 1, it's usually three hours at most. That day, it took the Flying Lady eight hours to make the trip, mostly because of the stops to knock back a few. After Big Pine came No Name Key and the No Name Bar.

Finally, they hit town in time for the nightly spectacular.

"Let's go right to sunset," Murphy said excitedly. "Buffett has to see sunset!"

Buffett was perplexed. They were talking about "sunset" as if it was a place.

But when he got to Mallory Square and saw the crowds gathering for the nightly ritual, he understood. Sunbleached guitar strummers played some James Taylor, old rummies blew conch shells to call the sun home, hippies did the free-form arrhythmic Grateful Dead dance, and an old man on a bicycle sold homemade conch salad. It was a working pier of creosote and concrete, but every evening, people flocked there for the best view in town, watching for that moment when the sun slipped beneath the horizon with a green flash.

Buffett soaked up the spectacle. The last beers from No Name were wearing off, so Walker suggested they hit a new bar as soon as the sun slipped behind the Gulf of Mexico.

It was a short walk to the Chart Room.

"Damn! It's Jerry Jeff!"

They got the standard greeting when they walked in the door. "Hey, boy—how *are* you?" Backslaps and hee-haws.

"Hey, everybody," Walker announced to the crowd, "this is my friend Jimmy Buffett. This is his first time in Key West."

Walker guided him to the bar, to introduce him to the bartender.

"Nice to meet you, Jimmy," Tom Corcoran said, handing him a beer. "The first one's free."

$$\boxed{9}$$

This Republic of Ours

I like to see a man proud of the place in which he lives. I like to see a man live so that his place will be proud of him.
—ABRAHAM LINCOLN

By his recollection, Jimmy Buffett hit every bar on Duval Street his first night in Key West. Murphy served as tour guide for Jimmy and Jerry Jeff, and she made sure they made it to the Key West Cemetery by dawn. The graves are aboveground crypts, and some of the large, prominent tribes have mausoleums so large one patriarch referred to the family tomb as "the condo."

For Buffett, it was another reminder of New Orleans. The two cities had a lot in common in terms of attitude and architecture. New Orleans bodies were also entombed aboveground, since the city was below sea level. This caused problems during torrential rains, and once, after weeks of stormy weather, diners at Commander's Palace, one of the finest restaurants in New Orleans, beheld the spectacle of bodies breaking through the rain-soaked walls of crypts and spilling out onto Washington Avenue.

No such accidents had occurred in Key West, but as he strolled through the grounds in the first light of day, Buffett began to develop another connection with the island town.

They went back to Miami and Buffett played out his residency at the Flick, but he had already decided that Key West was home. "Jerry Jeff and Murphy had not only given me a place to stay and a fun weekend in Key West, they had changed my life," he recalled.

He saved his Flick paycheck and caught a ride down the Keys, stopping at all of the same stops he'd made with Jerry Jeff and Murphy. In Key West, he bought a bicycle and purchased a new wardrobe at Goodwill—mostly flowered tropical shirts and Navy-surplus shorts. He took a ride on the Conch Train, which snaked tourists through the island, showing visitors the sights while guides on the P.A. system told stories of the culture. "It is still the best crash course in Key West history," Buffett testified.

Once he saw Key West, he decided where he wanted to be. This place was inspiration as much as it was home. "The most important thing about the place," he recalled, "was that it was completely virgin territory. Incredible characters, great bars. A different form of life, almost. It was still a wide-open town, where artists, straights, gays, shrimpers, sailors, criminals, and politicians all frequented the same bars."

In the early days, he often slept on Tom Corcoran's couch and ate Judy's spaghetti. There was a child now, a little boy named Sebastian, who would crawl up to the couch while Buffett sat there strumming his guitar and marvel at the man's thick blond hair and mustache.

Buffett smiled at the kid, figuring that with these new friends and this little boy smiling at him, maybe he was on his way up. Nashville was the bottom. Now, thanks to Jerry Jeff and Murphy—maybe her most especially—he had found the right place to start over.

He'd been born in Pascagoula on the Gulf and been raised mostly in Mobile on the Gulf, and here he was in Key West, the raised ridge between the Gulf and the ocean. Salt water was in his blood. He wasn't a country singer, at least not a shitkicker country singer. Nothing wrong with those, of course, and Jerry Jeff was just about the best of that breed. But that wasn't for him. He was becoming something else, he knew, and it was something to do with the water and this place.

He watched them in the kitchen, working on dinner. They had decided to do the bourgeois thing in honor of having a child, and so Tom and Judy had been married at the Cistern at Mallory Square, with Captain Tony walking the bride down the aisle. Sebastian was four months old. Everyone still talked about "the reception" (drunken bash, really) that followed at the Old Anchor Inn. Corcoran was fond of J.P. Donleavy's *The Ginger Man* and so named his son after the repulsively attractive protagonist of the book, Sebastian Dangerfield. He and Judy had a small home on Whalton Street, one bed, one crib, a cubbyhole kitchen, a living room with a cast-off couch and a Bell Telephone wire spool as a coffee table, complete with stained rings from beer cans and wine bottles.

Buffett often sang for free drinks at the Chart Room, and soon everybody knew Jimmy Buffett. He played at most of the venues on Duval Street, just him and his guitar, singing for beer and small change. If he wasn't bunking at Corcoran's, he was in McGuane's guesthouse.

McGuane urged Buffett to partake in other forms of recreation, and once, under the influence of McGuane and mescaline, Buffett sailed a sixteen-foot skiff out into the Gulf Stream and was all alone, out there fishing for marlin like a wigged-out Santiago from *The Old Man and the Sea.*

He developed an obsession for a beautiful blonde girl named Edith, who—recognizing that the name was pure *Leave It to Beaver*—went by the nickname Eddie. She worked at The Looking Glass, an upscale dress shop on Duval. The store had a stoop with a low wall rising up the stairs to the door. It was a perfect stone hammock for Jimmy Buffett and his guitar. He'd sit there and play for hours, mostly to be near his inamorata and to occasionally see her. He loved playing with her name, working "Eddie" into lyrics of standard songs and improvising to impress her.

Jan Toppino, owner of the shop, didn't mind Buffett as a person, but as a businesswoman, she didn't particularly like the long-haired boy sitting on her stoop. He was poorly dressed and, on occasion, aromatic. But she couldn't figure out how to get him to leave.

Besides, that's one of the reasons she had a husband.

"Hi, Jimmy," Paul Toppino said when he ambled outside. "How you doing?"

Buffett stopped playing. "Well, hi, Paul. I'm doing all right."

"Jimmy, you got to stop this," Toppino said. "You're fucking scaring away all the customers. Can't you play your music somewhere else?" He said it with a smile. Buffett took it with a smile. "It was all in good fun," Toppino said later. "Sort of."

And so Buffett moved on to another storefront and Eddie became another could-have-been in his life.

"Strangely enough," Buffett recalled, "when I first got to Key West there wasn't a real music scene." He wasn't a big fish in a small pond—he was the only fish, swimming solo. "It was open, new territory. It was a magical place."

Buffett found that as a songwriter, he didn't need to venture north of Stock Island for material. There was enough weirdness, depravity, and debauchery in Key West to keep him in business for years. Strolling down the streets late at night, after a gig, he'd pick up the ambient sounds of lovers quarreling, other lovers fucking, off-key singing, and spastic dancing. He could get it all just from a walk back to the McGuane guesthouse. Buffett loved that all these people who couldn't get along up on the mainland—rednecks, hippies, straights, homosexuals—all seemed to get along just fine in Key West.

Beyond the drinking and drugs and wrought-iron balconies, Buffett saw another, deeper connection between New Orleans and Key West. "There was much more of a literary presence," he said. "I had been a book reader for a long time—a great fan of Hemingway, Fitzgerald, and Faulkner. So that literary side attracted me because I loved reading and felt comfortable in that atmosphere."

Thanks to Murphy's introduction to the owners, Buffett became one of the regular performers at Howie's Lounge. "I thought if God was going to end the world, he would start with Howie's Lounge," he mused. Russell Chatham remembers that dive as one of his favorite haunts when he and Jim Harrison visited McGuane. "That's where we met Buffett," Chatham said. "He was singing in there for free drinks. Neither Jim nor I had two nickels to fucking rub together, and we were hoping that we'd get a free drink too."

Buffett also played at the Old Anchor Inn as an unknown and immortalized it as "the Snake Pit" in his song "My Head Hurts, My Feet Stink and I Don't Love Jesus."

Buffett played almost any venue in town, but the Anchor Inn was the place that best got out the crazy. In perhaps his only performance of what would become known as karaoke, Buffett—overcome with either inspiration or demon rum—leaped onto the stage when the Anchor Inn's juke began belching "The Candy Man," performed by Sammy Davis Jr. In full-blown Al Jolson mode, Buffett sank to one knee and began lip-synching the song, flailing his arms like an old minstrel-show entertainer. He leaped from the stage to the bar and—without spilling a drop of precious booze—hopscotched his way through an obstacle course of drinks, all in time to the music. He ended with an elaborate bow.

It was go-for-the-gusto, spontaneous entertainment, and Buffett was a take-no-prisoners performer. People took notice.

Soon, Buffett had his own apartment, then saved enough money to get a really good place, an apartment at 704 Waddell Street, cheek by jowl with the Casa Marina, the plush beachfront hotel Henry Flagler had built to congratulate himself for completing the Florida East Coast Railway. The upstairs apartment was seventy-five dollars a month, and the downstairs neighbor was a new kid in town—Chris Robinson, storyteller and bartender, soon to fall into the Chart Room crowd.

The place on Waddell had a semiprivate beach that was perfect for Buffett and Robinson.

"You could go swimming naked at noon," Robinson said. "I could go catch a lobster at lunch. At least fifty percent of the time, someone was making love on the beach. On every jukebox was 'If You Can't Be with the One You Love, Love the One You're With.' "

Buffett filed for divorce from Margie Washichek on September 20, 1972. He was able to finally live, without remorse, the life of a free man in paradise. He also became what he'd wanted to be from the moment he set foot on the island: a Freshwater Conch, just like Murphy. Soon he was accepted as part of Key West's hippie artist community, along with Jim Harrison and Tom McGuane.

Tom McGuane was riding high. *The Sporting Club* had earned great reviews and so the critics were ready when *The Bushwhacked Piano* was published in early 1971. McGuane was no longer an unknown. He had been declared The Next Big Thing.

The plot was thin and at times as far-fetched as a Pecos Bill tall tale. But, as with *The Sporting Club*, McGuane's wordplay was breathtaking. This was musical composition as much as prose writing. His sentences held the joy and wonder of a Bach air or a Clapton guitar solo. Here indeed, sighed the critics, was an artist of language.

In this counterculture novel, the totems of the ruling class were destroyed—in some cases, only metaphorically—by McGuane's protagonist. Nicholas Payne lived by this credo: "I've made silliness a way of life." McGuane cast him in the literary mold of Jack Kerouac's wandering Dean Moriarty or as an updated, smart-ass Huckleberry Finn. Confident with the invincible fury of youth, Payne disparaged all but self in a monumental trip that finished, significantly, at the end of the road, in Key West. At that point, unless he grew gills and adapted, he was doomed to exist in this culture he disdained. The only option was to change it, and that effort, even at his age, Payne realized, was futile.

When the book was published, the expected Hemingway comparisons were carted out as the reviews noted that McGuane had turned again to the man-against-man macho theme. Plus, he took the story to Key West, to Papa-land. Writing for the *New York Times Book Review*, critic Jonathan Yardley noted that McGuane's writing revealed "a passion for the manly world of the hunting lodge, the fishing expedition, the boys' night out."

But rather than being summarily blasted, as Hemingway and his acolytes often were by the American literary establishment, McGuane got a pass because of the sheer inventiveness and audacity of his prose. The *New York Times* blared Yardley's praise. McGuane's two novels were "the work of a writer of the first magnitude." And more: "His intelligence is as great as his style. His persistent thematic concern is the defilement of America, land and people alike, the advent of what he calls 'a declining snivelization.' "

Yardley wasn't the only one to ejaculate in print over the book. Most of the major publications noted flaws and predictability in the plot but raved over the wordplay, what the *New Yorker* called McGuane's "joyous inventions in the present tense."

In his eyes, McGuane saw gasoline pumps as the work of Stonehenge druids. Peripheral characters were measured as if sides of beef. In one celebrated passage—a scene at the Key West Booster Club Picnic—McGuane described the bounty prepared for feast: "Some of the wives had laid out tables of country fixings, jams and jellies and whatnot, in a sentimental materialization of the kind of quasi-rural bonhomie that seemed a millimeter from actual goose-stepping and brown-shirt uproars of bumpkin fascism." The over-the-top allusion is straight from the jaundiced mind of Nicholas Payne. You could argue the point, maybe. But the language brought forth the requisite *whew* of admiration for Tom McGuane, who smirked between the lines.

Comparisons to Hemingway were apt. Similarities to William Faulkner were evident. Some critics saw the bitterness of Mark Twain's later work (*The Mysterious Stranger*) as an influence.

But McGuane was distinctive. He was writing a rock 'n' roll literature and each burst of wordplay was like a lightning-fast solo on a Gibson Les Paul.

The Bushwhacked Piano crossed the finish line not because of its plot or insight into contemporary culture (though it had that) but because of the inventiveness and virtuosity of its creator. The American Academy of Arts and Letters honored the book with the Rosenthal Award for 1971.

Spring 1971 was a McGuane bifecta. On the heels of *The Bushwhacked Piano*'s publication, the film version of *The Sporting Club* was released by Avco Embassy Films. The critics formed a firing squad and the film was put down largely as a mess, an attempt to capitalize on the post–*Easy Rider* world of youth culture with gratuitous jabs at old farts and fogeys. Within the comic-strip structure of the film, McGuane's carefully preserved and rendered dialogue came off as funny in a way that was not intended.

Jim Harrison accompanied McGuane to a screening of the film. "It was a horrid movie," he recalled. They were in New York, and they were fairly drunk by the time the film started. "McGuane stood up and yelled a lot of rash things at the screen at the top of his lungs. There were a lot of people there, but Tom was a great big, bold guy and he didn't give a fuck."

Miserable though the film might have been, McGuane was too much of a gentleman to take public his criticism of the Hollywood people. After all, he had cashed the check.

Though the reviews were generally wretched, it was still an

achievement to have a book turned into a cinematic spectacle. Sure, this was the town of Tennessee Williams and his multiple film adaptations. And James Leo Herlihy lived here too—though he was pretty much a hermit—and Hollywood had turned his little novel into the 1970 Academy Award winner for best picture, *Midnight Cowboy*. But that was rarefied air. Few could exist at that altitude and now McGuane was climbing to that level. He sold film rights to *The Bushwhacked Piano* and was beginning to sniff out a plot about cattle rustlers in modern-day Montana for the Hollywood people.

Back in Key West, he was what they called *the shit*. Seemed to a lot of folks that the transition happened overnight. Big old shy handsome devil Tom McGuane, that workaholic nose-to-the-grindstone writer, was coming out of his shell, burrowing into the nightlife, and having a good old time. The girls began coming, those willowy girls with the long hair and unblinking, massive eyes. They began looking at McGuane too.

And he began to look back.

He decided his next novel would be about Key West, this new home. Perhaps this place was the last vestige of the sixties counterculture. He looked up and suddenly he saw a lot of people like himself walking the quiet streets—longhairs, stoned and giggling some of them, lithe and supple lasses too, who shed their clothes and their inhibitions when they approached Mile Marker Zero. This is where the disillusioned gathered to look for new illusions.

McGuane saw that it was a place to watch for the signs of a clash between the Old Values and the New World Order. It had all the drama of the country packed into the narrow space of the town. The narrative could not get too far-flung on the two-by-four island. The story would be set on the Rock, but it would be a story of the whole country.

Hollywood continued to beckon. It intoxicated.

Though he saw himself as a Serious Writer, he knew that such people rarely made a lot of money. California—that's where all the money was, in the hands of those producers and studio bosses festooned with gold chains and coke spoons.

Writing for film made sense if McGuane wanted to support his Montana–and–Key West lifestyle and buy himself time as a Serious Writer. Otherwise, he might need to do something he found horrible, like teach creative writing. That path was frequently death for a Serious Writer, but was often necessary for survival.

As for the switch to screenplays from novels—that was a piece of cake for McGuane. He'd studied at Yale Drama School and written a play. Now he just added the veneer of camera direction.

And for that, he made a lot more money. Noting the praise and honors heaped on *The Bushwhacked Piano*, he also cataloged his frustration. "It took two years to write," he said, "and earned me thirty-seven hundred dollars. I just can't live on that."

McGuane shrugged off the idea of a slow learning curve for filmmaking. "Anyone can learn the technical end of it in ten minutes," he said. "After that, it's just like novels: you have to tell a story."

So for the movies, he began working out a Montana story, the tale of two cattle rustlers who steal only what they need. They don't go for whole herds. They just kill a cow here and there and sell the meat to pay the rent.

And for his next novel, he decided on a Key West story, something that had to do with feuding fishing guides on one level but that was really about the clash of values and generations. Setting it on the small island, he ensured that the characters couldn't run away from each other, and confrontation was inevitable.

And suddenly, he was famous.

It wasn't just the book reviews or the news of movie deals. Mainstream magazines did features on him and his lovely wife ("a direct descendant of Davy Crockett," they brayed) and how this beautiful young couple lived on a ranch part of the year and in this island paradise the rest of the time. Another contract brought more money and the McGuanes moved again, to a yet grander house in the old-town section of Key West. The new homestead was now party central, presided over by the new and improved, aggressively social Thomas McGuane. Harrison and Chatham visited, as did Valdene. Writer Richard Brautigan, poet laureate of hippie America, also came to party.

But who could keep up? McGuane's mantra was *more more more*—more booze, more drugs, and soon, on the side, more women.

In the magazines, the young couple smiled into the wind—him with a flowing mane of far-out hippie hair, her with a beauty and perfection women envied and men desired.

But that life in paradise was ending, though neither husband nor wife knew it at the time.

"When fame hit," Tom Corcoran remembered, "the marriage was pretty much over."

McGuane had fully embraced the Key West lifestyle, with its booze and drugs and bleary hangover intensity of bleach-bright mornings. Writer Toby Thompson was working on a book about drinking, so it was no surprise that his path would eventually cross McGuane's.

Thompson came to Key West for interviews and observations. When he first showed up at the McGuane residence, Becky McGuane greeted him.

"She was small, blonde, cheerful, with an unthreatening sensuality and a steady diligence any man would work behind," he said. "She was charming; magically so. She had a way of listening to what you said that overstepped politeness. And she knew men, how to mother untamed herds of them."

McGuane obviously adored his wife. He was friends with Vaughn Cochran, a local artist who sculpted and painted—he had a gallery called Bahama Mama's, kitty-cornered from Sloppy Joe's—and he was also a potter.

McGuane said that since he and his family were doing the half-year-in-Key-West/half-year-in-Montana thing, they wanted something that was constant between the homes. *How about a dining table?* he asked Cochran. *Do you think maybe you can do something special, something we can pack up and take with us every season when we leave?*

Cochran thought for a moment. Like every red-blooded man in Key West, he found that his blood pulsed a little faster when he saw Becky McGuane. *I've got an idea,* he told McGuane. He explained it in great detail. If the McGuanes had been a married couple in Keokuk, Iowa, or Tucumcari, New Mexico, they might not have gone for it. *But this was Key West, man.*

Vaughn and his wife Cydall went over to the McGuanes and the four of them sat around, drinking a couple glasses of wine. Then Cochran got out this mold he'd brought over. Becky McGuane took off her clothes and lay down in the six-foot-long form. As McGuane and Cydall Cochran watched, Vaughn Cochran covered her body in clay, until he had made a ceramic cast of the whole magnificent spectacle. "I took the clay and put the clay all around her body, where the table surface would be," Cochran explained. "Then I poured plaster and the plaster I poured on top of her was the part would you see. I pulled the mold off and then poured the clay slabs into the mold and fired them."

It took Cochran a month to finish the thing, but when he was done, they had a table that was part Chinese mahogany and part Becky McGuane's body, as if she were holding up the table—nurturing, feeding her family and guests.

"It was one of the greatest sculptures I've ever made," Cochran said.

Latham, Corcoran, and Clark still held forth at the Chart Room, and were eventually joined by the new kid in town, Chris Robinson, who bartended part-time and smuggled pot for his main income.

Corcoran decided to branch out and so he started a small business, F.T. Sebastian Leatherworks, in a former gas station on Fleming Street, a half block from Duval. He came up with the designs for pillows, belts, purses, man bags, and wallets, and employed some local hotties to tool the leather to fit the customer orders. It was nearly a not-for-profit, but Corcoran liked it and he made just enough to keep the operation afloat.

As a retired gas station, the building had an overhang to protect customers and attendants back in the time when there were gas pumps on the concrete island instead of planters. McGuane asked if he could store his skiff there so he could do some repairs.

Sure, said Corcoran, always willing to do something to help out a friend.

Because it had once been a gas station, it had exterior doors to the *His* and *Hers* on the side of the building. McGuane would drop by, ostensibly to work on the skiff, and soon find himself enamored of one of the leather-tooling hotties, who all wanted the famous writer. Corcoran would look up suddenly, and find that he was the only one tending customers. He soon learned that McGuane had taken the *hottie du jour* to the men's room and was giving her the tuppenny upright against the bathroom wall.

On another day, a spectacular sunny Key West morning, McGuane was standing in front of his home on Ann Street when a girl in a bikini rode by on a bicycle. There wasn't much to the bikini and McGuane watched the wiggle as the girl pedaled toward Duval. He forgot what he was doing and started walking after her. *Why not?* he said to himself.

McGuane had certainly come out of that serious-writer shell.

"Tom went crazy, and just started drinking," Chatham recalled. "There was one day he just walked out of the house and saw that we were having fun and he wasn't. And he went crazy. He went down to a bar and that was all she fuckin' wrote."

Valdene remembered a similar moment, when McGuane shrugged off the drudge and went crazy.

"Tom was a big, strong, healthy American guy and there was a lot of fun that big, strong healthy American guys could have in Key West," Valdene said. "And did he enjoy that? Yeah, he did."

Of course, McGuane didn't own the copyright on sport fucking. Few libidos could compete with Russell Chatham's.

Chatham was such a sexual connoisseur and often so wildly successful with women that when he suffered that occasional dry spell, the whole town seemed to be aware of it, adjusting to the shifting deck of Chatham's carnal steerage. Once, the gulf between Chatham and his last sexual encounter was on the verge of becoming a sea of discontent and agony.

"We'd been there about a week," Chatham recalled of this particular visit, "and for some reason, I wasn't getting laid. I was getting hysterical. When you're desperate, you're fucked, because it shows, and then nothing's going to happen."

The needier Chatham appeared, the more he needed to get his confidence back. Like a masterful slugger in the abyss of a terrible slump, he couldn't think how he could get out of it. At his more paranoid moments, he wondered if the women of Key West were engaged in a conspiracy to frustrate him.

Chatham was distraught. "What am I going to do?" he asked Dink Bruce.

Then, as he looked into his friend's kind face, he saw the answer.

Bruce was helpful to a fault, a guy who could make things happen. He was skilled, talented, and knew everybody and everything. His father had helped Hemingway and they were great friends. Now, Chatham decided, it was time for Bruce to lend his special expertise to the new generation of artists in Key West.

"Here's what needs to happen," Chatham told Bruce. "We need a really good whore."

Bruce didn't associate with prostitutes. The women who disrobed for him so readily on his boat were amateurs, not professionals.

"I don't know any," Bruce shrugged. But then the lightbulb went off over his head. He did know the best lawyer in town, Jack Spottswood. "Jack defends a lot of these girls when they're in trouble," Bruce told Chatham.

Bruce called up Spottswood and asked him straight out. "I have a friend who needs to get laid," Bruce said. "Who's the best whore?"

Spottswood replied, "Hands down, it's Elena."

So Bruce arranged it and called Chatham. "Go to the house at two o'clock," he told him.

"So I'm waiting there," Chatham recalled fondly, "and this girl rides up on a bicycle."

The girl got off the bike, tethered it to the post, and smiled, introducing herself.

"Hi, I'm Elena," she said. "We'll fuck in a minute, but let me jump into the pool and cool off."

She undressed in front of Chatham, dove into the pool and swam back and forth a couple of times, then got out.

What followed became a major feature of Chatham's sexual highlight reel.

Back in Montana after a Key West trip, Chatham would resume his normal life as a serious artist, but that didn't mean he didn't find himself thinking about the island town.

"It was a world so different from my normal world," he said. "I hate heat. I hate humidity. And what that does is, it creates a lifestyle that's just not like anyplace else. You could feel it in the air: this was a place where people didn't wear very many clothes. You knew that at any second, the girl sitting next to you would fuck you. That doesn't happen in anybody's normal life. Try doing something like that somewhere else and you're going to take a fuckin' left hook to the face."

When he'd first come to the Keys in the late sixties, McGuane had toyed with the idea of being a fishing guide. This was before *The Sporting Club* was published, when he was still looking for a way to support himself while he fed his writing habit.

He figured guiding would earn him seventy-five dollars a day. He'd do that one day a week and write the other six. That would be all the money he'd need. To build a nest egg, he fished more than two months straight, seven days a week, and soon grew exhausted from the work.

But that crash course allowed him to know that world, and to speak of guiding with authority.

He never tired of fishing. He and Harrison and Valdene, along with occasional visitors such as Richard Brautigan, were serious about it. They went out on the flats, looking for permit, bonefish, or tarpon, rhythmically casting lines like maestros conducting orchestras.

Poling the skiff through the shallow water, it was like looking through blown window glass. The fishermen could see everything.

"What is most emphatic in angling is made so by the long silences—the unproductive periods," McGuane wrote. "No form of fishing offers such elaborate silences as fly-fishing for permit."

The sun and sky would blend into variations on themes of blue and green.

"You never see a painting that reminds you of what you see on the flats, where in one day, the light changes thousands of times," Harrison reflected. "It's like Brautigan said, 'Layers and layers, strata of lamina of blues and greens, south of the variations in the bottom from turtle grass, the coral to clear sand.' Any writer who is a romantic is fascinated with the tropics. *The Marquesas . . . Boca Grande . . . trout . . . barracudas . . .* you love the sound of those names. They sound so exotic."

The stillness, the blues, the greens, and the magnificent struggles of the fish—it was all breathtaking. For McGuane, this was "absolutely pure fishing."

McGuane had begun his book about Key West and fishing. He was too wrapped up in that world not to write about it. He explained the lure: "Places that are heightened, the way Key West is, the way New Orleans is, the way New York is, are intriguing to novelists. The novel is basically a social form. A novel is always being strained outside of its contours when it's made to portray a kind of solitude or nakedness."

On another occasion, he described why it was a no-brainer to write about Key West and its culture. "American writers love exotic atmospheres, and yet really don't want to live outside of the country," McGuane said. "Key West is one of those places that allows them to have it both ways."

Harrison likewise knew the appeal of the island. "You're at the end of America," he said. "It's the tropics and it doesn't, largely, have much to do with the rest of Florida."

McGuane began crafting a story of a dissolute young man, Thomas Skelton, returning to his hometown of Key West after a road trip and excursions into the world of drugs and sexual escapades. Quite suddenly, Skelton becomes a fishing guide. The story largely centers on his relationships with two more experienced guides: Faron Carter, suspicious but somewhat innocuous, and Nichol Dance, a menacing figure who threatens violence if Skelton goes through with his plan to open another charter business.

Skelton's fanatical and sudden dedication to chartering wasn't just because of his skill guiding on the flats. The sea was the only place where he felt free from the limitations of the stifling country.

Fortunately for Skelton, Dance's temper earned him jail time and Skelton took over his business temporarily. As a guide, Skelton was somewhat inept, and when Dance was released, he took back his skiff. Skelton turned to his family for help. His father was a self-declared invalid, so it fell to his self-made-businessman grandfather to subsidize the venture.

The three rivals then engaged in a deadly battle for fishing supremacy in the Keys.

It had the stuff of a standard adventure novel, but McGuane gave readers a clue he might be up to something more, that this novel might be about the clash of generations and values so obviously ripping apart the culture.

In his one-sentence prelude, he wrote:

Nobody knows, from sea to shining sea, why we are having all this trouble with our republic . . .

The between-the-lines sentiments subtly delivered to readers McGuane's observations about the collapsing values of the country in which he had grown up.

"I felt as if I had a fuel tank strapped on my back," he said. "I felt we were on the cultural nosecone of America, and I had to write about it."

McGuane said the experience of writing the book was unlike any other feeling he's had as an artist. "As I wrote," he recalled, "I could feel the cultural resonances humming up through the keys of the Olympia. It's the only book I've ever felt that. I felt I was in a parade." From the vantage of two decades, he realized, "It was different than anything I've done before and different than anything I've done since."

McGuane also described the book as "his metallic, extremist view of the world." Much like the main character, Thomas Skelton, McGuane was terrified by his family and his perceptions of them, which made the southernmost point of the United States that much more attractive.

"*Ninety-Two in the Shade* was written from a pretty druggy consciousness," McGuane said. "It's more in the language than the events. It reflects the fact that I felt I was in some sweeping cultural change in this country. I didn't want to make a journey to India or get stoned all day, but at the same time I was somehow or other one of the dissident elements in the society and I knew something drastic had changed. It was the tone of things, the voice of things, the kind of disconnectedness of lives against a background of connected lives— the lives of our parents and grandparents."

Ninety-Two in the Shade was published in the summer of 1973, and there was no doubt among the friends at the Chart Room, as well as the literary critics of America, that this was the Big One. With the subject, setting, and verbal economy of *The Old Man and the Sea*, McGuane was making his claim as his generation's Hemingway. Several big-time critics said as much, and those notices brought the book a lot of attention, which would come to be an albatross for the young author. Being the *next* anything else implies an inherent lack of originality.

The *New York Times Book Review* devoted its front page to the book, with a confident, long-haired author staring down the reader in a Jill Krementz portrait (another sign he had arrived, enshrined by the photographer to the literary stars). From the opening phrase, praise was heaped upon the writer. Critic Thomas Edwards laid out the inevitable: "Clearly this is Hemingway country. Not just the he-man pleasures of McGuane's men, but even the locales of the novels—up in Michigan, the northern Rockies, Key West (with Cuba just over the horizon)—recapitulate Hemingway's Western Hemisphere life and works. Yet male competition—less a matter of 'honor' than an instinctual commitment to what one has undertaken ('following through' Nichol Dance calls it)—makes an impressive kind of sense in McGuane. In a world where little is worth keeping, a man can at least keep his word."

Life continued to change for McGuane. Until then, he and his friends "fished quietly and seriously," and then "suddenly it was all over," he lamented. "It had gone public. It had turned into a horrible circus, and the passion, the mystique of the whole thing, went up into this sort of episodic loony tunes."

Being a writer on par with rock stars meant that over-the-top behavior was expected on occasion.

McGuane and his friends partied so hard in Key West that they decided to institutionalize the practice. Someone came up with the name Club Mandible (for some reason, they named it after the lower jaw) and they chose purple long-sleeved shirts as their uniform.

Everyone had a nickname stitched across the back of the shirt. McGuane was Captain Berserko, Tom Corcoran was Bwana Dik, and Judy Corcoran was LCDR (Lieutenant Commander) Bust. The real count, Guy de la Valdene, was Count No Account. Cydall Cochran was Faye Wray, and her husband Vaughn was Garnet Woolsey. Jimmy Buffett was L. T. Barko. Becky McGuane, aka Queen Bee, lent a regal presence to the gatherings.

Membership was not exclusive. "We just wore the purple T-shirts every night and went out drinking," Vaughn Cochran said. "If you were there, you were a member. It was nonsensical—no reason, no purpose."

Club Mandible had its own theme song, "Boogie" by John Hartford, composer of "Gentle on My Mind." It was a simple, nonsense song and fit the club's lack of purpose:

> *Hey babe, you want to boogie?*
> *Boogie woogie woogie with me?*

As Corcoran said, "It led to a whole raft of codified queries: 'Where's the boogie?' 'Want to go out and boogie?' " It was during this period of infatuation with "Boogie" that Corcoran and McGuane attended a performance at the Monroe County Fair by country singer Skeeter Davis. They stood in the back, but Davis made eye contact with McGuane and, drawn by his power, came out to say hello after the performance. After a few pleasantries, McGuane made his move.

"Want to ride the boogie trail?" he asked.

"No, darlin'," Davis laughed. "I got off that road years ago and now I'm a born-again Christian."

McGuane shrugged. "I was born right the first time."

Another requirement of being a literary rock star was owning newer and faster cars.

McGuane bought a Porsche 911, a symbol of superstar status, and crashed it while driving 140 miles an hour. Remarkably, he wasn't hurt. But the accident left him mute for a time.

"I kept thinking I had died," he said. "I kept thinking of all the things I hadn't done." This empowered him. "In Key West after the accident, I finally realized I could stop pedaling so insanely, get off the bike and walk around the neighborhood. The changes that came were irresistible, but it was getting unthinkable to spend another year sequestered like that, writing."

But he hadn't died. Later on, he would think that maybe he was just awakening.

10

Square Grouper

*The game is played out nightly in the inlets and beaches
of Florida's 1,200-mile coastline, along back-country
roads and at dirt airstrips. Fishermen churning home
to Miami through the Cape Florida channel may be
startled to find a white Customs launch bearing down
on them. Blue-shirted men with holstered revolvers play
a high-intensity beam through cabins and scan decks
with night-vision goggles. . . . To the south at Key Largo,
deputy sheriffs with high-powered rifles cruise through
mangrove swamps, on the prowl for marijuana runners.*
—TIME, MARCH 13, 1978

Marijuana had been around for years and was part of jazz culture
and of black culture. It seeped into the world of white middle-class
kids in the sixties, as dormitories lit up and the music blared: "Everybody must get stoned!" The Beatles smoked dope and spoke of
it freely. There were other drugs, of course, but by the seventies,
LSD—once so hot in the late sixties—had become, in the words of

one connoisseur, "the Studebaker of the drug market" used only by aging dilettantes.

Sure, there was hashish and mescaline and mushrooms and opium here and there, but marijuana was the meat and potatoes of the drug diet in the early seventies. And a lot of it came in through South Florida, especially the Keys.

But in the early seventies, there was more tolerance for that sort of thing in Key West. Buffett called it "an open town of smugglers, shrimpers and crazies. It was the end of the world."

Pot was part of the daily life of Key West. The town drew the arty types and they needed their inebriants. Hemingway had his rum and whiskey. McGuane and his friends had those, and added marijuana to the mix.

Marijuana was everywhere, and the Key West cops—some of them, at least—looked the other way. Colombians flew Piper Cubs full of pot to homemade landing strips hacked out of the undergrowth of the Lower Keys. Shrimpers took huge loads of it onto their little boats, storing them in the hold with their legitimate haul.

Everybody wanted it. In a resort town, it was hard to keep a business going, especially a family business, when tourists were gone half the year. *We got to put food on the table, man.* That was the rationale. *What's the harm in selling a little bit under the counter?*

Shrimpers doubled their pleasure by filling their boats with pot. They'd deliver loads of commercial American cigarettes to South America and then bring back pot on the return. Dope brought a better price than shrimp.

If they were at sea and the feds were closing in, they'd discreetly toss the bales off the boat, away from government eyes. If the feds saw it, there wasn't much they could do—at least nothing that would hold up in court. The floating dope was not in the possession of the boat's captain or crew. They called those errant bobbing bales "square grouper."

If the feds came up too fast, smugglers unable to outrun the Coast Guard had few options. "If capture is unavoidable," Tom Corcoran said, "there occurs an instant and practical definition of the price of freedom: sink the boat and get rescued. The purchase price of the boat plus cargo rarely exceeds lawyers' fees. Better luck next time."

Soon, every Bubba with a boat was out there unloading bales of dope from Colombian ships. Or the Bubbas got in their pickups and went out in the swamps, greeting the pilots who brought their little planes down in those tight clearings, barely missing the royal palms on the way in and coming to a stop just ten feet back from the mangroves.

The Key West economy was dependent on the pay cycle of the U.S. naval base and, to a lesser extent, on the fluctuating tourist trade. Marijuana provided steadiness and continuity.

"To live on an island this small, you need a different psyche, a different mindset," said a prosecutor who led an investigation of Key West's Bubba system for selling drugs. "Marijuana, in their mindset, was no different from shrimping. There is simply a different moral and legal system."

Coast Guard cutters from the Key West station would stop shrimp boats for spontaneous "safety inspections." If they found marijuana, the Guard would arrest the shrimpers, seize the dope, then fly a pirate flag on the cutter's mast. The seized dope would then show up for sale within a week on Duval Street.

Everybody wanted a piece of the action. In season, T-shirt shops thrived, selling shirts with rude or obnoxious slogans to tourists ambling in with wads of cash. In the off-season, the shops nearly had to peel customers off the sidewalk.

So selling marijuana was a way to keep the business alive and keep Mom and Sis and Baby Boy Phil fed. Besides, it was just marijuana. *Hell, wasn't much different between that and a cold Budweiser.*

Soon it was more than a little extra cash to tide people over.

When they realized how easy it was to deal with the Colombians and peddle the pot for them, shopkeepers got a little more brazen and upped their allotment. The business was fine, but now they needed a larger house, a faster car, a bigger boat. Check that: They didn't *need* it; they *wanted* it. They were getting greedy with the easy money.

Dope was good for the local economy.

Key West police had several options: enforce the law, look the other way, or participate and supplement their income.

Though marijuana growing, dealing, and trading wasn't officially endorsed by the Key West power structure, a lot of local businessmen and public officials either participated in the trade or at least allowed it to happen. More heads shook in the state capital in the more conservative parts of mainland Florida. This was all the evidence they needed that Key West remained a pirate culture.

Dope smokers were "stupid and immature," according to Florida's governor, Claude Kirk, who called on residents of all ages to provide a model of behavior for young folks. Every generation had its addictions and its vices. It's time to "rap" with the now generation, Governor Kirk told participants at a conference in Miami Beach in 1970 on drug and alcohol abuse.

"We will not begin to lick this problem with our young until we become as concerned over alcoholism being the nation's third-deadliest killer as we are over marijuana being its fastest-growing problem," the governor said. "It means taking a good, hard, honest look at our own indulgences."

Adult Key West—the drinking class—wasn't setting the sort of example Governor Kirk wanted. With the nightly sunset celebration and rampant leisure, the town's culture was built on relaxation, and relaxation meant alcohol: old-fashioneds, manhattans, gimlets, whiskey sours, mango sours, martinis, mai tais, mojitos, and all other varieties of booze consumed straight, and often.

The *Key West Citizen* carried front-page stories on the dope trade most every day: "Marijuana charges dropped," "Pot farmer is charged," and "$1 million in dope found in school," for example.

Still, the shrimp boats kept bringing tons of pot into Key West, where it was weighed, bagged, and sent up north in the trunks of Chevys and in the backpacks of college kids. Gainesville, the state's biggest college town, was the logical drop point. It was near the nexus of Interstate 10, which ran from the Atlantic to the Pacific, and Interstates 75 and 95, which covered the Midwest and the East Coast, all the way up to Maine.

Federal agents from the Drug Enforcement Administration couldn't find these good-old-boy flotillas and the low-altitude fly-ins. They estimated they were aware of and able to confiscate only about 10 percent of all the marijuana smuggled into the United States.

On the Key West end of the drug equation, the smuggler was usually a small-time operator, nearly a mom-and-pop storefront operation.

In 1973, seven amateur smugglers were arrested up the Gulf Coast in Steinhatchee, a small fishing village best known as the place to find king-hell scallops in season.

The "Steinhatchee Seven" (as they became known) had thirteen tons of marijuana on their boat. It was the largest pot bust to that point in American history. They wouldn't have been busted if they had had a better distribution model set up.

"We were the Robin Hoods of the day," said Steve Lamb, twenty at the time of his arrest as one of the seven.

Lamb oversaw smuggling from Jamaica, Venezuela, and Colombia. Everything went without a hitch until the big bust at Steinhatchee.

Problem was, that time they brought the dope in on a shrimp boat. For two days, the crew shoveled bales onto skiffs and dumped them on an island at the river's mouth. They were slowly moving the marijuana to waiting semitrailer trucks when the police found them.

Lamb and his crew were transferring the bundles to semis when the police pulled up.

"Busting us was the worst thing the feds could have done," Lamb said. "It opened the eyes of all the fishermen."

It empowered a lot of shrimpers and small-time operators to see what sort of money they could make in the dope trade.

Lamb and his partners each served two years, then went back into business.

"It was a perfect time to be alive and young and healthy and wealthy," Lamb said. "The fish bit better, the beer was colder, and the girls were prettier."

And the hauls were about to get larger, to meet the demand.

Whenever the feds did make a good bust, as they did at Christmas in 1973, they were aware that what they had confiscated could just as quickly be stolen back by the smugglers. When the agents confiscated thirty tons of weed (*a new record*) in South Florida, the National Guard was brought in to watch over it while it was housed in a Ringling Brothers circus tent until it was ceremoniously incinerated.

To Phil Clark, holding court at the Chart Room, smuggling was a "gentlemanly sport." Chris Robinson also tended bar there, smuggled weed on the side, and later became a successful fishing guide. He remembers Clark filling the small bar with his big tales of the pirate's life on the high seas, smuggling dope.

"Mostly it was marijuana, not cocaine," Robinson said. "It fit in with the Key West pirate atmosphere."

With a straight face, Clark often told people he was just a full-time shrimper. But to his close friends, Clark told stories in his fake Bahamian accent and bragged about serving time for smuggling in the late sixties. Behind the bar, slinging drinks, he mesmerized the Chart Room crowd.

Murphy was among the mesmerized. She'd gone off to Texas with Jerry Jeff Walker, but she wasn't there long—maybe a year—before she realized it wasn't working out, mostly because there was an additional woman in Walker's life. So she and her little boy came back to the town that had become home.

Clark was charismatic. Murphy didn't expect much more of a commitment from him than she had had from Walker. "By then he'd had about three wives and about eighty-five girlfriends," she said. She paused for a moment. "We got married in late '73."

He was charming, that Phil Clark. Didn't matter if you were man or woman or beast. Everyone loved him.

"Phil would stand at the bar and get so drunk he would almost pass out," Robinson remembered. "But he'd wake up and kick his little boot down on the ground and toss back another beer. He always had his shoulders back and had this great grin."

Clark was a delightful bastard, and when the tourists came through for a drink, looking for a recommendation on a place to stay, Clark was always quick to recommend the Pier House, the attached resort.

Usually, the tourists were fairly drunk by the time Clark sent them on their way to the front desk. "He would always get the tourists to check into the hotel," Buffett recalled, "and then he would charge all of *our* drinks to *them*."

When he wasn't slinging drinks, Clark was on the dock. He was a hirsute bloke: a beard like Jerry Garcia's, hair pulled back into a tight ponytail. Shirtless, he was like mohair, and he wore puka beads around his neck, tight jean shorts, and sandals. The men wanted to be like him. The women just wanted him.

Jimmy Buffett secretly wished he could be a pirate, like Clark. It wasn't the smuggling part that so attracted him; it was the Jim Hawkins/*Treasure Island* ambiance the man exuded. "He was a real pirate," Buffett said. "He had that kind of breath and those eyes."

Other friends suggested that Clark had been in another kind of nefarious pursuit—the advertising industry—and had reinvented himself, bogus accent and all, in the islands.

The thing about Clark was that no one knew for sure what the truth was, probably not even Clark. After a decade of reinvention and role-playing, he probably could no longer tell fact from fiction. And it was certainly a greater cachet in the mid-seventies to be a smuggler than an ad agency guy.

"I guess everybody would like to be a smuggler," Buffett mused. "It's adventurous, romantic, swashbuckling. There's something about going to sea—there's this mystery and romance—that I think is carried over in literature and music."

Smuggling had mystique. *High Times* magazine, the journal of the serious pot smoker, named Buffett the "smuggler's favorite" when he began recording his songs about life in the Keys. Buffett shrugged. "As long as I don't get arrested, that's fine," he said.

Conchs always had the live-and-let-live attitude, but there was something about the hippies that the old-timers found a little disconcerting.

There was the hair, first of all. Conchs weren't in any position to start lecturing people on hygiene. A lot of the old Conchs smelled of salt water and sweat, wearing clothes that would never again be clean. But hair was a political statement, kind of a *fuck you* to everybody.

The hair was like a passport. You might be new in town, but if you had long hair and you found yourself among the similarly hirsute, it was like a calling card.

Duuuude. Then the nod. *What's up?*

Thus was a Brotherhood of Hair born.

It looked as though the hippies were taking over in the early seventies. The U.S. Navy decided to close its Key West base, and the move was thought to be a disaster for the local economy. The city was used to the biweekly rhythms of the Navy's pay periods, when proprietors could count on the sailors getting too drunk and spending too much money. That's what kept a lot of local businesses afloat.

Now that way of economic life was ending. To the old-line, conservative Conchs, the symbolism was obvious: those damn, dirty hippies had won. The Navy with its duck whites had left and soon smelly barefooters were overrunning the place.

Tourism was not yet a big deal, so the local economy couldn't rely on it. "The town was not a great tourist destination then," Vaughn Cochran recalled. "At least, they didn't get normal tourists. They only got the ultra-hip people. The average family just didn't go. It wasn't a good family place."

That is, of course, unless your family was in organized crime. Drug smuggling was pretty out in the open, and the old Conchs associated that with . . . long hair.

The Key West police began being deluged by complaints from residents and shopkeepers in the Duval Street area:

"Help! A hippie is sleeping in my car!"

"There's a young man outside, taking a bath with my water hose. Get over here and arrest him!"

"I'm a laundermat owner and about two this morning, I found a group of hippies in the bathroom of the laundermat, taking baths. This has got to stop!"

In answer to these complaints, the police arrested thirty-two hippies in a twenty-four-hour period in December 1971. They were charged with vagrancy, even though several of them were residents of the town.

One year, a new-age entrepreneur had purchased the old Fogarty House and planned to rent out office suites to hip, young capitalists. The idea was a hippie mall. Instead, when neither the investor nor the tenants came through, it became kind of a crash pad. In came the cops, and hairy young folks were arrested and taken to jail.

Not long after that, a group of hippies moved up the Keys, to Rockland Key. There they established a roadside hippie-friendly commune to take care of travelers and avoid the hassles of Key West. But the old-timers complained and the Monroe County deputies swooped down, and, again, hairy young folks were arrested and taken to jail.

When the busts turned up marijuana, there was an eyebrow-lifting chorus of *I-told-you-so*'s from the old Conchs. Some were willing to look the other way, maybe even see if there was some way to make a little profit from this appetite for dope. Others would never relent in their hatred of long hair and all things related to it, especially marijuana.

All was not well in paradise. *Solares Hill* decided that Key West would not be able to remain immune from the poisons in the outside world.

The *Key West Citizen* continued chugging along, as most small-town dailies do. But the task fell to *Solares Hill*, the underground paper, the hippie paper, and its readers to try to lead the way to Key West's salvation.

11

A Year of Living Dangerously

Lust and greed are more gullible than innocence.
—MASON COOLEY

It was Guy de la Valdene who had the idea of making a film about fishing. Valdene's sister was dating a French filmmaker named Christian Odasso. During Odasso's visit to Key West in the summer of 1973, Valdene took him fishing and Odasso fell in love with the colors and the tranquillity on the blue water. He turned to Valdene and said, "We should make a movie."

It took months for Valdene to coordinate schedules to get McGuane and Harrison together for the film. From the beginning, he couldn't consider making the movie without them. For his part, Odasso insisted that if he was directing the film, he needed an all-French crew. By March 1974, cast and crew in place, the cameras started rolling.

The plan was to shoot fantastic fishing footage. But Valdene also wanted to show Key West: the Conch Train snaking tourists through the streets; the music and ethnic rhythms of Bahama Village; stoned conversations around the open-air tables as the Great Authors discussed the serious business of fishing. In between, there were shots of the hairy duo of Vaughn Cochran on washboard and multi-instrumentalist Gove Scrivenor on autoharp.

"We fished and filmed real hard," Valdene remembered. "We had a house on White Street and you had three or four French guys in there, and myself. And there was no serious naughtiness in those days yet. That came later. Well, there was a *little* bit—what am I talking about. But nothing really outrageous, I think, because we were so damned tired. But we did have fabulous French meals every night and a lot of wine, and then the next morning we'd be up at six thirty, filming all day."

They had everything they needed but the fishing footage. Getting the fish to perform on camera was difficult. Harrison was a master fisherman, but he had no luck when the cameras started.

"There were hundreds and hundreds of fish in Pearl Basin," Valdene recalled. "It was flat goddamn calm and they were finning all over the place and we could *not* get Jim to hook a fish! It was like, 'God, Jesus, Jim, *please!*' Here we've got the sun, the big orange sun, and a thousand fish, just imagine."

Most of the time filming was done on the flats, with two men on a skiff and the crew in an adjacent boat—Dink Bruce's—on a scaffold erected in the shallows. Only the necessary words were said. The crew made no disruptions. To contrast with the beauty and serenity, Valdene also filmed the raucous atmosphere on a party boat from Garrison Bight. Here, small sharks were reeled in and clubbed to death while tourists watched, occasionally splattered with blood and cartilage.

Since it was a film about stoned fishermen out on the flats, the footage of the tarpon leaping, wiggling in the air, was played in slow motion, accentuating the drugged-out elongation of marijuana time. Jimmy Buffett added a sound track of lilting music, all recorded during one stoned afternoon in a local studio.

When Valdene and Odasso finished the film (they took credit as codirectors), it was tough to find a distributor. *Tarpon* became much more than merely a cult film. It was a cult film within the subcategory of movies about fishing, specifically, tarpon fishing. To call it obscure is to call water wet. Yet fishermen still regard it as the holy grail of the form.

"Nobody had ever done anything like that before," Cochran said. "It was like Picasso painting a Cubist painting. It was an art film about fishing . . . completely revolutionary." Writer Carl Hiaasen, a skilled fisherman himself, called the film "a work of art."

McGuane's first screenplay to be produced was *Rancho Deluxe*, the story of modern stoned-out cattle rustlers, filmed near McGuane's ranch south of Livingston, Montana.

"I had the problem of making a living," McGuane recalled. "I'd do journalism. But the big chance of breaking out of the economics of that was writing a book and getting the screen rights sold, or getting a screenwriting assignment."

As it happened, producer Elliot Kastner bought the screen rights to *Ninety-Two in the Shade*. Immediately, McGuane told him, "This is going to be a hard film to get made. It's going to take some time."

Kastner was patient, so he asked McGuane, "Don't you have something that we can work on in the shorter term?"

As McGuane recalled, "I think I lied and said, 'Yes. It's called *Rancho Deluxe*.' "

Kastner fell for it, and then it was put-up or shut-up time. "I wrote *Rancho Deluxe* in three weeks," McGuane said. "That was dead easy."

Kastner was in love with McGuane. He locked him up for three movies—*Rancho Deluxe*, the film version of *Ninety-Two in the Shade*, and an as-yet-untitled movie that would star the reigning king of Hollywood, Jack Nicholson.

Rancho had a couple of hip young actors in the leads, Jeff Bridges and Sam Waterston, with Jimmy Buffett doing the music. Kastner signed Frank Perry as director.

Perry's record was inconsistent. First time in the director's chair, in 1962, Perry hit a home run with *David and Lisa*, a small-but-important film about two mentally handicapped people falling in love. He made some higher-profile films after that (*The Swimmer, Play It as It Lays, Diary of a Mad Housewife*) and even some quality television—most notably, a film of Truman Capote's beautiful story "A Christmas Memory." With conspiratorial eyes and a riverboat gambler mustache, Perry could look—in the right light—like Salvador Dali's American nephew. Actors loved him. He coaxed great performances from his cast and listened to their suggestions and interpretations.

That was one of the reasons Elizabeth Ashley signed on for a supporting role in *Rancho Deluxe*.

Ashley was a doe-eyed southern belle, born in North Florida horse country, raised in molasses-voiced Louisiana, and schooled for the serious stage. She did a short apprenticeship in television (*Ben Casey, Route 66*) and made a sudden impact on the big screen with her first film, *The Carpetbaggers*, the scandalous must-see movie of 1963. The next year, she held her own in the all-star film *Ship of Fools*.

Though she could have pursued a big-screen career, Ashley seemed more intent on stage work. She'd do prestige films, then series television. So that summer of 1974, when half of Key West moved to Montana for the filming of *Rancho Deluxe*, Ashley was preparing for the triumph of her acting career. She was from Tennessee Williams's Southern Gothic world and she understood his stories as few other actors could. Ashley was cast as Maggie the Cat in the American Shakespeare Festival's production of *Cat on a Hot Tin Roof* in Stratford, Connecticut.

She was pure sex on the stage. "I had to give every man in that audience a hard-on," Ashley said. "I had to bring my own private animal lust out of the closet and expose it on the stage."

After Stratford, the production was moving to Broadway. Word was out: Elizabeth Ashley was the definitive Maggie, better than Barbara Bel Geddes, who'd originated the role; better than Elizabeth Taylor, who'd played the part on film.

Trouble was, the theater in New York wouldn't be available until September 24. She had a six-week break before rehearsals began for the Broadway version of the show. That's when Ashley's agent told her about an odd little film they were making out near Livingston, Montana.

The director? Frank Perry. *Love him*, Ashley roared. Billy Fraker is the cinematographer? *Love him!* Montana? *Beautiful!*

She read the script ("funny and off the wall," she said) and had actually read the writer's first novel, *The Sporting Club*.

Lots of reasons to sign on to the film. "But mainly I thought the gig would be fun," Ashley said.

Her part was small. She played the trophy wife of the wannabe cattle baron vexed by two cattle rustlers. When she arrived on the Montana set, the movie was already half done.

She showed up one evening and immediately went to the abandoned Livingston store used by the production company for showing the cast and crew what film had been shot that day. Ashley slipped in the back of the store, looked for familiar faces and found Fraker. She started sizing up the rest of the room and her eyes landed on a tall, handsome cowboy.

"Who's that?" she asked Fraker.

"Tom McGuane, our writer."

During a break, Ashley managed a couple of minutes with McGuane, then went back to Fraker for more information.

"What's his story?" she asked.

"Married," Fraker said.

"Gotcha."

No work was planned for the next day, so McGuane invited cast and crew out to the Raw Deal Ranch for a party.

Becky McGuane greeted Ashley at the door. As they began creating their friendship, every time Tom McGuane came near, Ashley nearly lost control. She couldn't recall the last time she had been attracted to a man on such a basic, animal level.

McGuane flirted with her, as he did with any woman. His wife didn't seem to mind that he was gazing at every woman in sight with his half-mast eyes.

Nobody else on the set responded to him the way Ashley did.

McGuane came up behind her when she was bent over the pinball machine. He took her by the elbow and drew her outside.

He led her to a pickup truck, apparently not his.

"Let's fuck," he said.

"What?"

"I said let's fuck."

"I understand your meaning," Ashley responded. "I don't fuck married men. I adore your wife."

"We don't have that kind of scene," McGuane replied.

"I've never screwed a married man in my life," Ashley protested. She was considering it, however, but reasoned with herself. "If I was going to start, it certainly wouldn't be in his hometown with his wife and kid around."

"I screw everybody," McGuane told her. "Becky and I screw all the time. She's crazy about you."

Ashley took a day to think about it. The next evening, back in Livingston, McGuane approached her again. "I want to fuck you so bad I'm not going to take no for an answer."

They spent the night in his camper truck. In the morning, McGuane went home. A few hours later, Ashley was atop a horse, waiting to shoot one of her first scenes in the film, when Becky McGuane approached, calling her name. "Thomas told me all about last night," she said. "I think it's wonderful. Usually, he just screws those dumb cowgirl teenyboppers. He has the biggest crush on you."

Ashley was stunned. Here she was, a veteran of Hollywood in the free-love years and she had to come to rural Montana to find a couple with a radical marriage.

With Becky McGuane's approval, Ashley began her crazed affair with McGuane. Sex was "blood sport" to Ashley, and McGuane she saw as the center of the hurricane blowing through the middle of the seventies.

"He was Captain Berserko," she said. "The greatest kick in the world for him was breaking the rules, whatever they were. Becky once said we were like twins, that if he had been born a woman he would have been me and if I had been born a man I would have been him. We share the same character flaws. We are both creatures of excess. If you can't do it to excess, why bother to do it at all? We both want everything our way every minute."

The mad love continued all through the *Rancho Deluxe* shoot. By the time she was done with her part and ready to hit Broadway, Ashley figured it was over. There was no way that something this intense could survive all the way to the other side of the continent. As she told McGuane good-bye, Ashley laid out the conditions under which she would continue their involvement: "I want to meet you in motel rooms a couple of times a year and go off on two-week binges with you."

But back east, preparing for her role, it continued. There were nightly phone calls from both McGuanes. He came for a visit and the crazed lust continued. They went out for a matinee showing of *The Sting*, and Ashley and McGuane had sex in the front row of what they thought was an otherwise-empty theater. Only when McGuane got up afterward to go to the bathroom did they realize two little old ladies had been watching from the back of the theater.

Tennessee Williams came to the rehearsals and fell in love with Ashley, telling her emphatically that he felt blessed that she was giving voice to his words. "Everythin' you are doing is wonderful," he told her, "it's just wonderful."

Williams and Ashley enjoyed spending time together, letting their accents meander, so rarely were they in the company of other southerners. McGuane was still visiting and, since he knew Williams from Key West, they all got together for drinks. Williams was amazed at what the McGuanes were doing with Ashley. He withheld approval, but he did love the gossip.

He beheld their lust and told them, "I imagine that sex between a man and a woman is probably a very beautiful thing. But you have to understand it's somethin' that's beyond me. When I was still a very young boy, I was taken to a whorehouse for my initiation into manhood, and this woman made me look right between her legs. I don't know, all I could see was somethin' that looked like a dyin' orchid. Consequently, I have never been comfortable with orchids or women."

McGuane and Ashley thought they were exploring the next step in the evolution of male-female relationships. If they all agreed that they could love more than one person during their lives, didn't it follow that they could love more than one person at one time? This was the Tom McGuane rationale for having both his wife and Elizabeth Ashley. He wanted the sedan and the convertible. For a while, the women seemed to think that was possible. McGuane ran off for wild mad-monkey-sex weekends with Ashley, but he went home to his wife. And she was cool with it.

But then Becky McGuane began having fun with her half of the experiment. Warren Oates, a journeyman actor, part of Hollywood's "rebel crowd" that had taken up residence in Montana, had fallen in love with her. While McGuane was with Ashley back east, Oates took Becky with him to California for a mad-monkey weekend of her own.

McGuane flew into a rage. Ashley chewed him out for being hypocritical.

They all tried to talk about it on the phone. Ashley explained the new frontiers and the next step in the evolution of man-woman relationships.

Oates listened patiently. Then he said, "Bullshit."

"It's real simple," he said, "Becky and I love each other. You and McGuane love each other. Fine. Becky moves in with me. You move in with McGuane. Each of us has a civilized, sane relationship, and we all live happily ever after."

But it would never be that simple. After a week with Oates, Becky and her son flew east to be with Tom and Ashley. The whole time, McGuane had been pacing like a leashed tiger. When the plane landed, he was on his wife.

"I hope you enjoyed your little vacation," he spat. "And how is our good buddy Warren Oates?"

Again Ashley told him he was being two-faced. But at that moment, McGuane was behaving like a jealous fourteen-year-old and he couldn't hear her.

They spent the night together, though not, as McGuane had hoped, in the same bed. The next day, the McGuanes went back to Montana and Ashley returned to preparations for the Broadway production of *Cat on a Hot Tin Roof.*

They would meet again soon—in Key West.

Weird things happened in the seventies: hot pants, pet rocks, and *The Gong Show*. And in Key West, Florida, in the fall of 1974, a motion picture producer gave a million dollars to a guy who'd never directed a film before, and told him to go make a movie.

Elliot Kastner was producing *92 in the Shade*, his second McGuane-written film, and he was intent on finding a director who recognized the between-the-lines material in the story. It was about fishing guides, but it was also about the nation at large: the generational clashes, the disillusionment, the war over values. The best director for the job was Robert Altman, director of *M*A*S*H* and other counterculture films that had managed to reach wide audiences. But Kastner could not get Altman's attention. Altman had just finished making *Nashville*, another great "statement" film, and was the hottest thing in Hollywood. Next: There was talk of hiring Nicolas Roeg, who'd recently directed the über-hip *Performance*. But Roeg convinced McGuane that *he* should direct the film of his novel, and that planted the idea in Kastner's head.

"Any asshole can direct a movie," Kastner told McGuane, "and you're going to have to do it." McGuane was already well on his way to considering it for a number of reasons.

"The financing was in place," McGuane said. "Kastner owned the rights. But suddenly, he had no director. Nobody else was going to go out the window unless he supplied the director. I had never aspired to be a movie director. So suddenly, I have the job. You know how these movie deals go. You get a signing bonus and then when photography starts, you get the balance of the payment. I was economically strongly motivated to make sure this movie got made. It was pretty clear that if I didn't do it, it wasn't going to happen. So I thought, 'Well, this is seven weeks out of my life. It'll support me and my family for at least three years. I'd better do it.' "

Kastner was intent on McGuane finishing the script for that up-coming Jack Nicholson film. Kastner thought he might be able to team Marlon Brando with Nicholson. He'd produced two pathetic films with the great actor, but now Brando was in the middle of a ter-rific comeback after *The Godfather* and *Last Tango in Paris*. Brando was bankable again. Team him with Nicholson, Kastner figured, and that movie'll be a sure-fire winner.

But you need a script before you can make a film. So McGuane held the bargaining chip. *Let me direct this film,* he told Kastner, *and you'll get that Brando and Nicholson script.*

When he was making *Citizen Kane*, Orson Welles, another first-time director, said making a film was like having the best toy train set in the world. McGuane liked to quote that, dismissing the fact that he hadn't done a long apprenticeship as an assistant director or a director of photography. He'd had only one script produced. It was, in fact, the only script he had written.

Though a million dollars sounded like a lot, McGuane knew it wouldn't go very far. Luckily, he planned to shoot the film on a tight schedule in his hometown, using locations he knew well. With the Navy base closed, bringing in any kind of business, even a small-scale movie production, would be good for the economy. They could cash in a lot of chips, draw a lot of goodwill.

Peter Fonda was still one of the reigning kings of the New Hol-lywood. The son of film royalty, he had made his name as the writer-producer-star of *Easy Rider*. When he read the book *Ninety-Two in the Shade*, Fonda felt the character of Tom Skelton had been written for him. First, he wanted the rights to the novel as a producer. He was crushed when he discovered Kastner had beat him to it. Fonda was vacationing in Hawaii, but he called the mainland once a day to tell Tom McGuane, someone he hadn't even met, that he was the man for the part.

It was a coveted role. Both *Rancho Deluxe* stars, Jeff Bridges and

Ernest Hemingway on the porch of his home on Whitehead Street in Key West. He lived in the town for a decade and wrote many of his most celebrated works there, including *A Farewell to Arms, To Have and Have Not, Green Hills of Africa,* several of his greatest short stories, and the beginning of *For Whom the Bell Tolls.*
Credit: HistoryMiami

Tony Tarracino, owner of Captain Tony's Saloon. *Credit: Tom Corcoran*

Tennessee Williams in his gazebo, 1978. *Credit: Tom Corcoran* BELOW: Dink Bruce out on the flats. *Credit: Tom Corcoran*

Tom Corcoran with wife, Judy, and son, Sebastian, 1975. *Credit: Tom Corcoran*

Corcoran, not long before he left Key West, 1979. *Credit: Tom Corcoran*

Guide Gil Drake fishing with Tom McGuane. *Credit: Guy de la Valdene*

McGuane at the wheel of his boat, 1978. *Credit: Tom Corcoran*

Jim Harrison with a minor catch. *Credit: Guy de la Valdene*

Peter Fonda (left) and Warren Oates appeared as feuding fishing guides in *92 in the Shade*, released in 1975. *Courtesy of Thomas McGuane*

Margot Kidder was one of Hollywood's hottest young actresses when she filmed *92 in the Shade* with Fonda (right) in the fall of 1974. *Courtesy of Thomas McGuane*

Guy de la Valdene, French count and sportsman, 1978. *Credit: Tom Corcoran*

Hunter S. Thompson took refuge in Key West at the end of the seventies. *Credit: Tom Corcoran*

"Murphy" brought Jimmy Buffett to town. *Credit: Tom Corcoran*

Buffett, here in 1977, found his muse in Key West. *Credit: Tom Corcoran*

Valdene, McGuane, and Richard Brautigan (FOREGROUND) outside the Chart Room in 1974. *Credit: Dink Bruce*

Becky McGuane with a friend during the *92 in the Shade* shoot.
Credit: Tom Corcoran

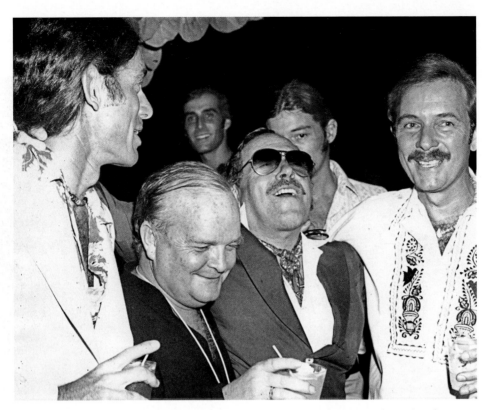

McGuane with Truman Capote, Tennessee Williams, and James Kirkwood at the *92 in the Shade* wrap party, 1974. *Credit: Monroe County Public Library / Key West*

Kidder and McGuane during their brief marriage in the mid-seventies. *Credit: Courtesy of Margot Kidder*

Elizabeth Ashley played Jeannie Carter in the film. *Credit: Getty Images*

Valdene on his North Florida estate, 2010. *Credit: Valerie Valdene*

Harrison at Pine Creek, Montana, 2010. *Credit: William McKeen*

Chatham in his Livingston gallery, 2010. *Credit: William McKeen*

Corcoran being feted at a writers' conference, 2008. *Credit: Nancy Gondak*

Thomas McGuane rarely returns to Key West and is in his fourth decade of sobriety and what he calls a "jubilant marriage." He lives on a sprawling ranch near a speck of a town called McLeod, Montana, and works in this cabin, writing the novels and stories that have placed him in the front ranks of American literature.
Credit: William McKeen

Sam Waterston, wanted to play Skelton. Warren Oates also wanted the part, badly enough to visit the *Rancho* set and impress Kastner by appearing uncredited in the film as Jimmy Buffett's harmonica player.

The competition steeled Fonda's resolve. "I was upset I didn't get the property," he said. "But I was damned if I was going to give up the part." In his head, producer Fonda had cast himself as Skelton and, as the consolation prize, he said Warren Oates could be Skelton's nemesis, Nichol Dance.

Now he just had to convince Kastner and McGuane. After a score of calls, Fonda finally scolded McGuane. "If you don't get Warren Oates to play Nichol Dance," Fonda told him, "you don't understand your own book."

Oates was sitting in the room with McGuane when he took the call. Convinced by Fonda's tenacity, he agreed to his casting suggestions. Despite coming right off the huge box-office success of *Dirty Mary Crazy Larry*, Fonda agreed to work for the union minimum, to keep the film's budget under control. If it was a success, Fonda had a deal to share in the profits.

In addition to Fonda and Oates, *92 in the Shade* had an impressive cast, including William Hickey and Burgess Meredith as Skelton's father and grandfather; young actress Margot Kidder as Skelton's free-spirited girlfriend; and Harry Dean Stanton as Faron Carter, the neutral fishing guide in the story. McGuane held the role of Carter's baton-twirling wife, Jeannie, for his favorite actress, Elizabeth Ashley.

Still, it seemed insane to hand over a million dollars, a skilled camera crew, and some of the most talented actors in Hollywood to a novice.

Second-guessers were around, but McGuane shrugged them off. Making a film was all about storytelling. He'd told the story in his novel. Now he just had to reimagine it.

Filming began, and complaints soon were coming on the set. With experience on both sides of the camera, Fonda bit his tongue. *You're cutting the scene too soon,* Fonda told McGuane. *Let the scene play out a little longer.* A more experienced director would know these things, he thought.

On his side of the camera, McGuane was having problems with his star. "Fonda was really very hard to direct," McGuane recalled. "He had a drug problem. He had a girlfriend from Hawaii who was so afraid he'd meet another girl that she would sit on the edge of the sets, watching—monitoring his every move."

Still, on the surface Fonda seemed perfect for Skelton, who was somewhat disconnected from the world. Despite his own reputation as a party animal (that was real marijuana he smoked on-screen in *Easy Rider*), Fonda was a thorough professional at work. He scoffed a bit at McGuane's view of the movie as another excuse to party.

"Warren, myself, and at least I know Michael Butler, the cameraman, were all very straight. It was Mr. McGuane himself who was going around hitting all the flowers he could find, a Mr. Bumblebee. He was being such a bad boy."

While Mr. McGuane was pollinating, both Fonda and Oates were madly in love with Mrs. McGuane.

The McGuanes and Ashley were having three-ways on the phone each night after her Broadway performance. Meanwhile, Becky continued her affair with Oates, while heartbroken Peter Fonda watched the woman he loved in a relationship with his best friend. A young actress named Margot Kidder was playing Miranda, the vibrant, sexual young woman in the film. It was obvious to everyone on the set that she had turned her director's head.

"I do remember when I first read the script," Kidder recalled. "I read this terribly well-written dialogue, not figuring out that films are about structure and the thing was totally unstructured, and I thought, 'Who is this writer? God, he's great.' I insisted on getting a meeting."

Kidder was sick the day of her audition, but she made an impression by passing McGuane a note: "I think you're a genius. I love your book. I want to be in your movie. Please call me." She was there because she admired the script, with its "great, zippy one-liners." McGuane's wit, she said, was "extraordinary." McGuane was also easy on her eyes. "There was the handsomest man I'd ever seen, with the finest body I'd ever seen," she recalled. "I pretty much fell in love right away."

Margot Kidder was a true free spirit of the times. "If you were of the sixties, there was such an innocence to the sexuality and the drugs," she said. "I was a sixties girl through and through. Us sixties girls had no hang-ups about sex." Such was not the case for McGuane and company. They were fifties men, she said, and that would end up causing problems.

"I'm all for social anarchism," Kidder said, "but chauvinism enrages me. These guys preyed on us sixties women, because, let's face it, we really put out. Then they expected us to wait on them hand and foot."

Free spirit to some, pain in the ass to others, Kidder was at least making herself known. On her arrival in Hollywood, she fell in with the talented cadre of young directors that included Steven Spielberg, Martin Scorsese, and Brian De Palma. Kidder and De Palma fell in love and the director wrote the film *Sisters* for Kidder and her best friend, actress Jennifer Salt. The film had blood, sex, nudity—all of the elements for which De Palma would become known. And it helped make Margot Kidder into the It Girl for 1974. She had a few other successful films, including *The Great Waldo Pepper* and *The Reincarnation of Peter Proud*. She also had no qualms about shrugging off clothes for the camera, and she was perfect for Miranda, the woman from whom Thomas Skelton could not extricate his heart.

As if he did not have enough on his plate, McGuane caved in when Kidder passed him that note.

So now here she was in Key West, sleeping with the director. The director's wife was having an affair with one of the stars of the movie while the lead actor pined for her. And now the director's mistress was about to fly into Key West to film her part.

"Shooting was chaos," Kidder recalled. She and Tom took the front bedroom in the McGuane home, while Becky took the back bedroom with her lover. "Tom would sit with Becky and me and talk about how there should be no jealousy. But then he'd quote Flaubert about needing to live a bourgeois life in order to be original as an artist. Through it all, Becky was heartbroken, even though she pretended not to be. She was the epitome of the 'devoted wife' and I adored her."

Becky McGuane was of a species that Kidder could not understand, and that's when she came to the conclusion that McGuane was a fifties man at heart. "There was a century between the fifties and the sixties," she said. "What I saw pretty quickly was a bunch of guys who hadn't gotten laid in high school. They'd gotten married young and [they] treated their wives like scullery maids." She saw the job description: "Being the little wifey, accepting their husband's affairs." Kidder had a strong, independent mother who'd raised her in Canada with the credo "Never trust a man."

At the moment, however, Kidder was too besotted to back away. Somehow, she managed to avert her eyes from the approaching train wreck. "We were so madly in love," she said.

Kidder was a bookworm and so she loved the company of not only McGuane but also of Harrison, Chatham, and the other writers who were in Key West, now circling around the movie set. To her, the men were all showing off for each other.

"Key West was a rather forced show that the guys put on for each other," she recalled. "It was all about Ernest Hemingway. Tom hiring Dink [Bruce]; that's all about Ernest Hemingway, because Dink's father had worked for Hemingway. It was just the seventies version of a jousting competition: who could take the most drugs and stay standing? They were all doing Ernest Hemingway the Second—on coke. But I don't think Key West was that very inspiring to any of those guys."

Kidder also saw it as a generational clash—the fifties men trying to have sex with the sixties women. "Those guys were very cynical about what they were doing and that they should be worshipped as gods by women," she said. "They'd strut around each other like peacocks and brag about how many girls they fucked. As a group, they were embarrassing. One on one, they were sweet, gentle guys, lost, gentle souls. Jim Harrison could open up and talk about being lost, depressed, or confused," she continued. "But he'd never talk that way in front of the guys. And there were two Toms. There was Captain Berserko, and then there was the Tom I loved, the sweet little boy."

To the outside world, *92 in the Shade* looked like an out-of-control movie production, with drug-gobbling actors and prolific sport-fucking, led by the wild, long-haired, libertine director. No one was trying to hide anything, so the stories leaked about all of the sexual escapades and partying. For the weeks the cameras rolled, the fun never stopped.

"I was involved in all of the drinking and other activities that went on *around* the making of the movie," Vaughn Cochran said. "In the daytime, they were making movies. I just partied with those guys every night. It was a tough pace to keep up. You know that line in that Jimmy Buffett song—'If I don't die by Thursday, I'll be roaring Friday night.' That was the absolute perfect description of what it was like to live in Key West then. In the morning, I was, 'I'm never doing that again.' By six o'clock it was, 'Well, fuck dinner. I'm going out.' "

Bleary-eyed and sleep-deprived, McGuane used whatever substances he could to keep going. For his part, he doesn't remember partying as hard as other members of the cast and crew.

"I don't think I partied at night," McGuane said. "I was too tired at the end of the day. Around that period, there was plenty of partying. I don't remember it as a big problem. What I remember is the producer saying, 'You have thirty-six shooting days and you're going to finish this film in that time whether or not you get brain cancer.' "

Still, McGuane readily admitted there was some degree of bedlam and lunacy on the film set. "I have some pretty good friends who were around when I was making *92 in the Shade*," McGuane said, "and they said I was insufferable; I'm sure they're right. The only excuse I can make is I think when you live in that world, you get a little remote, a little arrogant, and a little crazy."

Despite the fact that Oates was sleeping with his wife, McGuane helped coax a brilliant hedgehog of a performance from him as Nichol Dance. Maybe the Great Experiment he had cooked up with Ashley truly could work. Somehow, he and Oates were getting along fine.

Maybe, on the set of this film, they were establishing some new world order of relationships. That's what the seventies were about, right? Taking the ideals of the sixties and putting them into practice. No better place to do that than Key West.

"It was a wonderful time to be young," Kidder said. "The sixties didn't end until about 1976. We all believed in Make Love Not War— we were idealistic innocents, . . . despite the drugs and sex. We were sweet lovely people who wanted to throw out all the staid institutions [that] placed money and wars above all else. When you're young you think that's how life works. None of us were famous, we were broke. We didn't think they'd be writing books about us in thirty years. We were just kids doing the right thing."

Fonda was torn in several different directions. He was giving what would be regarded by some as a superb performance as Tom Skelton, despite his constant need to bite his tongue and not tell McGuane how to do his job. Meanwhile, he watched his best friend, Oates, cavort with the woman he now decided he loved, Becky McGuane. Fonda had been divorced only a few months from his wife, Susan, the mother of his two children, Justin and Bridget. But already he was mad for Becky.

Into the middle of all this stepped Elizabeth Ashley.

She had opened in *Cat on a Hot Tin Roof* on Broadway, succeeding in giving a devastatingly sexual portrayal of Maggie the Cat, panting for sex after her husband decides he's no longer interested. The performances in Connecticut had been remarkable. On Broadway, they were transcendent.

The difference, she decided, was McGuane. He had made her feel the kind of lust Maggie felt for her husband, Brick, before he cut it off. And she was cut off from McGuane, because of geography. He'd gone back to Montana, and then down to Key West to shoot *92 in the Shade*. He was holding a part for her for when her Broadway run was through.

But Broadway couldn't get enough of Elizabeth Ashley. *Cat on a Hot Tin Roof* was a hot ticket because of her onstage fire. "I knew all about Maggie's ache, Maggie's strut, Maggie's gut, Maggie's crotch," she said. "I didn't have to imagine them. I was living them out every day." She acknowledged a debt to McGuane for what he had done for her as an artist.

Now the producers wanted to extend the run of the show into the new year, but she had contracted to play this supporting part in *92 in the Shade*. She knew about Margot Kidder and knew she didn't want to go to Key West and have all of that paraded in front of her.

It finally took Becky McGuane's negotiating skills to get Ashley to get on the plane. "Elizabeth, you really do have to come," she said. "This is no way for it to end." Ashley negotiated a week off from Maggie.

When Ashley landed in Key West, there was no one at the airport to pick her up. After a long wait, McGuane showed up and tried to hug her when he got out of the car—but then he stopped. She was the Snow Queen, chilly and brittle.

She got in the car and they drove in silence. Finally, McGuane said that Becky had fixed her room, that she was staying with them.

"Absolutely not," Ashley snapped. She would go see Becky, then check into a motel. McGuane kept trying. No cracks in the ice.

"Elizabeth, this whole thing is getting way out of hand," McGuane said. "Don't you think we ought to talk about it?"

He looked at her and fell into caves of ice.

Later, at the motel, McGuane pleaded with her, but Ashley held to her resolve. "I was as cold and mean as an ice pick," she said.

Some of the auditions for *92 in the Shade* had been held in Los Angeles, and Ashley had let McGuane stay at her home, while she went back east for *Cat on a Hot Tin Roof.* She figured out the time-table in her head, factored in the little mash note from Kidder, did the math, and confronted McGuane with the classic accusation: *You fucked her in my bed, didn't you?*

McGuane admitted it. "A bed is a piece of furniture," he offered in his defense.

Nuclear winter arrived. Ashley was so furious she hurled a heavy lamp at McGuane, and he staggered back, suffering a slight concussion. Later, Becky McGuane told Ashley to laugh it off. "If there was ever a man who had it coming," Becky said, "it was him."

Somehow, McGuane and Ashley managed to hold it together for the week of shooting. They could speak as director and actor, talk about how scenes could be played. Kidder stayed out of the line of sight. But they did have one scene together.

Tom Corcoran recalled the tension: "In the confrontation at Cow Key Marina—Elizabeth Ashley versus Margot Kidder—they were vying over the affections of the writer/director. There was a constant danger of the cat fight becoming too real."

Then Ashley returned to New York and her triumph on Broadway.

When industry people wondered if McGuane knew what the hell he was doing, directing a movie full of stars cascading out of control, he always pointed back to storytelling. "A genuine fictional talent should be a robust thing capable of taking on challenges from journalism, screenwriting, or any other place where it finds itself," he said. "It became clear pretty fast that this was just another typewriter and I had to sit there and write as good a tale as I could." As a writer who enjoyed the tools of his work—words—as much as plot, he found the movie set to be another, larger playpen. "Cinema has enormously to do with language," he said.

Her part completed, Ashley returned to New York and her status as the toast of Broadway.

Warren Oates and Peter Fonda left for Texas when the shooting wrapped to begin making their new film, *Race with the Devil*. Oates knew that his relationship with Becky McGuane would not endure. He also knew that Peter was in love with her. "Flyer," Oates told his friend, "you know that Becky and Tom are getting a divorce."

Fonda immediately called Becky and begged her to come to Texas. By the time she arrived, he had filled her hotel suite with yellow roses. He proposed marriage that night. She didn't say yes then, but she did eventually.

McGuane flew off to London with Kidder. She was pregnant and soon to have his baby. He also had a film to edit, another screenplay to finish, and his "serious work," to which everyone told him he must return.

But the young author was in no hurry to do what everyone else told him to do.

"It was love for eternity," Margot Kidder said. "Little did we know it was love for a little less than three years."

12

Margaritaville

So many nights I just dream of the ocean
God I wish I was sailin' again
Oh, yesterday's over my shoulder
So I can't look back for too long.
—JIMMY BUFFETT, "CHANGES IN LATITUDES,
CHANGES IN ATTITUDES"

Tom and Judy Corcoran were part of a loose-knit tribe that had provided Jimmy Buffett room and board after his arrival in Key West in 1971.

The Corcoran home, with beautiful wife and adorable baby Sebastian, represented stability to Buffett. "I fed him," Corcoran recalled. "Jimmy had no money. He came home with me for spaghetti one night, and he picked up my guitar and started strumming a song he was working on. A couple nights later, I couldn't sleep, so I got up and started strumming the guitar, playing that song. I couldn't remember Jimmy's words, so I made up my own."

A couple of days later, Corcoran shared his lyrics with Buffett. "Damn, Corcoran," Buffett said, "you've got a song."

Corcoran was a great storyteller, and the resulting song, "Cuban Crime of Passion," was about a crazed love triangle that could exist only in Key West. "People get by and people get high," Buffett sang. "In the tropics, they come and they go."

Buffett was a musical and cultural sponge. He had grown up on the northern Gulf Coast, in Alabama and Mississippi, so he could speak the language of the water. But living hand-to-mouth in Key West introduced him to the people and places that were now infecting his songs. He soon found himself woven into the culture of the little town. He knew the bartenders, the shrimpers, and the smugglers.

It had been three years since the *Down to Earth* album and two years since Barnaby Records supposedly lost the tapes to *High Cumberland Jubilee.* As an artist, Buffett was in serious need of what the music industry called product. The original idea behind a music career had been to use it as a way to meet girls and make records. He was doing fine with the girls, but he didn't have any albums to press into their hands.

He still went on the road, doing small clubs and colleges, usually with just his guitar, Vaughn Cochran on washboard, and Greg "Fingers" Taylor on harmonica. Buffett had met Taylor in 1969, while playing a gig at his alma mater, the University of Southern Mississippi. In 1972, Taylor got in touch and said he wanted to come visit. "Just look for me on Duval Street," Buffett had told him. Sure enough, he wasn't hard for Taylor to find. When he saw Buffett, he was spread-eagled on a pool table in the Green Parrot. Buffett and Taylor joined with Cochran, and they formed the first version of what Buffett called the Coral Reefer Band.

Don Gant, a music executive at ABC Dunhill Records in Nashville, caught a couple of the small-club shows and began talking up

Buffett as a prospect for the label. No one else at the record company shared his enthusiasm, but Gant was adamant. As a former one-hit wonder, part of a band called Neon Philharmonic, Gant knew what it took to make a successful record. He described himself as "turned on" by Buffett's story songs about life in Key West. Gant was a persuasive fellow, and he managed to secure a $25,000 contract for Buffett to start his career again. Gant brought Buffett to Nashville at the end of 1972 and put him into the studio with some session musicians, and they quickly produced his reboot album for $10,000. Buffett worked fast and efficiently and used the leftover funds to buy a Boston Whaler he had had his eye on back in Key West.

The album he made, *A White Sport Coat and a Pink Crustacean*, was a blueprint for the rest of his career. Though it contained songs that could have been on any country singer's album ("The Great Filling Station Holdup," even "Why Don't We Get Drunk [and Screw]"), there were songs that no one else could do. No one else was mining the same creative territory.

McGuane knew this and was eager to write the album notes. In full lunacy mode, reminiscent of Bob Dylan's prose poems on his albums in the sixties, McGuane made it clear this artist was different:

> The folk orientation in recent music has always been selective
> and [a] little arbitrary. We are beset by the quack minstrels of
> a non-existent America, bayed at by the children of retired
> orthodontists about "hard times" and just generally depleted
> by all the clown biographies and ersatz subject matter of the
> drugs-and-country insurgence that is replacing an earlier
> song mafia. In fact, maybe your stereo has already shorted
> out with slobber anyway. Nevertheless, it does not seem too
> late for Jimmy Buffett to arrive. He is [as] dedicated as ever
> to certain indecencies and shall we say reversible brain dam-
> age; his duties toward the shadowy Club Mandible in Key

West have yet to be explained. And of course he has never washed dishes or owned a puppet show. Still, he was among the first of the Sucking Chest Wound Singers to sleep on the yellow line. And as a souvenir of some not so terrible times, this throwback altar boy of Mobile, Alabama brings spacey up-country tunes strewn with forgotten crab traps, Confederate memories, chemical daydreams, Ipana vulgarity, ukulele madness and yes Larry, a certain sweetness. But there is a good deal to admire in Buffett's inspired evocations from this queerly amalgamated past most Americans now share. What Jimmy Buffett knows is that our personal music history lies at the curious hinterland where Hank Williams and Xavier Cugat meet with somewhat less animosity than the theoreticians would have us believe.

The album's most conventional song, "The Great Filling Station Holdup," actually made a dent on the country charts, hitting a high point of number 58. The flip side of that record was "Why Don't We Get Drunk (and Screw)," a remnant from Buffett's days with Barnaby. The record company sent promotional singles of "The Great Filling Station Holdup" to disc jockeys with the same song on both sides. It pushed "Why Don't We Get Drunk" with jukebox companies, where it became a huge hit. Buffett called the song a "total satire," figuring one song ought to come out and say what all the rest of the songs only implied. "I was hearing a lot of suggestive country songs," he said, "in particular, Conway Twitty's 'Let's Go All the Way.' I figured I would write a song that would leave no doubt in anybody's mind. I thought back to a late night in an Atlanta diner where I was eating and watching this out-of-focus businessman trying to pick up a hooker."

Buffett wrote the song but on the record label it was credited to "Marvin Gardens," named after a prize property on the Monopoly

game board. Whenever he performed the song in concert, he pretended to introduce Mr. Gardens to the audience.

Despite the record company's ruse of putting "Filling Station
Holdup" on both sides of the promo single, disc jockeys on FM
stations—where the rules about playlists and lyrics were more lax—
simply played the album version of "Why Don't We Get Drunk." It
helped put Buffett on the map.

But the song merely made him appear to be a country singer who
chose not to be subtle. People who bought the album came away with
a different feeling for his music. "Cuban Crime of Passion" could not
have been conceived—much less recorded—by any other artist. He
showed his talent for melancholy reverie with "He Went to Paris," a
paean to Captain Tony, one of his new Key West friends. Two other
songs overtly addressed his love for Key West: "I Have Found Me a
Home" and "My Lovely Lady."

With the album, Buffett began crafting the image that would
serve him so well in his career. Guy de la Valdene's cover photograph
showed a slouch-hatted, bemused, and barefoot Buffett at Schooner
Wharf, perched on a couple of lobster traps. The title, a play on Marty
Robbins's old country hit "A White Sport (and a Pink Carnation),"
conveyed Buffett's gentle good humor.

"Jimmy was able to personify the lifestyle of Key West and it was
electric," Vaughn Cochran said. "The lifestyle was energetic. It was
the sun, it was being on the water every day, it was playing music and
partying. He captured all that and turned it into a product."

When it was released in June 1973, *White Sport Coat* was not a
huge hit, but it gave Buffett a higher profile. He still played on Duval
Street when he was home, but now he was getting booked as an opening act and traveling the country. He had been in the business for five
years and still felt he was in dues-paying mode. But at least he had a
record company that believed in him enough to not lose his recordings.

Still, the record company wanted Buffett to make adjustments.

He'd recorded *White Sport Coat* with Nashville studio pros, including guitarist Reggie Young and fiddle players Johnny Gimble and Vassar Clements. Even self-contained rock bands used session pros in the studio. (When the Byrds recorded their No. 1 hit "Mr. Tambourine Man" in 1965, the producer decreed that only one member of the band, leader Jim McGuinn, played well enough to be recorded.)

There had never been a question about the two Coral Reefers, Cochran and Taylor, performing on the album. Buffett did what Don Gant wanted. He was the producer, and he wanted the smooth sound of the session pros.

Now that Buffett was making modest tours, representing the record company (*Ladies and gentlemen, put your hands together for ABC Dunhill recording artist Jimmy Buffett!*), the executives felt they could say something to Buffett about his "band"—like maybe he needed to get a real one.

Vaughn Cochran became the Coral Reefer equivalent of Pete Best in the Beatles. "In the end, ABC Dunhill thought Fingers was OK, but that I didn't fit in," Cochran said. "Washboard didn't fit the look. Harmonica did. The band began growing into something more conventional."

It took a while to build. Buffett started bringing another guitar player along on tours, a guy named Roger Bartlett. But that looked like a duo, not a band. Taylor was around to join them onstage and gradually, over the space of a couple of years, Buffett began to assemble his group. Buffett and the newly expanded Coral Reefer Band opened shows for a diverse lot, from Frank Zappa and the Mothers of Invention, to Lynyrd Skynyrd, Delaney Bramlett, Three Dog Night, and Hoyt Axton. He was getting a lot of exposure to wildly different audiences, but it's unlikely fans of Frank Zappa left the concert and ran off to buy an album by the Buffett kid.

Still, Don Gant was pretty sure the Buffett kid was on to something, that there was something unique in his songs.

A tragedy also helped Buffett's career. Buffett had gotten to know Jim Croce when he'd come to Key West to play. Croce became hugely popular in the early seventies with the story songs "You Don't Mess Around with Jim" and "Bad Bad Leroy Brown" and lovely ballads such as "Operator" and "Time in a Bottle." Buffett and Croce were friends and Croce, though a major star, would sometimes play sideman to Buffett in the Chart Room. He liked Buffett's songs. The two men seemed to have a lot in common.

On September 20, 1973, Croce was killed in a plane crash on his way to a concert appearance in Texas. He left behind a wife, an infant son, and a career full of promise. Buffett was devastated.

Both musicians were with ABC Records. What Croce had shown, in the space of a year, was that there was a market out there for sensitive-singer-songwriters-who-could-also-be-up-tempo-and-who-couldn't-really-be-classified. Croce had nearly single-handedly created that audience. Now ABC wanted to slip Buffett into that slot.

Gant got Buffett back up to Nashville as soon as he could, and booked time at Woodland Studios in October 1973.

The sessions went well—again, with studio pros such as Doyle Grisham and Tommy Cogbill, that much was expected. During the last day of recording, Buffett nailed his version of Lord Buckley's "God's Own Drunk." While the "lightweights" celebrated the end of the sessions with champagne, Buffett and drummer Sammy Creason decided to get a bottle of tequila and a couple of straws.

"We went at it and in fifteen minutes we were just knee-crawlin' drunk," Buffett recalled.

There was no entertainment in their hotel's bar, so Buffett banged on his acoustic guitar and Creason destroyed the drums left behind by the lounge act. They were drunk and incoherent. They were also hungry, but the kitchen at the King of the Road Motor Inn was closed.

Out in the parking lot, Buffett couldn't find his rental car, so he climbed on the hood of the nearest car and surveyed the lot. Turns out he was wearing golf shoes. They were secondhand golf shoes with the cleats removed, but there was still enough residue of cleat to mess up the finish of a fine car, such as the one on which he was standing.

It belonged to a man attending a law-enforcement convention at the King of the Road. In fact, it was the car of one of the principal speakers: the tough-talking sheriff Buford Pusser, whose life story had recently been turned into the movie *Walking Tall*, which electrified drive-in moviegoers of the South, in the heart of Cracker America.

And now Buffett was standing on his car, messing up the finish. Sheriff Pusser took note.

There was no time for introductions. Buffett had no idea that he was dealing with the biggest bad-ass in American law enforcement in 1973, the redneck version of Dirty Harry. "I just thought he was some ex-football player turned counselor," he said.

"Son, you stay right there," Pusser ordered. "You're under arrest."

Buffett turned around. "You can kiss my ass," he responded.

Buffett jumped down and joined his friend in the now-located rental car. Pusser followed them and stuck his head into the driver's-side window, inches away from Buffett.

"Would you like for me to turn this car over?"

Creason promised Pusser that if there was any damage to his car, to just let the folks at ABC Dunhill know, and they'd pay for it. After all, this fellow—he nodded at Buffett—was a major recording artist.

"No, they won't," Buffett yelled at Creason. Then he looked at Pusser. "I'm still gonna beat your ass if you don't leave us alone."

This was too much for Pusser. He reached inside the car, grabbed Buffett by the hair on the back of his head, and held him in place.

"I had a big bald spot on the back," Buffett said. "I looked like a monk for about three months. "

They couldn't leave because the rental car was an AMC Gremlin and one of the safety features of the Gremlin was a device that would not allow the ignition to turn over until the seat belts had been buck-led. But Buffett was too busy holding on to his hair to strap in, and Pusser was repeatedly punching Creason in the nose.

"Sammy, I don't wanna die in a Gremlin," Buffett cried. With all of his strength, he buckled his seat belt and pulled out. Eventually, Pusser had to let go.

They drove to a nearby restaurant, Charlie Nickens Bar-B-Q, to nurse their wounds and consume pork products. But then they re-turned to the King of the Road, still wary that the crazy man—they still had no idea who he was—lurked in the bushes. For protection, they got out the tire iron, brandishing it as they walked the gauntlet of prosecutors in the lobby. When Buffett got up to his floor, he real-ized he'd lost his room key.

Creason was too nervous to make that walk again, so he handed Buffett the tire iron. Buffett stuck it in his back pocket. As he stood at the front desk to get his replacement key, he felt someone slide the tire iron from his pocket. He turned around and the big bastard was there.

"I whipped around and I said, 'Look you, that was for my protec-tion, and you started this whole thing. I didn't mean to get on your car and I'm still gonna beat your ass if you don't quit bothering me.' "

Then, two good-natured police officers took Buffett by the arms and led him to the elevator. "Son, we *would* call the police and have you arrested," one of them said, "but we figure you're just lucky to be alive because that was Buford Pusser."

Now Buffett understood. "Oh. Eighth floor please."

When the album *Living and Dying in 3/4 Time* was released in Feb-ruary 1974, it again propped up Buffett's laid-back island image with Valdene's cover photo. He was perched on the bow of a half-sunken smuggler's boat, ironically named *Good Luck*. There was a bigger budget this time and so there was a gatefold cover, which was given over to a painting of a psychedelic Key West sunset by artist Rick Bibby. The music inside the album was a mixture of lilting ballads and somewhat standard country fare.

But it gave Buffett his first hit single. Musicians from Artie Shaw to Simon and Garfunkel to Kiss had written songs about the loneliness of the musician's life on the road. Few were as evocative as "Come Monday," which took the form of a reassuring phone call from a performer to his lover back home.

Buffett by now had a steady girlfriend, a model named Jane Slagsvol, whom he'd met when she came to Key West on vacation. He'd seen her making a call in a phone booth outside the Chart Room in the fall of 1972. He'd come out of the bar to introduce himself when she hung up, and now she was the woman he wrote songs about.

Dressed in strings and Nashville ultrasmooth backing vocals, "Come Monday" had the elements of country-music schlock, but Gant as producer and Buffett as artist managed to hold on to the essential, simple truth of the song. In the hands of a conventional singer—Ronnie Millsap, let's say—"Come Monday" would come off as pure cornball, but the swallows and recesses in Buffett's voice, as well as its sleepy clarity, matched the soaring, sentimental melody.

Buffett was visiting London when he realized it was a success. "I heard it on the radio and called the States and got the good news," he recalled. "I guess that was when I realized I might be able to keep my phoney baloney job for a while."

The problem with Buffett was that no one in the industry could figure out how to classify his music. It wasn't conservative enough to be country, and the subjects of his songs wouldn't please the George Jones crowd. He did not quite match Jim Croce as a comic-book storyteller or as a sensitive-new-age-guy poet. And Buffett's music didn't have the stirring in the groin that the rock crowd wanted.

Originality was a blessing and a curse.

Despite having a modest hit, Buffett was still a cult artist. He traveled the circuit of small halls and big clubs (Max's Kansas City, Nashville's Exit/In, The Troubadour in Los Angeles). Gant kept pushing him to write and record, but Buffett was intensely loyal to his friends, so when Guy de la Valdene asked him to write a score for *Tarpon*, his fishing documentary, Buffett obliged, delivering the music in a day. Later that summer, McGuane insisted Buffett do the music for *Rancho Deluxe*, and also appear in the movie as a singer in a bar. Not much of a stretch there, but still, the Buffett kid was a relative unknown. To turn over the sound track of a movie to an untested one-hit wonder didn't seem like the prudent thing to do. But McGuane had hypnotized producer Elliot Kastner and he could get whatever he wanted, and he wanted Buffett to do the music.

Before the end of the year, Gant had gotten Buffett to record another album, one that firmly planted Jimmy Buffett and Key West in the public consciousness. *A1A* was named for the highway that connected Key West to the mainland. It also contained one of his greatest songs about the town.

"A Pirate Looks at Forty" was Buffett's love song to Phil Clark. Buffett was twenty-eight. To be forty was inconceivable. And yet, here was Phil Clark, behind the bar at the Chart Room, still living the life.

Suddenly, the Key Westers realized that Buffett was taking their day-to-day and packaging it for mass consumption. Buffett was serving the chamber-of-commerce function for the mass audience of hippies, college kids, daydreamers, and people who imagined a paradise with cold drinks and pretty women in tiny swimsuits, and a life monumentally perfect and serene.

He was picking up some far-flung fans as well. The governor of Georgia, Jimmy Carter, made inroads with younger voters when he began quoting Bob Dylan in his speeches. Now, as a long-shot candidate for the presidency, he was proudly proclaiming Jimmy Buffett and the Coral Reefer Band as the Carter family's favorite entertainers. Carter's honest but ill-advised slip of the tongue during that campaign (telling *Playboy* magazine that he had committed adultery in his heart many times) cost him some points in the polls, but he had no problem aligning himself with an artist who so well endorsed hedonism and whose band's name wink-winked at marijuana as an influence.

It's one thing to have a cult following, even if a presidential contender is a member of the cult. It's another to truly be a success. But that was waiting for him.

As the presidential campaign was winding down—with Carter as the Democratic nominee—Buffett was in the studio recording the album that became *Changes in Latitudes, Changes in Attitudes.* It was his most thoroughly realized album to date, in that every song was part of his vision of the Key West life. The Eagles couldn't have made that album. Neither could James Taylor or John Lennon. Buffett had created a milieu that was his personal, artistic property.

The month that Buffett and the Coral Reefers played at the inaugural ball for President Jimmy Carter, the album was released and Jimmy Buffett left behind cult status and became a major figure in American popular music. He also provided a boost to the Key West economy.

When the Navy pulled out, it was as if the city had been gutted like a swordfish on the rack at Murray Marina. The guts of the fish—in this case, the economy—lay all over the dock.

Now, because of a song, there was a new influx of tourists. Instead of only the extremely wealthy and eccentric, there were more middle-agers, more middle-classers, and more office-cubicle-daydreamers on their vacations who pointed the car south on U.S. 1.

Buffett's song "Margaritaville" became his biggest hit, reaching

No. 1 on *Billboard* magazine's Adult Contemporary chart, No. 8 on the Hot 100 chart, and No. 13 on the Country Singles chart. Beyond that chart success in early 1977, the song began to build a hard-core audience of fans that few other artists could claim. The Grateful Dead's army of fans, the Deadheads, were unmatched in pop music, but Buffett's fans, soon to be known as Parrotheads, were a similarly devoted legion. During the 9-to-5, they were daydreamers in cubicles, secretaries and middle managers who dressed in JC Penney and drove sensible compact cars. But when a Buffett concert was announced, they donned tropical plumage, made blenders full of umbrella drinks, and went to the arena to commune with the Great Man.

Buffett began building his music empire on the basis of "Margaritaville," but it did not have its foundation merely on ticket sales. He built his fortune on his summer concert tours. Like the Beach Boys, Buffett was an artist who identified himself with a particular environment and season.

"Margaritaville" seemed a lightweight confection, but like the best of Buffett's songs, it worked because of the details in his storytelling. The song told of a hangover, of half-remembered words and deeds, and of a lethargic, blissful life. In between, there's the imagery of "all those tourists, covered with oil," those sensory feelings of stepping on a pop-top, smelling the shrimp, beginning to boil. "Wasting away again in Margaritaville," he sings. "Some people claim there's a woman to blame." Something's troubling the singer, but he's not going to worry about it too much.

Fuck it—let's have another drink.

And that was the era encapsulated. In four minutes and twelve seconds, Buffett had bottled up the essence of Key West in an effervescent, maddeningly memorable pop song. We live from day to day, with peaks and valleys of inebriation and sobriety.

Fuck it—let's have another drink.

Buffett had tapped into the Lost Chord of the Tropics. The song didn't use reggae, the dominant Caribbean sound of the time, but instead had a vague echo of calypso, a sound whose time in the mass marketplace had peaked nearly two decades before with Harry Belafonte's records.

So now Buffett presented those office proles with a new World of Oz, Margaritaville (Key West), just 130 miles down that two-lane blacktop from Miami. The song didn't mention Key West by name, nor did any of the bars or hangouts get a shout-out. But everyone knew where Margaritaville was.

Buffett was often asked if he ever tired of singing the song. "The answer is no," he said. "It has paid the rent for a long time and seems to put a few minutes of joy into this troubled world when sung by fans at a show. I feel very lucky."

Here they came. Suddenly, all of those moms and pops who ran businesses in Key West, the ones who'd been gnawing their fingernails ever since the Navy pulled out, saw salvation. The good times, the fat times as a Navy town, seemed all gone a few months before, but now there was a different kind of tourist and the money was coming back, and coming back at a much higher level. This financial windfall wouldn't depend on a two-week cycle of Navy paychecks. This was steady, heavy income. How heavy depended on how much they drank.

The old Navy base found new life, and a new name, as Truman Annex, after the president who had visited the island most often. Coincident with the Buffett-inspired tourists was an influx of homosexual visitors, who knew that the island's live-and-let-live attitude gave great latitude for the gay lifestyle. Soon, gay couples were taking out extended leases on the condos being carved out of the old Navy quarters in Truman Annex.

The worker bees who came to Key West to find a few moments of that "Margaritaville" euphoria gave new life to resorts in decline. Sloppy Joe's wrapped itself in Hemingway mystique, selling T-shirts emblazoned with Papa's image as preserved by Yousuf Karsh. Soon, visitors could schlep back up to the mainland with 100 percent cotton proof of their visit to Margaritaville.

The title song of that breakthrough album of Buffett's best summarized his philosophy of life. Back on his first Key West album, he had sung, "I have found me a home." The rules were different in Key West. Buffett used that sentiment in his music, but with a twist that made the song more universal:

> It's these changes in latitudes, changes in attitudes
> Nothing remains quite the same
> With all of our running and all of our cunning
> If we couldn't laugh, we would all go insane

In the space of five years, Jimmy Buffett had gone from scruffy street singer, chased away from his perch in front of a Duval Street dress shop, to a performer who filled football stadiums. He had come to Key West as a failed country singer, had found his identity, and had now presented himself to the world as the human embodiment of the island life. He'd been on the run from a bad marriage when Jerry Jeff and Murphy brought him to town, but now he had married that girl in the phone booth, and their wedding was attended by rock 'n' roll royalty. They were starting a family, and if there was one thing that Jane Buffett knew, it was that Key West was no place to raise a child.

13

The King of Gonzo

*Paradise can be found on the back of horses, in books
and between the breasts of women.*
—ARAB PROVERB

When Jimmy Buffett began making big money, he figured maybe it was time to start spending time away from Key West.

Chris Robinson, his downstairs neighbor on Waddell Street, saw the change happen just as "Margaritaville" was all over the radio. Having a hit song about Key West was death to an artist who might want to hang out in the town that inspired the song. Suddenly, everyone was in love with it, and everyone knew who he was. Tourists came down U.S. 1 and expected Buffett to greet them at the city limits. They figured he played at most of the bars on Duval and expected to see him walking the streets in his cargo shorts and flip-flops, with a Corona in his hand.

"That place in Key West got a little too easy for people to knock on the door with a six-pack of beer and come play with him," Robinson said. "Jimmy slowed down living up there. He was living in Aspen mostly."

Jane Buffett had decided that Aspen, Colorado, would be a better place to raise children, and so they set about making their lives there. Like Key West, it was a resort town, but it wasn't as stifling as being on a small island. Instead of being the only celebrity in town, Buffett would be one of hundreds. *Look! There's Jack Nicholson! And over there—it's Robert Wagner and Natalie Wood! Oh! Which Kennedy is that?*

Buffett held on to his bachelor-era Key West apartment and had Chris Robinson look in on it. He'd use it when he visited and occasionally he gave the key to friends who had planned a fishing trip or laid-back time down there.

Tom Corcoran got a call from Buffett, asking him to keep a look out for a special guest who might need some extra help. He was a friend from Aspen and he was going to stay at the Waddell Street apartment indefinitely. He wasn't old or feeble or anything, but he was the kind of guy who demanded an extraordinary amount of assistance just to function on a daily basis. The smallest parts of life were a struggle.

Can you help me out? Buffett asked.

Sure thing, Jimmy, Corcoran said. *No problem.*

Then he hung up the phone and broke into a cold sweat. *Jesus Christ,* Corcoran thought, *Hunter S. Thompson's moving in. How am I going to survive* this?

At that moment, Hunter S. Thompson was the most famous writer in America. Yet he was not writing.

He had suffered a massive writer's block since the introduction of cocaine into his daily diet in 1974. He had gone from an erratic but productive correspondent to an unreliable writer who routinely missed magazine deadlines.

In the early seventies, he had been the meal ticket for *Rolling Stone* magazine and had done much to put it on the map with his "Fear and Loathing in Las Vegas" serial and his coverage of the 1972 presidential campaign. More-traditional writers admired the audacity of his writing, known as "gonzo" for its pure balls-to-the-wall approach to journalism. The generation then in college tried to imitate his style and watched his every move. To a million college kids, he was a god.

Then he decided to try that drug he'd been putting off trying for so long. It knocked him off his perch.

In 1974, *Rolling Stone* had sent him to Zaire to cover the fight between Muhammad Ali and George Foreman. Not only was Thompson unable to write a word about the fight, he didn't even attend it, instead floating in his hotel's swimming pool, into which he'd dumped a massive amount of marijuana. The day after the fight, writer George Plimpton—who *had* attended the Ali-Foreman bout—showed up at Thompson's hotel to check on him, to see why he hadn't been at the fight. Thompson told him about floating in the pool of marijuana and how the only other soul he saw at the deserted hotel sat by the pool, staring at him, probably wondering if the strange man on the air mattress was dead. "Maybe he thought I was a corpse," Thompson told Plimpton. Plimpton asked if the experience of floating in marijuana held any kick. "It's not the best way to obtain a high," Thompson mused, "but a very luxuriant feeling nonetheless."

Thompson went to Saigon in 1975 to cover the end of the Vietnam War for *Rolling Stone.* Yet despite the adrenaline rush of being in a war zone, he produced mere squibs of copy compared with the massive angry screeds that had first put him on the literary map.

Rolling Stone had also subsidized a 1976 trip to New Orleans for

Mardi Gras, hoping for more "Fear and Loathing" magic. The magazine paid all expenses for Thompson, Buffett, and friends Montgomery Chitty and Bill Dixon. The four had a tremendous, drunken time. And not a word was written.

If Jann Wenner, the editor of *Rolling Stone*, had not so loved his star writer, that would have been the end of Thompson's career. Still, Wenner kept trying to coax Thompson back to the fields of productivity.

Thompson's first great years coincided with his marriage. He'd been with Sandra Dawn Thompson for nearly fifteen years by the late seventies, and she had supported him emotionally and spiritually through the writing of his first three books, *Hell's Angels, Fear and Loathing in Las Vegas*, and *Fear and Loathing on the Campaign Trail*. She was largely unaware of his prolific infidelities for most of that time. He told himself that, as he was an on-the-road journalist, all desirable women were fair game.

Thompson was a voracious drug user, but he had stayed away from cocaine until 1974. Then he could not get enough. Not only did the drug affect his writing—which became an even more agonizing experience for him—but it also ate away at the foundation of his marriage. He wasn't as careful as he had been in covering up his affairs. When his wife came across a tape recording of Thompson with another woman, it was over.

The marriage ended, and it ended ugly. A deputy sheriff was called to their home outside of Aspen, to ensure that when Sandy left, her husband caused her no harm. A long, bitter divorce war had begun. Thompson was happy to accept Buffett's offer of his place in Key West. He needed to get away from Colorado and he needed to get away from this stifling identity he had created for himself.

Thompson and Buffett had a lot in common. Both were prisoners of personas they had created. Buffett's fans believed him to be a lovable lush, a happy-go-lucky party boy. He was some of that, but he was also extremely well read, serious about art and literature, and an astute businessman.

Thompson had created an exaggerated version of himself as a drug-crazed madman, nearly foaming at the mouth with rage over the right-wing rulers of the country. That was an enhanced version of reality. Thompson was in person a southern gentleman, extremely well (self-) educated, and serious about his work. By the mid-seventies, he began to feel trapped by his image. He had even become—against his will—a character in Garry Trudeau's popular *Doonesbury* comic strip. He had officially turned into a caricature of himself.

So among the cocaine, the divorce, and the suffocating image, Thompson was ready for a change. Buffett recognized this and handed him the keys to a new life in Key West. "I was angry," Thompson said. "I was, frankly, going through kind of a mean divorce situation and Buffett said, 'I've got a good apartment [there]. Why don't you take the apartment for a while, get out of town, hang out down [there]?' "

For Thompson, a man with a serious Hemingway fixation, Key West was a great place to chase that literary he-man dream. His borrowed home had a narrow stretch of beach and was just a couple of blocks from Hemingway's estate on Whitehead Street. Just as Hemingway set the agenda for those who followed in his wake, Thompson was Alpha Dog for his generation of writers. Artist Ralph Steadman, a frequent Thompson collaborator, said that the time in Key West allowed his old friend to indulge in the fantasy of "being Hemingway."

Thompson shared McGuane's great talent for putting the right combinations of friends together to create new friendships. Corcoran did that as well, so he took it as part of his Buffett mandate to make sure Thompson met the right people.

In addition to hanging out with Corcoran, Thompson got to know his duplex-mate, Chris Robinson. Robinson and Buffett had been good friends, and when the singer had married in Aspen in 1976, Robinson had made the trip and been introduced to Thompson on his home turf. "Here comes this guy in a suit, with wing-tipped shoes, semi-bald and short hair, the straightest-looking guy in the world," Robinson recalled. "And he was handing out acid to anyone who wanted some."

Another Florida friend at the wedding, Dan Mallard, said Thompson had not officially been invited because he inspired fear among friends. No one knew what sort of wide-screen epic prank he might plan. Even without an invitation he showed up, and in addition to the acid, he enlivened the reception by bringing a dog that had been sprayed by a skunk.

"He kept the dog under the table," Mallard said. "No one saw the dog, but they sure as hell smelled him."

Thompson and Robinson had prime real estate on the tiny two-by-four island. "We lived right next door to Louie's Backyard, a *real-fine* four-star restaurant," Robinson said. "Their exhaust fan used to come up right next to the upstairs window of Buffett's place, and I guess the kitchen burned something one time and all of this smell was coming over and so Hunter had this tape of all these S&M sounds . . . erotic orgasm sounds. And Jimmy had these big speakers— hundred-and-some amp JBL speakers. And Hunter put on the tape and cranked that thing up and aimed the speakers over at the restaurant: *'Oh! Oh! Oooh! Oh my God! Jesus!'* We were just howling and all those poor people next door were trying to dine." Day-to-day life as Thompson's housemate wasn't challenging. He was not the outrageous character that Garry Trudeau portrayed.

"Hunter would rant and rave up there, but I learned not to try to out-gonzo Mr. Gonzo," Robinson said. "He would get up in the morning—well, not the morning, he'd get up in the afternoon—and watch all of the different stations and read all the newspapers. Then we'd go down to the water and sit there and smoke a doobie together and have a nice conversation. The only time Hunter would get bizarre is when someone would try to out-bizarre him."

Like many Conchs, Robinson held a variety of jobs, eventually be-coming a successful fishing guide, as the owner of Big Kahuna Char-ters. Also like many Conchs, he spent time in the dope-smuggling trade. After getting pinched by the Coast Guard for smuggling a small amount of marijuana ("They *did* drop the charges," he pointed out), Robinson amused himself in a local wood shop trying to figure out some way to keep Coast Guard wives happy while their husbands were out busting dealers. He studied how the wood shop's antique jigsaw worked. It had a steady up and down motion that reminded Robinson of vigorous, pile-driving intercourse. With the jigsaw as inspiration, he used scrap parts from bicycles and lamps and con-structed something about the size of a clothes dryer, attaching an old metal tractor seat covered in heavy vinyl. He then affixed a latex ap-pendage rising from the center, a dildo with settings for two-, four-, and six-inch strokes. As a decoration on the front of the machine, Robinson carved a mahogany mushroom-shaped penis head.

The machine was operated with a handle that allowed the rider to control the speed of the insertion of the dildo.

"It came up on a ten-speed sprocket and, man, that worked better than we could," Robinson said.

Thompson wasn't known for doing much with his hands other than writing and shooting guns. He was fascinated by Robinson's craftsmanship and admired the assembled apparatus in the wood shop.

A few nights later, he pounded downstairs and beat on Robin-son's door.

"Chris! Chris!" Thompson yelled. "I've got this woman upstairs and she's asleep in the bedroom. I want her to find your machine in the living room when she wakes up."

Thompson and Robinson carried the machine from the wood shop and up the narrow covered stairway to Thompson's apartment. When the woman awoke, the presence of the sculpture achieved its intended effect.

It became Thompson's new favorite toy, and he kept it in his apartment for months, inviting friends over in the evenings to watch young women ride it.

"The two-inch stroke was the better stroke," Robinson remembered. "You had good penetration and although it was a shorter stroke, you could put the seat down so it went up farther. It just had enough play in it and had enough noise that the rhythm of the sound got them excited. It was kind of like a freight train: *'Choo Choo!'* We had girls breaking into the house to ride this thing."

But Thompson was not always a randy bachelor when he visited Key West. Although he was still suffering the agonies of divorce, Key West was also where he began one of the most important relationships in his life.

Laila Nabulsi was a beautiful young woman working on the hottest show on television, *Saturday Night Live.* From its debut on October 11, 1975, the program had defined the weekend for young Americans. It was the epitome of appointment television; people went out of their way to watch the show. Part of the attraction was its cast of Not-Ready-for-Prime-Time Players, including Chevy Chase, Dan Aykroyd, and the unpredictable John Belushi.

The show quickly earned a place in public consciousness, lobbing catchphrases into popular culture almost weekly. Nabulsi was a segment producer and a good friend of Belushi and his wife, Judy Jacklin. She often got drafted into Belushi projects, including the skit-turned-band that Belushi and Aykroyd had created, the Blues Brothers. There were a lot of continuing skits on *SNL,* from the *cheeseburger-cheeseburger* diner to the killer bees to the samurai desk clerk. The Blues Brothers had been conceived as a one-off skit, but when Aykroyd and Belushi announced they were taking the act on the road during the TV show's hiatus, Nabulsi became road manager. It wasn't a vanity project for hotshot TV stars. Guitarist Steve Cropper and bassist Duck Dunn, two of the greatest musicians in rock 'n' roll history, signed on to be sidemen. Nabulsi was friendly enough with Belushi that he felt comfortable asking her for favors.

One night in 1977, a couple of years into the show's run, he called to ask her to drop by his apartment and pick up a jacket from his front closet. When she brought it by his dressing room, it was the usual crazed preshow scene.

"There was this guy lying on the couch," Nabulsi recalled. "I didn't know who it was. I just remember thinking, 'Uh-oh.' I had this feeling like a bomb dropped. I kind of knew from the second I saw him that I was either going to love him or hate him."

Belushi and Aykroyd had made a cross-country road trip the summer before and invited themselves to Thompson's farm outside of Aspen. They'd befriended Thompson and even talked of making a film of his masterpiece, *Fear and Loathing in Las Vegas*, with Aykroyd as Raoul Duke and Belushi as Dr. Gonzo. Nothing came of it, but a friendship began. Thompson once said that John Belushi was "more fun in twenty minutes than most people are in twenty years."

Now, a year later, Thompson had come to watch a taping of the show, but after meeting Nabulsi, he decided to linger backstage. Later, at the Belushis' apartment, Thompson talked with his hosts but would not allow Nabulsi out of his line of vision.

In the morning, she walked home to her apartment and he followed. "Suddenly," she said, "he was in my apartment and wouldn't leave." They ended up spending the next two weeks together, mostly at Thompson's hotel, the Gramercy Park. "I knew right away he was the most original person I'd ever met," she continued. "Plus, he had quite a physical presence—very good looking. He was very funny, but I didn't get his humor right away. The first night I met him he went into the bathroom in John's dressing room and when he came out I asked if he was okay and he said, 'I was weeping,' and I thought he was serious. In the hotel we were talking and he would wander into the living room and make wailing noises. I thought he was crazy and I was trying to figure out how I was going to get out of this room. Then he would come back into the room and be perfectly normal and then go do it again. I was completely terrified. Finally I yelled, 'Stop it!' and he started laughing and said, 'I'm just looking for my lighter.' And after that moment, I got him."

Belushi was also from the broken-mold school of humanity and was one of Nabulsi's close friends, but knowing him and his eccentricities still did not prepare her for the Hunter Thompson Experience.

"I had never met anyone who looked like that or acted like that," she said. "He would answer the phone screaming, *'What?'* I had never met anyone who did things like that. He was such a wordsmith and he had a lot of fun with words."

Once, during those two weeks at the Gramercy Park, she heard him speaking on the phone, and there was something in his voice that puzzled her.

"The way he was talking to them made me ask who he was talking to," she recalled. "He said, 'Sandy.' And I asked who that was and he said, 'My wife.' And that was that." Nabulsi was horrified. She hadn't known who Thompson was when they met, much less known anything about his private life. There had been no mention of a wife for the two weeks they were together and he certainly didn't act like a married man.

"That was the end of it," Nabulsi said.

A year later, one of her *Saturday Night Live* friends invited her to a party. As she stood in the lobby of the building waiting for an elevator, the door opened and Thompson fell out. Later, alone together in a bar, he told her that he was in the middle of a divorce. Not long after that, they were at Buffett's place in Key West. "He was very happy in Key West," Nabulsi remembered. "That's when Hunter and I really started."

Thompson filed for divorce on February 9, 1979.

Nabulsi was his compass, but Thompson could not avoid the complications of a divorce. His soon-to-be ex-wife wanted to sell their home, a hundred-plus acres called Owl Farm, and split the profits. Thompson was aghast; he *was* Owl Farm. To argue in court that it was a part of his being, he even used *Doonesbury* strips as examples: Uncle Duke was portrayed at Owl Farm. How could she separate him from his womb? Thompson was still making payments on the farm and the place had a $450,000 market value. He felt entitled to keep it. They also squabbled over his gun collection, his wife's lawyers suggesting that it be sold and that she get half the profits. He had a lot of electronic equipment and other personal effects as well. She wanted to sell everything to dispose of the evidence of their lives together. Thompson wanted his life to go on as it had, just without his wife.

In the middle was Thompson's fifteen-year-old son, Juan. He lived with his mother, and though his father had been a phantom presence in his early life (Juan was awake and silent when his father was asleep, and Juan slept while his father worked), they were nonetheless close; Thompson loved his son and Juan fiercely admired his father.

Sandy Thompson felt a rightful claim to a goodly portion of her husband's assets. After all, she had been functioning as his editorial assistant/typist/research assistant/caretaker for nearly twenty years. Thompson's income for the last full year of their marriage (1978) was over $100,000. He lived mostly hand-to-mouth. Even when he was at his peak of fame in the early and mid-seventies, he was constantly badgering editors to be paid for stories and reimbursed for expenses.

In the four years since the end of his coverage of the Watergate scandal for *Rolling Stone*, however, he had written only five major articles.

It was retread time. Though he could manage (at most) one article a year, Thompson was about to have his greatest commercial success as a writer—a success owing, in part, to his writer's block.

Jim Silberman, Thompson's editor at Random House, had left that company to form his own publishing imprint, Summit Books. One of his first major titles was *The Great Shark Hunt*, a long-delayed anthology of Thompson's writing.

Thompson was one of the most famous writers in America, but he was always cash poor. Finally, he felt he was on the crest of a new financial wave with his new hernia book (more than six hundred pages). *The Great Shark Hunt* drew a lot of attention and sold rapidly to his built-in audience: all of those fans who had been waiting for something new from Thompson for most of the seventies. Finally, there was a book, though much of it was old. Many of the pieces were from his days as a *National Observer* correspondent in South America in the early sixties. The anthology also drew generous excerpts from his books *Hell's Angels*, *Fear and Loathing in Las Vegas*, and *Fear and Loathing on the Campaign Trail.*

Alas, the book had apparently been edited with a shovel. It was difficult to figure out the organization. David Felton, a former colleague at *Rolling Stone*, called it "probably the worst-edited and most self-indulgent work since the Bible. There doesn't seem to be any order." The early writing, Felton said, was "flat and uninspired."

Thompson didn't seem to mind the criticism; in fact, he seemed to agree with it. "I thought it would be pretty fun to see the development from [his career in] the Air Force to the [Muhammad] Ali piece [from 1978]. It seems like I've been writing the same thing, really, since I was eighteen years old. . . . I'll stand by this," he shrugged. "It's messy. It's fucked up."

Still, *Shark Hunt* drew several strong reviews, with most critics taking the chance to assess the first twenty years of Thompson's published writing, much of which had been difficult to find. *The New*

Republic compared him to Mencken and admired him for writing about moving targets. *The Nation* suggested that Thompson's view of modern America was truer than that of more conventional journalists. And conservative William F. Buckley said Thompson elicited "the same admiration one would feel for a streaker at Queen Victoria's funeral."

The Great Shark Hunt meant money, and Thompson needed it desperately. His paychecks were few and far between, and when his wife's lawyers asked for their share of the *Shark Hunt* advance, Thompson's attorneys said the money had already been spent.

He was in Key West, taking a sabbatical from publishing, figuring that anything new he wrote while still married would be considered joint property, of which his wife would be entitled to 50 percent.

In the introduction to *The Great Shark Hunt*, Thompson confessed to standing at a crossroads, pondering whether to make a swan dive into the fountain outside the window of his publisher's office, where he was writing his author's note: "I have already lived and finished the life I planned to live—(13 years longer, in fact)—and everything from now on will be A New Life, a different thing, a gig that ends tonight and starts tomorrow morning. So if I decide to leap for The Fountain when I finish this memo, I want to make one thing perfectly clear—I would genuinely love to make that leap, and if I don't I will always consider it a mistake and a failed opportunity, one of the very few serious mistakes of my First Life that is now ending."

He was at his continental divide. Suicide was all around. In place of an author photo on the back of the book, there was a Ralph Steadman illustration of Thompson with a gun to his head. The introduction was a suicide note for the First Him, the one who had been so suffocated by his own celebrity that he could no longer do his work, the one who was seen as a pied piper for drugs and debauchery. He wanted to get rid of that Him.

So it was no surprise that he found his release in the place once known as Thompson's Island. He could spend time in Key West, among his new friends, and not have to perform or become the Beast for audiences who demanded it. In Key West, he and Nabulsi could stroll the streets unmolested. He could drink at the Full Moon Saloon. With friends like Chris Robinson and Tom Corcoran, he could do what he could not do when he was on display as Hunter S. Thompson: he could relax.

"It's a decadent place," Thompson said of Key West. "*Decadent*. And it is a place where there is essentially no law, and people don't grasp that. See, I came down here with the right kind of mindset. I was angry."

Dink Bruce, slender as a shadow, was the local character closest to being bonnie prince of a royal family, by virtue of the Bruce family's friendship with Hemingway. Soon Thompson sought him out. The King of Gonzo was skilled as a writer, but couldn't do much else. Bruce, on the other hand, could fix a leaky pipe as well as produce an oil painting of a wild-island nude that could be mistaken for a Gauguin. Thompson, frequently helpless and needy, looked to Bruce for help.

By his count, Bruce figured the three times he came closest to death were at Hunter S. Thompson's hands in Key West.

First, there was the midnight that they were waiting at a red light in Thompson's cream-colored yacht of a car. The light changed. *One beat. Two beats. Three beats.* "Hunter, are we going to go?" Bruce thought Thompson might've nodded off for a moment. But just then a car roared through the red light. If Thompson had taken off when the light changed, both of them would have been peeled off Flagler Avenue. Although he showed no sign he was aware of death barreling toward them, Thompson seemed to have a mystical ability to know when to act and when not to act.

The second time came when Bruce had taken Thompson out on his boat to explore the mangroves choking the shore up the Keys. Thompson was interested in drug smuggling, having learned the stories of how shrimpers hid in the undergrowth to meet the arriving seaplanes of pot. It was all research for a story or maybe a screenplay, but they got too close to the real thing. As they were idling through the inlets, they heard a noise and sudden gunfire. Bruce felt a passing bullet comb the fine hair on the rim of his ear. Needless to say, he grabbed the throttle and they hauled ass. They had obviously encroached on a real smuggler. It was someplace Dink Bruce would likely never have gone if it hadn't been for the persuasive powers of Hunter S. Thompson.

Then there was the time when Thompson decided he needed a boat. He demanded that Bruce, who knew all things nautical, accompany him to the marina. Thompson tore down the road in his massive car, paying no attention to pedestrians, speed limits, or cops. Bruce suggested that they go to Boog Powell's place up on Stock Island. Powell was a retired slugger for the Baltimore Orioles who had come to Key West and opened a boat showroom and a marina. It was near closing time, so Thompson hurried through the streets, but when he hit Boog Powell's parking lot, he sped up instead of slowing down to find a parking place. "Hunter!" Bruce yelled. "Jesus!"

Thompson gunned the accelerator, aiming straight for the door. The massive old ballplayer stood on the other side of the glass, watching as Thompson braked and turned the car 90 degrees, leaving Bruce shaken, so close to the entrance that he couldn't open the passenger door.

Dink Bruce learned what everyone who knew the King of Gonzo already knew well: being Thompson's friend was dangerous.

Oddly, Boog Powell was not fazed by Thompson's arrival and was happy to sell him a boat. But the most important and long-lasting acquisition purchased that evening was a bullhorn. Thompson saw it on the wall and immediately fell in love.

He took it outside to test it and shattered the tropical calm of the Stock Island evening.

First, he tried the alarm setting. *Good.* Second, he set it on "screech." *Excellent!* Then he set it for voice.

"You fucking pigs!" his amplified voice screamed at the innocent burghers. "You'll never take me alive!"

It became his favorite toy.

Corcoran and his wife, Judy, were expert at cobbling together livelihoods from a variety of functions and income sources. Both had been in the Buffett orbit, and they had no trouble circling Planet Hunter. Thompson used his immense charm to lure Judy into working as his de facto secretary, even though she had a full-time job at a local real-estate office. Though he wasn't on a magazine deadline, it was still a lot of work to be him, and he made lists for Judy Corcoran in the way that he used to plot out his wife's duties: "Judy: Miami Herald, bank, Visa, booze, screwdriver." On another day: "Beer, Kaopectate, garbage bags, eggs, milk, lighter fluid, Kleenex, toilet paper. *Yell at me.* Say we have to go."

Tom Corcoran was often doing a number of jobs, which meant that sometimes they needed someone to look after Sebastian, their ten-year-old. Enter Uncle Hunter. When it was time for Corcoran to head off for his *job du jour* and Judy wasn't home from the office, Thompson often pulled up in the Corcorans' postage-stamp yard in his rented cream-colored Buick, with his new toy, the bullhorn. "Sebastian!" he would announce, feedback echoing down the quiet streets. "I have arrived! Turn on the network news!"

The Corcorans had no problem with Thompson watching Sebastian at either their house or his place on Waddell, once the sex machine was removed. On one occasion, Corcoran asked Thompson to put away a pistol he'd left on the coffee table, and Thompson was embarrassed about his oversight. Being around Sebastian reminded him of his own son and the shreds of his marriage and family.

"Hunter was always 'Doc' to the kids," Corcoran said. "Sebastian felt that Hunter was a guide of sorts, the voice of some kind of weird rationale to have a good life."

Chris Robinson remembered the fun Thompson had with his bullhorn. From the small beach on the property, it was hard to look up into Thompson's apartment because seagrape trees obscured the view. Occasionally, trespassers waded through the shallows and used the private beach.

"So this family came over and they were just making noise and they had their kids and their Kentucky Fried Chicken and they were just all talking," Robinson recalled. "So Hunter gets on the bullhorn and it sounded like such authority: 'Get off the beach or I'll cut your fucking throats!' And those people were looking around, wondering what's going on. And then a little while later, out of the trees: 'Get off the beach or I'll cut your fucking throats!' After about three times, they left. He just loved that megaphone because of the sound of authority."

Nabulsi was close to Thompson for more than twenty-five years and said he might have been his happiest when he was on the island. "In private life, in Key West, we had lots of quiet moments," she said. "He wasn't always performing. Hunter would get really nervous about speaking engagements or the public being around or having to perform. His speaking engagements were pretty wild because the kids were crazy with anticipation. The reason he was always up at night is because that's when he would write because it was quiet."

Still, being Hunter S. Thompson meant occasionally being noisy. He drove his Buick convertible through Key West's quiet streets well above the speed limit.

"He didn't care if people were crossing the street," Robinson said. "He'd be clenching that cigarette holder and he'd be screaming, 'Get out of the way, you bastards!' You know how slow it is in Key West and everyone's just slowly crossing the street and he's just plowing down the street when he was going somewhere."

Good news and more money arrived from Hollywood during one of his times in Key West residence. Film producer Art Linson came through with a check for the film version of one of Thompson's articles, a eulogy for his old friend and crusading Hispanic attorney Oscar Zeta Acosta. Acosta had disappeared in 1974, and in 1977, Thompson wrote a twisted and brutal article about him in *Rolling Stone*. He filled the piece with libel, he said, in order to draw Acosta from hiding. When the article appeared and Acosta remained silent, he knew for sure his friend was dead.

This odd but deeply affectionate portrait of the mercurial Acosta was being turned into a film called *Where the Buffalo Roam*. In addition to the money Thompson earned for selling the original magazine article to the movies, he also got a $25,000 fee as a consultant, which meant that he had to judge whether what was on-screen resembled the real man.

Desperate for money, Thompson didn't seem to care much about the movie, as long as he got paid.

John Kaye's screenplay telescoped several events in Thompson's life into a short period, with his relationship with the "Oscar" character (renamed Lazlo in the film) as the narrative tissue. Actor Bill Murray was cast as Thompson. He was part of the writer's crowd, since he was in the *Saturday Night Live* cast and close friends with Nabulsi. Preparing for the role, Murray lived with Thompson and Nabulsi and, at times, she said, it was like standing between mirrors. Murray was such an expert mimic that he absorbed Thompson's personality. For nearly a year after finishing the film, he still carried many of Thompson's mannerisms, particularly his gutteral nonstop speaking style. But superb performances took the film only so far. The whole script was heavy-handed comedy. Despite the efforts of Murray and Peter Boyle (cast as Lazlo), the film was a cheap cartoon.

Thompson had shown deep sensitivity and hurt in his epitaph for Acosta, but that was lost in the cartoonish film version, bogged down in leaden comedy. Even Garry Trudeau, who had appropriated Thompson's image in his *Doonesbury* comic strip, was alarmed when someone sent him a draft of the script. Although he didn't know Thompson and they had exchanged only brief notes, he sent him a reprimand: "I don't know how much they paid you to authorize that piece of shit, but it wasn't enough. If you must have your reputation trashed, at least have the integrity to do it yourself." Thompson quickly responded to his nemesis: "What lame instinct prompts you to suddenly begin commenting on my material? You've done pretty well by skimming it the last five years. So keep your pompous whining to yourself and don't complain. You'll get yours."

Mocked in print by David Felton for allowing such a weak film to be made from his life, Thompson threw up his hands. "I don't know why people are so concerned about my image," he told Felton. "I'm an egomaniac. *I* should be the one concerned about my image. Why are you and Garry Trudeau so worried about this film hurting me? *I'm* not."

Thompson received his check for the film while he was in Key West and began spending it as fast as he could, and having some fun as well, writing Corcoran a check for a million dollars with "cocaine" in the subject line.

Since he could not get Thompson to write for his magazine, *Rolling Stone* editor Jann Wenner tried to interest his star byline in doing something for the movies. Wenner was making a film production deal. Thompson had written his voice-over narration for *Where the Buffalo Roam* and the movies intrigued him. Escaping to screenwriting would allow him to leave behind the persona that cast a shadow over his work and life.

One problem: Thompson had never written a screenplay. He'd

digested what he'd learned from Harrison and McGuane and also latched onto Tom Corcoran, who was intent on writing for films.

Corcoran had studied with the best, being close to McGuane when he wrote the *Rancho Deluxe, 92 in the Shade,* and *Missouri Breaks* screenplays. He'd also picked up tips from Paul Schrader, who'd written *Taxi Driver* and *American Gigolo,* when he had come to Key West to polish the *Raging Bull* screenplay.

Thompson realized his buddy Corcoran could help with the technical details, and he agreed to try to jump-start Wenner's first venture into film. Schrader gave Corcoran good advice, which he relayed to Thompson: "Writing the screenplay is easy. Writing the treatment is the way you sell it. Here's how to do it. Don't write any more than twenty-nine pages. When they [film producers] see thirty pages, they get scared."

Thompson immediately perked up. He often described himself as a lazy hillbilly and so twenty-nine pages was nothing. He and Corcoran decided to write about drug smuggling in the Keys. He'd been interested in the intricacies of the practice from the moment of his arrival. He'd thought about doing an article, but the idea of trying a new form of writing was very appealing. Plus, a drug-smuggling movie was the sort of thing *Rolling Stone* might likely produce. Corcoran and Thompson's good friend Montgomery Chitty, an expert fishing guide, took Thompson out on the flats, through the mangrove channels, showing him how to operate a boat like a smuggler, finding the sorts of places smugglers might use to bring in their dope and wait on the buyers.

On the basis of the treatment, Wenner sold the concept to Paramount Pictures. Thompson and Corcoran called the screenplay *Cigarette Key.* Thompson clipped smuggling stories from the *Key West Citizen* and pinned them on a huge cork bulletin board Robinson had made in his apartment.

Thompson didn't want to be dependent on Chitty and Corcoran, so Robinson also tried to teach him to drive a boat. With some of the *Buffalo Roam* money, Thompson bought the seventeen-foot Mako Dink Bruce had suggested.

Robinson said Thompson knew only one speed on the boat: *wide-open.* Robinson advised him, "Hunter, just keep the wheel straight when the boat goes in the air."

One night, after Thompson had been out on the reef doing marine research and eating psychedelic mushrooms, he was trying to return to port when his boat got loose in Murray Marina. "It went airborne," Robinson said. "He and [a woman] had been out there on the reef and it was a full moon and it's really hard to get in at night in that marina. So you have to be kind of straight. But Hunter *was* a professional and he could do all kinds of things while on drugs. So he was backing up to the dock where he was going to leave the boat and [the woman] was on the back of the boat and he just was backing up and then kind of hit it in *forward* to stop the boat, but gunned it too much and she fell in the water, the boat just took off. He went over backwards, the motor hit him on the back of the head and *he* fell in the water and so this boat was in the marina, *loose.* I guess he gave it pretty good throttle as he fell backwards—he didn't *mean* to do that—and the boat, the torque of the engine, will make it turn and go in a circle. So this thing jumped the fuel dock and came back around in a circle and he's yelling, 'The bastard's trying to get me!' And he had to go down, under water. It ran around several times, knocked consoles off of other boats, just did a massive bunch of damage and then it got stuck on the fuel dock going, "*Whaaaaaaaaangggg!*" And he's screaming at [the woman] to turn it off and she's mad at him, because she thinks he did it on purpose and finally, after everything's settled out, he got the boat, set it in there, set the center console on it like nothing happened—'cause nobody was at the marina, since it was midnight—and *left.* So when folks came by in the morning, they thought some burglar had gone crazy and vandalized the place—until they saw the bow of Hunter's boat and saw all of the chunks out of it, where it had done all this damage. The marine patrol came over that day and we had to wake him up. We had to get him up and convince him that it was *very important* that he talk to the marine patrol. He had to do some kind of community service, make some speeches or something."

Thompson and Corcoran both hunched over the typewriter in Buffett's apartment, finishing *Cigarette Key*. "We made up the characters and came up with a few opening scenes and all of that other stuff," Corcoran recalled. "The smugglers [in the story] set up navigational lights in the mangroves that they could operate. They could run through the mangroves by activating these lights. When we started writing the script, his work habits were going down the tubes and his relationship with Laila was building, fast. He was head over heels in love with her and not caring at all about work. And so the work fell to me. I started writing and okaying things with him, and not okaying things with him."

Wenner was excited to hear that the script from Thompson might be arriving via Mojo Wire—Thompson's nickname for the early version of the fax machine that he carried around—and stayed in the office until the wee hours, as the machine slowly belched out pages. Corcoran took Judy and Sebastian on a vacation, and when he returned, Thompson offered payment for his large part in producing the treatment.

"Hunter had bought a Yamaha," Corcoran said. "That was to be my pay for working on the script—a Sony television and a Yamaha 650."

He also got a shared story credit on the screenplay: "By Hunter S. Thompson and Tom Corcoran." (In the end, Thompson delivered the much less powerful Yamaha 300 to Corcoran, who good-naturedly shrugged off the slight. He eventually noted the short-changing twenty years later in one of his novels.)

The film was never made because Paramount killed the deal. Hollywood was beginning to feel pressure to clean up its act in the early just-say-no days of the Reagan era, and a movie centered on drug smugglers was a hard sell.

Feeling indebted to Corcoran, Thompson gave him the idea for another film, which he called *The Mole.* "What Hunter dreamed up was an idea about a mole in the CIA who doesn't do anything until he gets to the very top, then he starts raising hell," Corcoran said. "I read a bunch of John le Carré novels really fast and I wrote a treatment on the thing."

One day, he was in the Alabama kitchen of Peets Buffett, Jimmy's mother, helping with post–hurricane cleanup, when Tom McGuane called from California.

"Tom Corcoran's here," she said into the phone. "Why don't you say hello?"

McGuane wanted to know what Corcoran was up to. He told him about *The Mole.* "Hang on," McGuane said. "I'm in Jeff Berg's office. Tell him that story."

Corcoran didn't know it at the time, but Jeff Berg was the president of International Creative Management, one of the largest entertainment firms in the world. Berg liked the story enough to offer Corcoran $10,000 for the treatment. That kind of money was a windfall to Corcoran.

He called Thompson and left a message on his answering machine: "*The Mole* has been sold," he said.

The next day, Thompson called back. "How did you know?" he asked.

Corcoran was confused, so he started telling the story about being in the kitchen of Peets Buffett and getting on the phone with McGuane and laying out the whole CIA-espionage plot to the Hollywood honcho.

As it turned out, Thompson had "taken back" his story idea, without telling Corcoran, and sold it to the studio making *Where the Buffalo Roam.*

Corcoran lost his first chance at big money as a writer. "Hunter was too naïve in those days to see what they were pulling on him in Hollywood," Corcoran said. They dangled the contract as another way to control the writer. There was no plan to ever make the film. (A happy ending came a year later, again in Peets Buffett's kitchen. Corcoran was on the phone with McGuane, reminding him of what had happened and how Hunter's "deal" was a no-go. McGuane was in Montana, but Berg was visiting, sitting there in his kitchen. Acting as de facto agent, McGuane resold *The Mole* to Berg, this time for $20,000. Corcoran wrote and sold the script. That was a good payday, but the script, like so many others in Hollywood, was never produced.)

During his time in Key West, Thompson briefly escaped from his image, his former wife, and the numbing emptiness of divorce.

When Nabulsi was not around, he'd move in on other women. *Come away with me*, he'd say, *and we will live like dolphins.*

It was in Key West that he met Russell Chatham. "In those days, it was kind of a much smaller scene," Chatham recalled. "Hunter was there, and he and Jim Harrison and I fished. That's how we got to know Hunter. Of course in those days, there was an awful lot of drinking and drugs involved. That colors the experience."

Chatham's huge canvasses and lithographs were selling for thousands, and his patrons included an army of Hollywood hipsters led by Jack Nicholson. He had the sort of fame few artists attained.

Along with fishing, cooking was a highlight of Chatham's annual trips to Key West, and Harrison routinely spent whole days preparing meals. Hunter usually just observed. "Fucking Hunter couldn't even make himself a cup of coffee," Chatham snorted. "He liked to *eat*. In those days, even though he was doing drugs and drinking, he did a lot of exercise too."

Montgomery Chitty was a longtime friend of Thompson's, who

had also come to know Harrison, McGuane, and Chatham well. He lived near Thompson in Aspen, but he was a Florida native and so he escaped the mountains for a few months in the Keys each year for fishing.

Harrison was back in the Keys, having just spent four months in Hollywood learning how to write screenplays. He had recently sold his novella *Legends of the Fall* to Hollywood, thanks to his friend and benefactor Jack Nicholson. Harrison invited Chitty and Thompson to join McGuane, Chatham, Valdene, and him for dinner. The Boys had all gathered for their annual Key West trip, and Harrison was working on a complicated Chinese meal that took three days to prepare.

From the moment Chitty and Thompson arrived at Harrison's rented place, Thompson was in the kitchen, asking Harrison and McGuane questions about script writing and agents and the nuances of film storytelling.

"Notorious most of his life for living hand to mouth, always searching the mail for the next check, Hunter decides then and there that the real money is in Hollywood, writing scripts," Chitty recalled. "This will be his financial salvation."

By four in the morning, dinner deep into digestion, Harrison finally took Chitty aside and begged him to take Thompson home. His relentless questions were driving Harrison and McGuane insane.

As Chatham got to know Thompson, he observed how different he was from his public image. "He was a much deeper, more serious person than the public I think even now suspects," Chatham said. "I think anybody who knew him, who actually took the trouble to know him, knows that. But as far as the general public is concerned, I think their view is that he was some sort of loose cannon, did a lot of drinking, and took a lot of drugs. That was true, but fundamentally, he was a very serious person."

––––––––

Hunter Thompson called her "Norma Jean," and when he met her at film director Bob Rafelson's house outside of Aspen, she was barely twenty. They began a crazy, aching affair that covered the years of his marriage crumbling and on into his deep relationship with Laila Nabulsi. (Though he seemed incapable of fidelity, he nonetheless kept a close bond with Nabulsi the rest of his life.)

But the Norma Jean relationship had one of its many flare-ups during his Key West years.

"Hunter S. Thompson was one of the sexiest men alive," she said. "Hunter was able to bring out primal male-female polarity in an ingenious and natural way. I just wanted to be dragged into his lair by the hair, bear down, make babies, and live in the service of my man."

Thompson was different, Norma Jean said, because he "got five times the juice the rest of us got, and thrice the wattage."

Their affair traveled from Aspen to Los Angeles to New York and Key West over a half-dozen years. At one point, when Norma Jean was living in Manhattan, Thompson spent the evening painting a black swastika on the buttocks of her roommate, who was a nurse. It needed to be dark, he told her, so her patients could see it through the uniform. "This'll get the adrenaline going," he said.

Once during that trip, Norma Jean was with Thompson at One Fifth Ave, a popular New York nightspot in the seventies. They were at a large table with people from the *Saturday Night Live* universe—writers, performers, and producers. Thompson abruptly got up from the table and left the club, returning a half hour later. He threw a big shopping bag onto Norma Jean's lap.

"I opened it to find a collection of the most exotic dildos, vibrators, brightly colored sex toys, lubes, and gels," she said. "He'd slipped over to the Pleasure Chest and did some shopping. He chose a T-shirt too, a white shirt with big black letters across it that read 'Beat me, fuck me, cum all over my tits, tell me that you love me, and get the fuck out.' It was shocking, I mean shocking. He was absolutely delighted with himself, and, without missing a beat, I pulled it out and down over my dress, and proceeded to stand and walk around to the other tables telling the diners how romantic my boyfriend was to give me such a sweet gift over dinner."

"Pay no attention," Thompson told the other diners. "She's on the way to a mental institution, hopelessly insane, mad, crazy bitch."

That was the trip during which Thompson met Nabulsi. That was it for Norma Jean for a while, but they resumed their crazy love affair in Key West.

Norma Jean said Thompson loved staging catfights.

"He'd somehow triangulate things and pit women against each other for his favor," she said. "I was out of my mind jealous in those early years."

Writers, like rock stars, had groupies, and there was no shortage of starfuckers in Key West. During the Laila Nabulsi period—when she was working in New York—Thompson brought Norma Jean to Key West, to stay with him at the Buffett apartment.

It was not a relaxing holiday at the beach for Norma Jean. "I stayed up five days straight, trying to keep the groupies away," she recalled. She collapsed from exhaustion but awoke to discover Thompson in the next room with another woman.

Ever since he was a child, Thompson had been getting people to follow his orders. As a boy, growing up in Louisville, Kentucky, he was chairman of the board for the neighborhood. As an adult with raging testosterone, he was still able to get people to do things they would never do in real life.

"Women put up with treatment they'd never allow with anyone else," Norma Jean said. "Men put up with the same scorching. Hunter was absolutely brutal with Bill Murray. Everyone gets burned; and everyone gets blessed. It's a queer thing."

Somehow, though, she always found her way back to forgiveness.

"That early morning in Key West when I woke to find the girl with Hunter in the next room, I saw red. Adrenaline was pounding in my veins and I leapt at him scratching and punching," she recalled. "I was a featherweight and he was a giant. He pulled a huge clump of hair out of my skull. I screamed that I was going to kill myself. Breaking free, I ran down the stairs, him in hot pursuit. I lunged into the surf, which was at the doorstep, and pushed my way into the ocean, flailing and wailing. Moments later Hunter reappeared on the beach, gun in hand. He's swaying from six days of sleep deprivation, rage, alcohol, a female visitor upstairs. I'm rolling in the surf. That moment, that single defining moment, may have been the funniest in our relationship history. He has the gun pointed right at me, at fifty yards away or more, and yells out, 'Don't worry; I'm just going to wound you.' The world stopped right then. Suspended in that moment of seeing death facing me, I saw only *the play of consciousness.* I understood the fine line between insanity and divinity. The rough surf, the cold water, the dawn, Key *fucking* West. Hunter and I shared a loving peaceful day that day."

Still, Thompson wrestled with identity issues. Key West provided him peace and quiet and a retreat from celebrity. He could drink at the Chart Room or the Full Moon and fans—if they recognized him—generally left him alone.

But the peace and quiet in the Keys didn't help him solve his essential problem.

When the British Broadcasting Corporation sent a camera crew to interview him the year before, Thompson had put his finger squarely on his problem. He had created a persona that was a blessing—hell, it's what put him on the map as a writer—but it was also a curse.

People expected him to be Raoul Duke, the mad-dog character he portrayed in his writing.

"People I don't know expect me to be Duke more than Thompson," he lamented to Nigel Finch, the interviewer. "Most people are surprised that I walk on two legs, and the idea that I would have a wife or a child or even a mother comes as a surprise. . . . I am living a normal life. Right alongside me, this myth is growing and mushrooming, getting more and more warped. When I get invited to speak at universities, I'm not sure if they are inviting Duke or Thompson and so I'm not sure who to be. I suppose my plans are to figure out some new identity—to kill off one life and start another one."

His legions of fans awaited his next major work. Thompson had yet to break through his writer's block. He brooded over his problems with identity. His marriage had crumbled, but his books sold furiously and his audience continued to grow. But in Key West, with his new friends and with Laila, he had found a home, where he was content to not be Hunter S. Thompson anymore.

14

Bum Farto and Ping-Ping

Maybe one day I'll be an honest man
Up till now I'm doing the best I can.
—Iron Maiden, "Wasting Love"

It became local legend. Jimmy Buffett used to wear a T-shirt in concert that bore the inscription "Where is Bum Farto?"

To audiences in Dubuque and Des Moines, that shirt must have seemed some kind of put-on. But in Key West, a name like Bum Farto didn't really stand out.

Key West is a town that relishes nicknames. Just ask Binky Weech, over at the American Legion. There's also Kiki, DumDum, Booger, Beefy, and Zero. You're not really accepted as a part of Conch culture until you have a nickname.

Everyone in town knows Dink, and there are a couple of theories about how Benjamin C. Bruce became known by that name. Both stories involve Ernest Hemingway.

Hemingway was great friends with Toby Bruce, and so even after he left for Havana, he stayed in touch, remained close to the family, and often visited Key West. When the Bruces were pregnant, Hemingway began referring to the child, still in utero, as "Dink." It was a common name at the time for a sidekick, often used in movies.

But there was another story. Hemingway was visiting and the little boy was running through the sprinkler, to cool off on one of those hot off-season days. The boy was naked, of course.

"Jesus," Papa Hemingway supposedly said, "will you look at the dink on that kid?"

That's the story Dink Bruce prefers.

Nicknames were a major part of Key West life, so it's no surprise that the town had a fire chief named Bum and a charming marijuana smuggler named Ping-Ping.

As long as he could remember, he'd wanted to be a fireman. He grew up across the street from the downtown Key West fire station. He was there so much, he became the firehouse mascot, and the old Conch firefighters nicknamed him Bum.

His first job after graduating from Key West High School in 1937 was working in the embalming room of the Lopez Funeral Home. But within two years, he was a fireman.

Joseph Farto was born in 1919 to a Cuban émigré named Juan Farto, who ran one of the finest restaurants in that era of Key West's history, the Victoria, on Duval Street. He had the restaurant for several years but then in 1937, when he was cash poor, he sold the building to Josie Russell, Hemingway's pal. That's when Russell was moving his bar, Sloppy Joe's, from Greene Street a half block over to Duval. Hemingway and other loyal drinkers carried the furniture to the new site. The original Sloppy's eventually became Captain Tony's, and the Victoria became, as the reconstituted Sloppy Joe's, one of the major tourist attractions in Key West.

Juan Farto continued to eke out an existence working in Key

West's restaurants, but his life had peaked with his years at the Victoria, and he was bitter in his new role of employee rather than employer. Bum Farto had no interest in following his father into the business, so closing the Victoria meant nothing to him. He just wanted to be a fireman.

In 1964, six years after joining the fire department, Bum Farto was its chief. Rarely has a fire chief been more distinctively dressed.

He wore red or shades of red exclusively: red pants, red shorts, red socks, red jackets, red shoes, red leisure suits, red skivvies . . .

All of the red was accented, of course, with gold chains and bracelets and watches and rings. He also wore rose-colored glasses, literally and figuratively. His fire chief badge was studded with rubies and he often sported a red leather cowboy hat custom-made by Tom Corcoran.

He was a friendly lug, with a broad face and ears hung like overripe figs on the side of his head. His smile was affable and offered evidence of imperfect dentistry. It was hard to be mad at him. He was, in the vernacular of the times, happy doing what he was doing.

Now that he was on top of his hometown's social strata, Farto started to show off a little more. He bought a Cadillac El Dorado convertible in electric lime green. In his red ensemble, speeding down the street in his decked-out lime-colored Conch cruiser, he looked like a mobile advertisement for margarita flavors.

Like most natives of Key West, he loved high school sports, especially baseball. Because his car was so desirable, it was also a target. So before a home game for the Key West Fighting Conchs, the groundskeeper would open up the gate and let *El Jefe*—that's what Farto called himself and asked all others to call him—park along the foul line, down from the Conch dugout. He watched the game from the dugout, dispensing his advice and sage wisdom.

He had cards printed which read:

KEY WEST FIRE DEPARTMENT
PHONE 6-2828

WE REGRET TO INFORM YOU THAT WE HAD
TO EFFECT FORCIBLE ENTRY IN ORDER TO
EXTINGUISH THE FIRE IN YOUR CAR.

Chief J. A. FARTO   Captain- - - - - - - - - - - - - - - - -

The fact that the chief had these cards printed suggests there was a rash of unattended car fires at the time. Though an unattended car fire might be a by-product of the marijuana trade, the cards were mostly about Farto's joy in seeing printed evidence of his power and authority.

He had plenty of responsibility. The fire department employed forty firefighters, and it had three stations and five fully equipped trucks. Thanks to President Richard Nixon's revenue-sharing plan, the fire trucks were fitted with state-of-the-art equipment, including hydraulic ladders and eardrum-piercing sirens.

Farto provided well for his family. They had a deceptively large home at 1601 United Street. It looked modest from the front, but he was continually adding on to the home and it stretched *back back back* to the end of his lot. Farto's stealth Taj Mahal was just a block and a half from Tennessee Williams's home. The household income was boosted by Esther Farto's work, and she helped pay for the home renovations. She was the principal cake maker at the Perez Brothers Bakery. Of course, *El Jefe* was supplementing his income in other ways, or so went the rumor.

Eventually, Farto got cocky, like a lot of the movers and shakers in the town's business community and its power structure.

They said he sold marijuana. Complaints were filed with the governor's office in Tallahassee, and the by-the-books Reuben Askew asked the district attorney's office in Broward County to investigate. Broward is the county north of Dade County, home of Miami, and two counties north of Monroe, county of the Keys. Apparently Askew had doubts about the effectiveness of drug enforcement the farther south he went in the state.

And then *they* said Farto moved from marijuana to cocaine.

Once Farto started selling cocaine from the firehouse, if indeed he did, the game was over.

Cops and agents from the Drug Enforcement Administration might look the other way for marijuana. Hell, they might even be in the trade themselves. But cocaine was different.

Everyone seemed to be doing it in the late seventies. There were all of those *Saturday Night Live* references about coke, and even Johnny Carson would generally have at least one cocaine-related joke in his *Tonight Show* monologue each night.

But still: marijuana was one thing, cocaine was another.

Cocaine was more expensive, so the stakes were higher and the suppliers weren't a bunch of good-natured hippies or stoned-out college kids. Coke suppliers were usually bad-ass motherfuckers, and they weren't selling a little dope; they were passing around sums of money that equaled the gross national product of neighboring South American countries. You didn't fuck around with them.

That is unless you were Bum Farto, the invincible man in crimson. Bum Farto—to hear Bum Farto tell it—could do no wrong.

And then one day, dressed all in red, he walked out of his house, got into his lime green Cadillac, and put his key in the ignition.

Immediately, a car screeched to a halt behind him. Another pulled up in front of him, the driver stopping so suddenly that he bobbed forward in the seat. Farto was blocked in.

The feds had come for Bum Farto, and they took him to jail.

In February 1976, Farto was convicted of selling cocaine to an undercover narcotics agent at the fire station.

Then Farto jumped bail, rented a car, and drove off into mystery. He was last seen in Miami, and then never again.

Or was he? For years there were sightings. *He's in Central America. He's in California. He's living the high life.*

But others were certain he was a victim of drug dealers, that he'd become part of the concrete edifice of the rebuilt Seven Mile Bridge.

Not everyone is sure the conventional wisdom is really all that wise. Tom Corcoran has his doubts.

"Bum was not an exemplary human," Corcoran said, "but I don't think he was in the business." Sure, Farto loved his red clothes, his jewelry, and his women. But that was the limit.

According to Corcoran, the feds figured he was low man on the IQ totem pole, so they targeted him.

"They wanted to bust everyone around him for looking the other way and importation," Corcoran said. So they exploited his weaknesses. "Step One, a black man offered to sell him jewelry of questionable sources. Step Two, the man told him he would cut the price if paid in equivalent cocaine instead of cash. Step Three, Bum knew where to get it, so he fell for it. Step Four, Bum was so dense that he agreed to do the deal in front of May Sands, the school for retarded kids. Step Five, the cops told the media that they also found a sawed-off shotgun under the front seat of Bum's chief's car. That, in itself, is pretty smart about what a fireman might encounter in a worse-case scenario."

But Corcoran is open to being convinced that Farto was guilty and had been caught red-handed, so to speak.

Years later, Corcoran met an agent who was in on the bust and told him his theory that Bum Farto was nothing more than an extravagant patsy. "He said they had proof of Bum selling," Corcoran said. "What quantities, he didn't say. Oh, we may never know. But I doubt he was a 'pusher,' as an earlier generation called it."

A decade after his disappearance, Farto was declared legally dead. This was so his wife—or widow, depending on what you believe—could probate his will. Despite all the fuss made over the missing *El Jefe* being declared dead, the law-enforcement community still considered it an open case and they assumed they would bring the man in red to justice some day.

Declaring the missing chief dead allowed Esther Farto to proceed with adjudication of his will. She was left about $2,000 in insurance policies and his pension, worth roughly $4,000 to $5,000.

She said she had not heard a word from her husband, to whom she had been married for twenty-one years. They had no children.

Nelson Jamardo went to work for Charley Toppino and Sons when he was fifteen years old. He was a yard boy, doing whatever he was asked to do—washing trucks, painting, working as a mechanic's assistant, and cleaning the construction company compound.

He became known as Ping-Ping. George Toppino, one of the five brothers who ran the company, gave him the nickname. Jamardo was so skinny as a teenager that Toppino said if you flicked him, he'd make a "ping-ping" sound. The name stuck.

Ping-Ping's uncle worked at Toppino's, so he got the kid a job for a dollar an hour. Ping-Ping ended up working for the company for more than half a century.

He had been raised in the Upper Keys, in a close Cuban family. "The Keys were the Keys," he said of his childhood. "It was beautiful. There was no construction. It was very laid back."

He moved to Stock Island, just north of Key West, while still a boy and watched the sleepy island turn into a den of iniquity and, later, into a playground for the rich and the very rich.

"Developers started developing things," he said, "and there was a lot of change." Since he worked for a construction company, he was part of that change, though Toppino's concentrated on infrastructure—building and rebuilding roads, building high schools, then tearing them down three decades later to build new and better high schools.

Through it all, Ping-Ping saw the changing clientele of Key West. "The Conchs now are priced out," he said. "The downtown's gotten so expensive. There are very few Conchs in Key West anymore. The Bubba system that used to run the town, that's vanished."

Bum Farto was part of the system. So were Manny James and Jimmy James. They're all gone now. Ping-Ping is now foreman at the Toppino's plant on Highway 1. A dignified old Cuban gent with close-cropped white hair and a thin mustache, he speaks slowly, in a husky voice with a strong accent.

"The Bubba system was simple," Ping-Ping explained. "If you had any problem, you knew the chief of police, you knew the judge. The locals took care of each other. It was just for the Conchs."

The Key West he came to know in the fifties had few gay people. "They was still in the closet," he said. Other than President Truman, there weren't a lot of visiting celebrities then—or if there were, the Conchs didn't care.

To Ping-Ping, Dink Bruce was a celebrity. To a lot of other Conchs, Ping-Ping was a celebrity. Captain Tony was a celebrity. The movie stars and rock 'n' roll singers who visited didn't faze the Conchs, who would get more starstruck over Captain Tony than they would over Mick Jagger.

Thanks to Phil Clark and Tom Corcoran, the local people soon had a place to hang out, the Chart Room. There wasn't a sign that said "No Tourists," but the bar gave off a Bubbas-only feeling.

Of course, it wasn't all Mayberry around town. Ping-Ping remembers when drugs worked their way into the social structure.

"At one time in the seventies, they used to snort coke at the tables," he said of the Chart Room. "They'd be smoking pot openly, and it was no big deal.

"Most of the fishermen, the commercial fishermen, they got involved in smuggling. I'd say 50 to 60 percent of them was involved. Some police looked the other way," he said. He paused, then added, "Some participated."

It seemed that everyone was doing it. By the mid-seventies, Ping-Ping had a family and had trouble supporting them on his paycheck, which clocked in at around $16,000 per year. So that's when he went to work as a smuggler.

It was easy to get started in the business.

"It came from Colombia," Ping-Ping said. "Sometimes, we sent shrimp boats there to get it. We'd meet the shrimp boat out in the ocean and bring it in on crawfish boats. On a shrimp boat, you could hold thirty, maybe thirty-two thousand pounds. We'd meet them with a couple, two-three boats and do it in two nights."

When the boats made it to the Lower Keys, Ping-Ping had to manage a series of delivery and drop-off points.

"We'd maybe unload it up the Keys," he said. "Sometimes, it was Key West, in the fish houses. Maybe you'd rent a house from someone because it was on the water, and use it for just that purpose, for unloading."

Once it was prepared for sale, then Ping-Ping had to oversee the distribution and shipping.

"There were sellers that would come and get it or it got shipped out on trucks, or cars, or vans," he said.

It was a pure, simple business. No one got hurt—at least, not on purpose. It wasn't a "gentleman's trade" in the classic sense, but it had a bit more dignity—or so Ping-Ping thought—in that era.

"In them days," he recalled of the mid-seventies, "we're talking strictly about marijuana. There wasn't no war going on, no guns, nothing hard, you know what I'm saying? It was a handshake. That was it."

Then things changed.

"Cocaine's when it got worse," he said. The feds got serious about the much-ballyhooed War on Drugs and got some souped-up equipment. "They got the hydrofoils and started going after the cocaine." As if the new Batman-like drug agents weren't enough of a problem, the coke-dealing Colombians weren't like the pot-smuggling Colombians. "When you dealt with cocaine, you were dealing with a different group of people," Ping-Ping said. "With pot, you made a deal and there was no gun, nobody coming to shoot you. It was an honest business."

Ping-Ping wasn't a stoner. He wasn't going home every night and firing up a fattie. He smuggled dope because he wanted to support his family. The $16,000 didn't go far enough.

"If you took in three–four bales of marijuana for yourself, it wasn't no big deal," he said. "You take twenty pounds out of two thousand pounds, it was nothing. With cocaine, you do that, they're going to come after you."

Ping-Ping led a pretty big operation that was shipping thousands of pounds of marijuana out each week to the drop points upstate such as Jacksonville or Gainesville or Tampa. Those towns were connected to the network of interstates that could quickly get the Colombian pot across the country and into the lungs of college students everywhere.

All of this was done as moonlighting and didn't really interfere with his day job at Toppino's. He lay low, but one day he made a move that attracted the attention of the feds.

It was the day he walked into a Miami Mercedes dealership and paid cash for three fine automobiles. That's a hard thing to pull for most folks, especially those earning only $16,000 a year.

He didn't just buy cars, either. Ping-Ping bought a share of the Bevis-Lewis Chevrolet dealership in Key West.

Eventually, he was busted up the Keys, in Big Pine. In 1980, he and his partners, known as the "Big Pine 29," were charged with smuggling 36,000 pounds of marijuana.

When he guided his boat to the dock at the Cohen house on Big Pine Key at four on the morning of November 8, 1980, he made out in the dim light what looked like a car waiting at the off-load point. Ping-Ping hesitated, but his partner said, *Don't worry*. Ping-Ping briefly considered that he might be the victim of a setup, but he was a trusting soul.

Agents of the United States Customs Service, the Florida Marine Patrol, and the Monroe County Sheriff's Department busted Ping-Ping and twenty-eight others during the off-loading operation. The agents "observed two large truckloads of marijuana bales just outside the house and a substantial amount of marijuana residue within the enclosed garage area." The federal agents estimated that the pot in Ping-Ping's smuggling operation that day was worth $9 million.

Ping-Ping had been under surveillance for some time. He had been busted in 1979 when federal agents found thirty-three tons of pot on his shrimp boat *The Selena* in the Gulf of Mexico. Amazingly, he was not charged, which made him feel invincibile.

Agents watched Ping-Ping's earlier operations from mosquito-infested mangroves, quietly studying how the soft-spoken smuggler and his team worked. After gathering what agents considered sufficient evidence, they busted an off-load in progress. Detectives observed two "speedy, shallow-water boats ideal for carting marijuana bales" cutting through the predawn waters off Big Pine Key. When one of the boats pulled up to the dock at the prearranged meeting place, two men were there to take the line and secure it to the pier. What the smugglers didn't know was that the casually dressed ne'er-do-well types were actually federal agents Steve Coletti and Mike Barber.

Another group of agents crept up on the house that was to be the site of the pot delivery, and "thumping noises" inside "deepened their suspicions" that bales of marijuana were being tossed to the floor, while loud rock music played. When the agents burst into the house, they expected a half-dozen potheads. Instead, there were nearly thirty people crammed into the space set aside for the dope processing.

"Amazingly," the *Miami Herald* reported, "a dizzying array of suspects began diving into trucks, under couches, into a canal." One suspect was arrested in a crawl space under the house. That day, twenty-three arrests were made; six more followed the next day. In all, twenty-nine men were charged with marijuana smuggling, as part of a "conspiracy to knowingly and intentionally possess with attempt to distribute" marijuana. All pleaded not guilty.

The trial was the biggest drug case in the region's history. When the defendants were being booked on the day of the arrest, Monroe County sheriff William Freeman was frantic. "Where the hell am I going to put them?" he asked. "The Holiday Inn doesn't check as many people in and out a day as I do."

Ping-Ping was singled out in the indictment and identified as the ringleader. His life came under the greatest scrutiny and the *Miami Herald* took note of his many extravagances. Ping-Ping liked his toys.

"The Lower Keys home of Nelson [Ping-Ping] Jamardo," one story noted, "is equipped with sophisticated parabolic microphones to detect intruders. His investments include automobiles and boats, houses and land. He reports a modest income far exceeded by huge expenditures of cash."

The trial was front-page news in Key West, but also dominated newspapers from Miami to Pensacola. None of this attention was well received by the defendants, even the mild-mannered Ping-Ping, who went after an aggressive reporter.

Ping-Ping was in custody and leaving court when *Miami Herald* reporter Robert Rivas approached him. "Rivas was reportedly waiting to take pictures," the *Herald* later wrote, "when Jamardo and three others allegedly 'rushed' at him and threw him to the ground.

Jamardo then reportedly picked up Rivas' camera and threw it at his face."

Ping-Ping remained the central figure throughout the trial. His lifestyle had been so over-the-top that it was easy to prove he'd done something in addition to his job at Toppino's.

The defense attorneys for the Big Pine 29 feuded, and because of screwups by the arresting agents and the prosecution, there was a possibility of a mistrial. But Ping-Ping and his cohorts were convicted and sentenced. Ping-Ping was ordered to serve twenty-one years in prison. He was first sent to Tallahassee, but then to a prison in Texas.

Because he'd worked there since he was a teenager, Toppino's promised him that his job would be held open until his return.

"Jail wasn't too good," he said. "When you go to jail, an old man told me one time, you can't be in there and your mind out in the streets. You have to keep that inside your soul. You get used to it and you make the best of it."

During his prison term, his marriage dissolved. "After three or four months inside, she started going out with someone else. My second son was three or four months old when I went to jail."

He served seven years, eventually being released for his superlative behavior behind bars.

He was distraught over the end of his marriage. "I'd had enough," he said. "I was going to leave the country, but my mama, she was worried I'd never see her again."

He'd made a lot of money. "I bought a house at Geiger Key, a couple of boats, some cars." His eyes glaze a bit at the recollection. "At that time, everything was crazy. You walk up to a guy with fifty thousand, sixty thousand dollars cash and you pay in cash."

The feds seized his property, and there was the jail time. But he'd had a lot of fun with his money. "I spent it," he said, eyes brightening. "I spent it on property, cars, things I love. It was coming in so fast, so I spent it."

He knows he's lucky, unlike Bum Farto. "He knew a lot of people in Key West," Ping-Ping said of Farto. "He was in a position to know the chief of police, the city manager, the city attorney . . . He knew too much and I think they was afraid he was going to talk. I'm willing to bet that he is not alive."

Those smuggling days are long gone. With his white hair, dignified bearing, and gravelly Cuban accent, he doesn't look at all like a drug kingpin, but more like a retired professor of Latin American studies.

As promised, his job was kept open for him, and so Ping-Ping came back to Toppino's, where he now supervises a small maintenance staff, including the handsome young kid out there washing cars, painting, cleaning the construction company compound, doing everything Ping-Ping used to do.

That's his teenage son.

Ping-Ping had lost enough for one lifetime and he was determined not to lose anything after getting a second chance.

Ping-Ping was right about the cocaine. The merchants reflect the drugs they sell. Marijuana smugglers were by and large laid-back, heavily lidded *dudes*. Coke traffickers were at the other end of the spectrum, bleary-eyed, intense, and often homicidal. Colombians had been sending their product to North America for years, content to let it be distributed by Cuban drug gangs. But then they decided to get rid of the middlemen.

The late seventies saw a flowering of cocaine culture, fueled by celebrities with their not-so-veiled references to nose candy on television talk shows, wearing shirts open down to the ying-yang, with gold-plated coke spoons dangling around their necks like crucifixes. Marijuana was for everyone. It was the people's inebriant. But cocaine was a status symbol of wealth, and when the cost was raised, the stakes went through the roof.

Key West became awash in cocaine and would remain so for decades. Coke use peaked in the eighties before it, and random sex,
began their dual declines in the era of AIDS and President Ronald
Reagan's declaration of war on drugs. But the island, isolated as it
was, never fully let go of cocaine or LSD or any other drug of which
the mainlanders had tired. Key West was content to be fashionably
out of fashion.

15

Redemption

My daddy . . . was a very simple man, and he didn't leave
me a lot. But what he did tell me was this: "Son," he said.
"It is possible to become so defiled in this world that your
own mother and father will abandon you, and if that
happens, God will always believe in your own ability to
mend your own ways."
—Bob Dylan, 1991

Tennessee Williams made it to the wrap party for *92 in the Shade*. So did James Kirkwood, a part-time Key West resident, then a year away from winning the Pulitzer for *A Chorus Line*. Most of the hip folks in town showed up and mingled with the movie people. It was a public crowning of McGuane as a literary light of his generation, a multimedia threat who now wrote screenplays and directed films. The crowd spilled out onto the Afterdeck at Louie's Backyard, next door to the duplex Buffett and Chris Robinson shared. The party went on well into the next day.

But when the celebration was over, McGuane had to finish the movie and finesse the disorder in his life. At that point, the film was a somewhat confused mass of storytelling choices that needed to be made.

In writing a novel, the choices were not simple, but at least they were more clear-cut. At the end of *Ninety-Two in the Shade*—boom, the hero dies, end of book.

But when it came to reimagining that story as a film, McGuane couldn't decide what he wanted. Did he want it to be clear that Nichol Dance shot Tom Skelton? Did he want to freeze-frame it and make people wonder? Or did he want Dance and Skelton to embrace and with an *aw, hell* shrug off their territorial battles over their dueling charter businesses?

He couldn't decide, so he made all three endings. Depending on where you saw the movie or when you saw it or how you saw it, you might get a different ending each time.

If you saw it at all. In reality, *92 in the Shade* was a tough one to find in the theaters.

The film was buried, due to lack of enthusiasm, bad press about the production, and poor distribution.

Skeptical reviewers lay in wait for McGuane and his *Citizen Kane.* The cowboy–fishing-guide prodigy was due for a critic's lashing. He had been mighty, so now must he fall. Most of the critics reviewed McGuane's life, not his film.

The Becky-Tom-Elizabeth-Margot-Peter sexual switcheroo had made the press, and while Peter and Becky Fonda rode off into the sunset, Tom McGuane and Margot Kidder began their relationship in the public's unforgiving eye. McGuane officially became fodder for gossip when the whole Hee-Haw Gang ended up in the pages of *People* magazine.

In the "Couples" section of the magazine, *People* ran a piece with a characteristically cumbersome *People* title—"Tom (McGuane) & Margot (Kidder) & Peter (Fonda) & Becky (McGuane) & Whoops"—

that played on the title of a popular mate-swapping film of a few years before, *Bob & Carol & Ted & Alice.* Now, the article said, Hollywood life was imitating art.

The article began:

> By the time he had completed his third novel, *92 in the Shade,* Tom McGuane was tired of being continually declared the Hemingway of his generation. Sure, he had found that writing fiction made him "happiest, but it doesn't pay spit, so a boy has to do other things." In the 1970s that could only mean making movies—and the messing around that inevitably seems to accompany it.
>
> Thus, when *92* was ready to shoot, McGuane had already apprenticed on the screenplay of the current western *Rancho Deluxe* and in the gossip columns opposite Elizabeth Ashley. Tom arrived on the Key West set of *92* in the fall of '74, established enough to direct as well as write, not to mention attracting Ashley into a minor part. His wife, Becky, a stoic direct descendent of Davy Crockett and of a dozen years' marriage to McGuane, was in town with their son, Thomas IV.
>
> Then leading man Peter Fonda arrived freshly divorced from his own wife of 12 years, and as McGuane wryly recalls the ensuing marital merry-go-round: "I went behind the bleachers for a hot dog, and you couldn't tell the players without a program." McGuane's Becky fetched up with Fonda. Tom himself ended, not with Liz Ashley, but with the movie's free-spirited co-star, Margot Kidder. . . .

The article poked fun at a bunch of movie-star oddballs run amok in the crazy lust incubator of Key West and did much to buttress the mantle McGuane tried so hard to avoid. McGuane, the reporter noted, "is finishing up his next novel and hewing to his Hemingwayesque life of backpacking, hunting and trout fishing." At another point in the story, the *People* writer breathlessly reported that McGuane "bagged an antelope an hour after dawn in a deep ravine and spent the next three hours hauling the 100 pounds of meat on his back four miles home." One of the accompanying photographs showed McGuane hanging up a buck for curing, as if to underscore the manly-man Papa H stance. Asked about the connection, McGuane denied the resemblance "except maybe geographically."

"Like Papa," *People* pointed out, "Tom winters in Key West."

Kidder was shown with their new daughter, glowing with the plutonium of new motherhood, and, the article noted, "the folks a mile down the road" were that other happy couple, Peter and Becky Fonda.

The hurricane of gossip around the partner-change mowed through any possibility the film had of reaching a wider audience. It became that film made by the libertines who swapped wives and slept around.

It was a film with prolific flaws. "It was a film without structure," Kidder said, "which means it was not a *film*. I tried to make my scenes work, but it was so embarrassing when I saw it for the first time." She had several successful films under her belt, but even when she felt things careening out of control on the set, she had declined to offer suggestions to McGuane. "Nobody gives Tom advice. Tom knows everything."

In the aftermath of the film's poor reception, McGuane began to consider dropping out of the movie world, even though the paychecks were good. With the seed money from Elliott Kastner, he'd written *The Missouri Breaks* for Marlon Brando and Jack Nicholson, but he didn't have a lot of interest in seeing the film through to completion. This time the director was Arthur Penn, who'd made *Bonnie and Clyde* and *Little Big Man*, among other excellent films.

What should have been a masterpiece, a virtually harmonic convergence of writing, acting, and directing talent, instead became a jangled mess. For his part, Marlon Brando showed up on the Montana set apparently determined to try out a variety of accents and sexual orientations in his interpretation of the role of a bounty hunter. At one point, the Brando character went out on a killing spree in a gingham dress, as if he planned a picnic, not homicide. Jack Nicholson was disappointed in both Brando's odd acting choices and his lack of interest in serious work. Nicholson also had some frustrations with the script, and during the 1975 production, when he looked to McGuane for help, he found that he was off in England with Kidder, editing *92 in the Shade*. So he called in his old friend Robert Towne, a screenwriter best known for *Chinatown* and *Shampoo*. Towne made major changes to McGuane's script.

The original screenplay was poetic and perfect in a way that such things rarely are. McGuane's descriptions and stage directions were as well crafted as his literate dialogue. His view of the West was somewhat Elizabethan in tone, and his characters spoke at times with regal cadence.

The story concerned a horse thief named Tom Logan, played by Nicholson. A regulator—that is, a hired gun—named Lee Clayton is brought in to bring the wild territory under control. Brando played Clayton.

The film was populated with the sorts of oddball peripheral characters McGuane had presented to the world in *Rancho Deluxe* and *92 in the Shade*.

In an exchange that would be unlikely in a John Wayne western, Logan engages in a dialogue with the female lead, Jane Braxton, played by Kathleen Lloyd.

> JANE: We're kind of starved for news out here. We just hear about grass.
> LOGAN: What's wrong with grass?
> JANE: Samuel Johnson said, "A blade of grass is a blade of grass, tell me something about human beings."

LOGAN: I don't understand that.

JANE: It means that Samuel Johnson was as bored as I am with nature. We had a famous painter of natural scenes out here last year and he painted up about ten square miles of canvas and he never painted a human face. Too bad he wasn't here to paint that boy Sandy hanging up so decoratively in front of the mountains. Sandy's pink tongue and white face would have just set off the deep greens of Montana so handsomely. It'd have made the damnedest bank calendar.

Nicholson seemed to be the only one of the principals intent on trying to make something out of McGuane's script, but with the odd performance of Brando and the permutations of Robert Towne, some of McGuane's musical language was lost in the cacophony. The beautiful, lyrical writing was published, unexpurgated, in a mass-market paperback of the screenplay, not the usual treatment given a scenarist's work.

One scene that managed to survive Towne's rewrites and all of Brando's twitching was the final confrontation between Logan and Clayton.

We *hear* meadowlarks and feel the blue suffusion of morning. Lee Clayton's sleeping face *fills the screen*: Repose.

His eyes open suddenly as we *hear* Tom Logan's voice.

LOGAN: (*offscreen*) Do you know what woke you?

A long pause as Lee Clayton shakes his head slowly.

LOGAN: (*offscreen*) Lee, you've just had your throat cut.

Still but total terror fills Lee Clayton's face. Finally, the eyes are empty of life and motionless.

Though McGuane was tempted by Hollywood and its money, his triple assault on the movie business—particularly his stint as a director—left him disenchanted.

"This will sound like I made it up, but the whole thing made me think it was a much less interesting, much less intense experience than writing fiction," McGuane said. "Everything you wanted to do came with such impediments. Say you want to shoot so-and-so coming out of the bank. Well, you've got to block off the streets . . . and everything is so complicated. I admire people who can hold their concentration in the face of all that, but to me, the creative excitement was nothing like writing."

Soon, another bloom was off another rose for Kidder, who played Miranda in *92 in the Shade*, had a child with McGuane, and then married him.

"I fell in love with the director," she recalled, "and moved to Montana and had his baby, so that was kind of what I took away from that experience. It [the film] was fun. I was so in love I couldn't see straight, so I didn't notice that it was being incompetently directed and didn't make a lot of sense."

The problem with the marriage was that the career ambitions of husband and wife did not intersect.

"After we got married," Kidder recalled, "we moved to Montana and he expected me to turn into a submissive ranch wife and serve the great writer. That kind of put an expiration date on that particular project."

Years later, Kidder recalled, "I was totally unsuited to Tom. I never wanted to be a wife. I couldn't think of a worse job on the fucking planet. But I did love Tom and will always love Tom."

The McGuane-Kidder marriage was soon dead, though the child they had together, Maggie McGuane, would keep them bound the rest of their lives. "We did make a beautiful daughter," Kidder said. "Maggie was beloved. When I first held her, I looked at Tom and said, 'Oh, so this is what love is.' I could see it hurt him. That's not the sort of thing you should say to your husband."

After a brief sabbatical from film to attempt the Montana-housewife role, she was offered what would become her career-defining part as Lois Lane in Richard Donner's big-budget film *Superman*, which introduced Christopher Reeve in the starring role. The part required that Kidder relocate to London for six months during filming. When she broke the news to McGuane, "he looked at me kind of funny," she said, "asked me if I was going to do it and when I said yes, I woke up the next morning and he's packed all my things and moved them outside."

Still, the attraction had always been strong. "I was so addicted to him," she recalled.

By the middle of the seventies, after the marital whirlwind and sexual and substance excesses of Key West, McGuane was numb.

"I just didn't feel anything happening for a long time," McGuane said. "I just didn't have a point of view, except I felt things were going downhill like lava that's just ten degrees short of solidifying. It's moving all right, but what is it?"

Then, within eighteen months, McGuane experienced a trifecta of tragedy. His father died, his sister died, and his mother's health deteriorated seriously, and she became addicted to painkillers.

"My mother was a very troubled person," McGuane said. "She had alcoholism, prescription drug problems, and she'd been such a great girl all of her life, and to see her deliquescing into this condo-dwelling crazy, it was hard. She was just a great girl and my father was really not a nice guy. He had some good sides to him. Very hardworking, but a lifelong alcoholic. Never missed a day of work in forty-four years, but an angry guy. Mother was a lighthearted, literary, comic Irish girl, and a beauty. She was a famous beauty in her day. But she got dragged down by the facts of her life, and by the end, she was a pretty sad case."

McGuane began to wrap himself around what had happened to him in the last few years and try to shape the disparate emotions and charred dreams into a narrative. It had been a long time since he'd written a novel, a full five years since *Ninety-Two in the Shade*. That life was over. That wife and son were gone. Another wife and child had come and gone. He had flirted with Hollywood and a career in film. He had blown through the foul recesses of the town's nightlife and become the fully formed king of nocturnal pain, Captain Berserko. The imagined Club Mandible hellion had come to life as a raving banshee on Duval Street. Tom McGuane could be very mean when he wanted to be, and those moments came when he was at his drunkest.

Valdene recalled the differences in drinking with his friends. Chatham, for example, could become even more charming with every sip. McGuane was another story.

"Something would tweak in his head," Valdene said, "and he would get aggressive. It was difficult. He wasn't a fun drunk at all."

In addition to the family history with alcohol, McGuane's temperament didn't mix well with booze.

As Valdene saw it: "He was such a wired-up person and he is so intelligent that when you put that wired-up guy with alcohol and take him to a bar, where there are a bunch of assholes to begin with— and all these assholes are fucking drunk, well, something's going to happen. In my case and Jim's case and Russell's case, 99 percent of the time, we'd sense something changing with the people in the bar and just say, 'That's fine, do whatever you want.' Tom couldn't do that and that was a problem." Often, there were bar fights.

It wasn't that McGuane was unaware of the problem. At one point, he told Valdene that he needed to make changes.

"I have to stop drinking hard liquor," McGuane told his friend.

"Why don't you switch to wine?" Valdene suggested.

"That's an idea," McGuane said.

But McGuane was unfamiliar with moderation. When Valdene saw him next, he was drinking wine from a tumbler.

He was that rare serious writer whose name was known even

to those who didn't read books. He was flying at Hemingway's brain-numbing altitude. Once he'd made it into *People* magazine, it was all over. He was a rock star of writers, and he moved with a faster crowd.

This was apparent when he attended the 1977 wedding in Aspen of his good friend Jimmy Buffett and Jane Slagsvol, the girl Buffett had seen making a phone call outside the Chart Room.

The future Mrs. Buffett had encouraged the singer to buy a home in Aspen, something away from the debauchery of Key West, something that might be a little more family friendly, in case they wanted to begin spawning children. Yet the week of the nuptials in Aspen is remembered by all who participated as something that would make the orgies of ancient Rome look like a 1957 punch-and-cookies mixer.

McGuane recalled the week of hard drinking and drugging that led up to the Buffett bachelor party, a day before the actual ceremony. As the party started, a naked girl was wheeled in on a gurney, wearing only whipped cream and a terrified smile.

"She's got big eyes and she's obviously scared to death," McGuane remembered. "There's whipped cream all around and things like that. And all these hungover people could give a shit less. She rolls into the room in this state of stupefied silence. Tom Corcoran walks over and says, 'Honey, you're going to be crazy about high school.' "

Hunter S. Thompson attended that party, though most people in attendance don't believe he was invited. Even in the world of rock-star excess, the King of Gonzo could be too much. Women— clothed women, not jump-out-of-the-cake women—had also infiltrated the party, including Thompson's wife, Sandy.

"We're stretched out on a couch and Hunter's wife was very animated, dancing around and trying to get someone to make a pass at her," McGuane said. "She was visualizing an orgy. No one's paying any attention to her at all. This is like five o'clock in the morning and Hunter walks in and she's undulating around and bumping and grinding and Hunter says, 'That's enough for one day.' He leads her out and—it's on the second floor—and I walk out on the balcony and Hunter and his wife are on the balcony and she's tearing him a new asshole. He's kind of hunched over, trying to get away from her, and she's after him, yelling, 'You son of a bitch! Goddamn you, mother-fucker!' It was such a scene."

McGuane was one of the serious writers Thompson most admired. Thompson even had "Ninety-Two in the Shade" etched on a gold plate and fastened to the back of his desk chair, so it was behind him as he wrote.

But for McGuane, the Thompson persona of the mad-dog, drug-crazed Valkyrie overshadowed his work.

"Hunter was so imprisoned in his public persona that he would get very nervous if you talked seriously about anything, so he might say, 'MuhGwayne. Read your fuckin' book. Jesus fuckin' Christ!' And I'd say, 'Thanks, Hunter. Good-bye.' And that would be it."

Now McGuane wanted to write a novel that somehow wrestled between covers all of the craziness he'd seen. He chose as his protagonist a fictional rock star who'd come home after a fame binge. His name was Chester Hunnicutt Pomeroy and he was returning to Key West, determined to win back his one true love.

It was a world McGuane could easily understand: pain, excess, public humiliation, embarrassment, and the machinery behind the making of a music star. He'd seen much in his association with rock 'n' roll royalty, such as Jimmy Buffett and his friends in the Eagles.

The resulting novel, *Panama*, was published in 1978, five years after *Ninety-Two in the Shade*. Where the earlier book had received effusive praise, made the front page of the *New York Times Book Review*, and been nominated for a National Book Award, this book was treated like stale dogshit.

Many of the major reviews read as if reading the book was not re-quired to critique it. The publication of *Panama* was an opportunity for a referendum on the life of Thomas McGuane. So savagely was it treated that friends shrunk away from the author.

"It was a disaster when it came out," McGuane admitted. "It was dedicated to Jim Harrison and I think he was embarrassed by being associated with it. I think he was ashamed that his name was on it. Later, he came around when its reputation started to emerge and he said it's a great book. At the time, he really wanted me to get his name off of there."

Misunderstood by critics, baffling to those discovering the author for the first time, seen as an apologia by others for his years of excess, *Panama* was a tough sell to the reading public.

And, as had often been the case with McGuane's work, critics seemed to completely miss or misunderstand his humor. Pomeroy's over-the-top descriptions of rock stardom, his fractured relationships with women, and his challenging family battles all had echoes of McGuane's life. So too did the redemption of the fictional character match his creator's.

After the disasters of the previous half decade, McGuane was due for something good. He'd lost his father, his sister, and his mother. "And I lost my mind," he added.

"He was out of control," Chatham recalled. "Tom is lucky to be alive, frankly. So he's this kind of sole survivor of his family. He's fought tooth and nail for whatever it is he has."

In the aftermath of his two divorces and the deaths in his immedi-ate family, he was numb with guilt and regret.

Like so many divorced fathers, he missed seeing his children at the breakfast table. "I had a very close relationship with my son," McGuane said, "and when his mother and I got divorced, he was only ten years old."

Beyond that, his habits had changed for the worse. "I went from being somebody who had about three drinks a week into somebody who was at least on the cusp of alcoholism. The worst part of it was the personality change I had when I was drinking. That lasted about forty months and I saw the handwriting on the wall. I say 'on the cusp' because I found it so easy to give up drinking. It was a very negative part of my life."

Margot Kidder thinks McGuane has turned himself into a villain in his memory. "He thinks he was far worse than he was," she said. "I've seen him dead drunk, seen him coked out of his mind, and he wasn't an asshole at all. He could be *mean*, and that part wasn't fun. But the booze relaxed him enough where you could get into the center of his heart."

For McGuane, the change began when he met Laurie Buffett, sister of his best friend. Jimmy Buffett had told his sister to look up his friend "Tom the Writer" when she visited Key West. The change in McGuane's life was nearly immediate, though his new bride—and they were married before *Panama* was published in 1978, making her the third Mrs. McGuane in as many years—did not insist that he give up drink and drugs.

There was a clear Buffett family influence. It was getting to know J.D. and Peets Buffett, the parents of Jimmy, Lulu, and Laurie, that gave McGuane a model of what a marriage was supposed to be.

"I really loved the Buffett parents," McGuane said. "They were working people, really good people. My father-in-law had worked in the shipyard all his life and his son became a rock 'n' roll star." It was that foot in reality and foot in fantasy that intrigued McGuane about the older gentleman. He saw that the elder Buffett appeared to have his head screwed on straight, despite the overwhelming fame that had infiltrated his family's life.

But the most drastic change came one New Year's Eve when the Buffett children and their mates were gathered with the parents for the holiday.

"We were at the house in Montana on New Year's Eve," McGuane recalled, "and we had too much to drink and the next day everybody had a hangover. So we're watching the ball games and my mother-in-law made a big pitcher of Bloody Marys and as soon as I had one, I was drunk again, and I just hated it. My father-in-law had just bought a carton of Lucky Strikes and he lit up and said, 'Jesus, I wish I could quit smoking.' I picked up his Lucky Strikes and opened the door—there was a great snowfield out there—and tossed the Lucky Strikes out. I said, 'You quit smoking and I'll quit drinking.' "

And that was it.

McGuane was strong enough to not backslide when friends produced wine or whiskey at dinner. He could decline graciously and not covet their glasses as they sang with joy after the meal. He had the vigor to withstand the beckon of alcohol because he had seen what it had done to his family.

But avoiding temptation was one thing; inviting temptation was another. Thus, he began staying away from Key West.

"It had become kind of a grim place," McGuane said. "So it's not Key West's fault necessarily. But the party was over by the late seventies. People were dispersing, going elsewhere. It had been a hippie town. It had been a run-down town, turned into an opportunity town for late sixties, early seventies hippies, then it turned into a gay town. A gay town and a hippie town are not the same thing."

But looking back, McGuane would not want his life unraveled and Key West removed.

"I'm thrilled it happened," he said. "I have a great marriage, based on Key West. It's a well that I can go back to from time to time. It's a well of unencumbered idealism. We thought we could re-create American society. Those hippie fantasies were still in place. More and more, when I talk to people my own age, we consider ourselves old hippies, we're glad we were hippies. We were glad to have the values we acquired while we were hippies. They're still high quasi-religious standards about how to live with other people."

Key West was what it was, he thinks, because of what the country as a whole was like at the time. Richard Nixon was president, the nation was mired in an unwinnable war, and the generations were at a stalemate.

"I think we were able to look out at the Nixonian world and really feel that the only possible explanation for it was that we lived in a completely different country than the one that Nixon lived in and represented. We hoped that our vision would become the dominant United States of America. For the time being, there were at least two countries, and we weren't in his."

And so McGuane and his new bride settled into ranch life in Montana. No more did he follow the half-a-year-here, half-a-year-there schedule. Becky and Peter Fonda lived not far away—close enough, in fact, for young Tom McGuane IV to walk between the homes of his parents, across the hay fields. And Margot Kidder also made sure that Maggie McGuane would know her father. Tom and Laurie McGuane also had a daughter, Anne.

Somehow, Tom McGuane had escaped a dangerous paradise.

16

Evacuation

*For everything you have missed, you have gained
something else, and for everything you gain, you lose
something else.*
—RALPH WALDO EMERSON

McGuane's sobriety didn't affect his friendships with Harrison, Chatham, and Valdene. They were all supportive and at first cautious about drinking in his presence, but he assured them they needn't change on his account. He had made his decision and he had the support of his new wife and family.

McGuane's resolve was steel, and he withstood temptation. But as he spun off into another orbit, he was not with the other three as much. And there was also that moment, when the seventies had ended, when the rest of The Boys decided maybe it was time to stop going to Key West.

"We just looked at each other and said, 'Maybe we can't do this anymore,' " Valdene recalled.

They would always be friends, but those friendships would be played out in Montana, where Chatham and McGuane lived, or in Arizona, where Harrison had his winter cabin, or on Valdene's splendid estates in Palm Beach and his huge hunting property in North Florida. As the old song said, "If the good times are all gone / Then I'm bound for moving on."

So that's what they did.

A mass exodus from Cuba began in April 1980 after a plunge in that nation's economy. President Jimmy Carter, in a magnanimous display of southern hospitality, opened his arms. Over the course of a few months, ten thousand Cubans fled the island, many of them freed from prisons and institutions for the criminally insane by Cuban president Fidel Castro. Many landed in Key West.

When it began, Tom Corcoran's journalistic instincts kicked into high gear. "I hopped on my motorbike and rode up to Garrison Bight and got in touch with a buddy of mine who was a charter captain, and I asked if he had space on the boat and I asked if I could go along," Corcoran said. This was the period when he was still putting in several hours a week babysitting Hunter S. Thompson, but the story was too big to set aside.

He made arrangements to photograph the boatlift for *Newsweek*. "I went home and packed and got on the boat and we were pulling away, and . . . I don't know if I have a photograph of it, or just a photo in my mind: it's my wife and son, who was ten at the time, and Hunter and Laila standing on the pier. We were about fifty yards off the pier at Garrison Bight and I thought to myself, 'There's something wrong here. Hunter should be on the boat.' I was going off to do something outlandish; to go off and cover this Cuban boatlift, and Hunter's standing on the pier. At that point, I think he was so in love with Laila that he didn't want to give up an hour."

Though he still saw himself on his self-imposed sabbatical, Hunter

Thompson's instincts required him to be part of an event, or at least *feel* that he was part of it, so he began drafting a novel inspired by the boatlift, which he called *The Silk Road*. He did not finish it then, but published three scenes from it a decade later in his *Songs of the Doomed* collection. Still, being so close to the biggest news event of the day and *not* being part of it ate at him. It was a signal that he needed to get back in the game and that it was time for him to end his respite in Key West.

The boatlift was the biggest thing in the country at that moment and ground zero for the story was Key West.

Keith Graham was a twenty-eight-year-old photographer for the *Miami Herald* who volunteered to cover the boatlift and its impact on Key West. He lunged for the assignment, so in love was he with the town.

Some of the stories broke his heart.

He remembered photographing an eighty-six-year-old woman, obviously feeble as she gingerly stepped off the boat at the docks in Key West. Her sixty-five-year-old daughter held her mother's shoulders. They had both come on a rickety raft that miraculously survived the ninety-mile trip from Cuba.

The old woman was crying when Graham saw her. She said something, which Graham asked a bystander to translate. "I've come to die in a free land," the woman had said.

One morning, a month or so into the boatlift, he recalled looking up and seeing a different sort of face. Key West had always been a small town of benign locals and exotic visitors. Now Graham saw something new.

"The town is different today," he told his editor on the phone. Suddenly the streets were fetid with strolling criminals. Most of them moved on and enough of them landed in Miami to forever change the politics and culture of the town. It had morphed from a congenial town full of retirees in yacht-sized El Dorados to a town best known for its crime, nightclubs, and conspicuous excess.

After those first two months of the boatlift in 1980, the assignment turned into an indenture for Keith Graham. He worked fifty-five straight, grueling days, with no weekends. He was so in love with the assignment at first that he had told his editors he could keep costs down by staying with friends. So there had been few charges for food and lodging. But after fifty-five days, he was drained. *I need help*, he told his editors on the phone. *Send someone down*. When no one showed, Graham said he was going to check into the Casa Marina under a fake name and ring up enormous room-service charges that the *Herald* would have to pay. Still, no reinforcements arrived.

He wasn't bluffing. He checked into the Casa and spoiled himself with sleep, food, and beverage. Then he decided to do something he'd always wanted to do.

He knocked on the door at 1531 Duncan. No answer. Another knock, no answer. *Hell, it is Key West*, he figured. So he opened the door and called out.

"Tennessee?"

"That's right! I'm here," came a voice from deep within the house. "I'm out back."

Wearing a peach-colored silk kimono, Tennessee Williams was sprawled in all of his magisterial glory on a chaise longue by the pool with the rose tattoo at the bottom.

"Mr. Williams, I'm Keith Graham from the *Miami Herald*. I just wanted to come by and talk about this boatlift."

Williams arched his eyebrows and smiled to himself. "Well, well," he muttered. Then he called out, "Bruce!" An impossibly well-proportioned young man in a swimsuit emerged from the house. "Please get our young guest whatever he wants to drink, and

I'll have another." Williams hoisted his well-used glass and urged Graham to sit down.

Graham had always thought that Tennessee Williams was the great American writer, a man whose every work was another piece in a massive landscape of tragedy. Here he was, alternately brooding and jovial, sitting by his pool on a June afternoon when all hell was breaking loose down at the docks.

Graham knew he would never have gotten past the doorman if he'd tried to see the great dramatist at his New York apartment. Even if he'd sighted him at a Broadway opening, he'd never get close enough to even gasp his name, let alone have a conversation.

The swamp alligator in the kimono held court, basking in the golden light of a late afternoon, talking about the boatlift, the weather, and the capriciousness of the human heart. Keith Graham thought, "This could happen nowhere else. This could only happen in Key West."

Tom Corcoran had a tentative connection at *Newsweek* named Vernon Smith, the Atlanta bureau chief. Smith was coordinating coverage of the boatlift, and Corcoran promised him some dramatic photos of the action at sea. Corcoran thought that when his pictures of the boatlift were printed in *Newsweek*, it would open a lot of doors. Unfortunately, another photographer got his art to the picture editor four hours before Corcoran's work arrived.

That was the way things were going for Corcoran. After a decade in town, with a wife and son, he didn't have a lot to show. He and Judy went to parties and she was the only woman without a Rolex. A lot of his friends had gotten into the smuggling business, but Corcoran had avoided that path. Instead, he'd bartended, been a disc jockey, run a leather shop, and written songs. He had collaborated with Buffett and Thompson but did not have a lot to show for those ventures.

There had been the temptation to smuggle marijuana. Corcoran was good on the water—hell, he was a Navy man, after all—and he and Buffett had sailed a lot together. Buffett once called from the road and asked Corcoran to meet James Taylor and sail with him from St. Barth's to Montserrat for a recording session. There was plenty of room on the boat for extra cargo, but that wasn't Corcoran's style. Deep down, he was still a boy from Ohio.

As they noticed the changing times in Key West, Buffett mused to Corcoran about how simple twists of fate altered the trajectory of their lives.

"If I hadn't had 'Come Monday' and you hadn't had Sebastian, we'd probably be out on those boats," Buffett said.

The innocent days of any-Bubba-with-a-boat were over by the end of the seventies. But it wasn't just missing—or avoiding—the boat on pot smuggling that had Corcoran questioning his choices. There were a lot of factors at play.

Number one, of course, was his son. "He was ten, and Key West had changed radically," Corcoran said. "Key West was a different place by the end of the seventies. It had turned into a place [strictly] for grown-ups. I did not foresee a good experience for him if we stayed."

The second reason had to do with the economic changes. Key West had been trying for decades to lure tourists to town. During the Great Depression, the Works Progress Administration had hired writers and sent them south to write about the glory of the Keys. Stetson Kennedy was one of the WPA writers who came to work and stayed to play, marrying a Key West girl. He became a student of Key West's history and folklore, and his work remains one of the best sources on the city and its crazy lust.

Finally, at the end of the seventies, here they came: college kids on spring break, young professionals throwing off work for a week to get mad drunk on Duval Street, and homosexual tourists needing that live-and-let-live attitude. Key West was a safe port.

"It was just part of the trend of the time," Corcoran said. "America was discovering the Keys; Americans were discovering the coast in general. Everybody was trying to escape to the ocean. That's what made Buffett so successful then; he caught that wave."

But what was good for the town wasn't so good for the people who'd been calling it home.

"The immediate impact for me," Corcoran said, "was that rents went up."

The third factor in the Corcoran relocation was the *we-could-have-been-contenders* feeling he and Judy shared. Both had college educations, yet they were doing leather-tooling here, odd jobs there. Judy worked for a real-estate firm. They were living hand to mouth, doing work well below their abilities, and as they got out in the world and saw how their old friends were doing and the position they had earned in life, they began to think that if they didn't start to play catch-up, they would fall irrecoverably behind.

"Judy and I felt we had squandered our educations," Corcoran said. "I couldn't make a living as a photographer and Judy couldn't get a worthy job."

Corcoran knew that he had talent as a writer and photographer but that he would never earn his worth as long as he stayed put. "I wasn't making the kind of money I should be," he said. "I saw the people outside of Key West and how they were living. Our hippie days had been glorious, but we felt them getting tarnished by people making money hand over fist, scamming and smuggling marijuana. The opportunity for us to improve our lives was not facing us down in Key West. It was somewhere else, and we had to have some hope of improving our lives."

They started looking around for a new home, some place more affordable. Their only criterion was that their new home had to be in the South and near the ocean. They narrowed the choices to Beaufort, South Carolina, and Fairhope, Alabama. Corcoran knew the Fairhope area well because it was near Jimmy Buffett's parents.

In mid-September 1979, Hurricane Frederic hit the Gulf Coast and caused major damage to the home of J.D. and Peets Buffett, near Mobile. Jimmy Buffett asked Corcoran to do him a favor and help his folks dig out from the storm. Corcoran was happy to help, and that visit planted the seed in his mind of that area being a good place to live, perhaps a good place to raise a child.

Buffett came to visit, to see how things were going. He and Corcoran went to a bar to toss back a few, and they met a woman and began talking about the area. Corcoran asked about the housing market.

"I'm a property manager," the woman said. "I've got the perfect place for you."

She was right; it was perfect. It was a condominium on the water in Fairhope, complete with a pool. It was going to be vacant the following June, she said, and she'd pencil him in.

So Corcoran was pretty sure when he stepped off the boat after his night at sea covering the boatlift that he was breathing his last gasp as a Key West resident. He and Judy had decided to move when the school year ended in May. A new life, a safer and more prosperous life for his family, awaited in Fairhope.

By that time, things were looking up. Corcoran had collaborated with Hunter Thompson on the screenplay for *Cigarette Key*, their story of drug smuggling in the Keys, and he had also taken Thompson's espionage story and written a film treatment called *The Mole*. That one—temporarily, at least—held the interest of Hollywood, and being on the right track was all the encouragement Corcoran needed at that point.

Things were better in Fairhope. Judy Corcoran got a job in a sporting goods store but soon was hired as the office manager for a construction company with high-profile projects, such as the remodeling of the Grand Hotel in Point Clear.

Corcoran found himself in a congenial community of writers but without some of Key West's deadly temptations. Thompson came to visit and to ask for Corcoran's help in lashing together his out-of-control manuscript for *The Curse of Lono*. The thin story of the book grew from Thompson's trip to Hawaii to cover a marathon, but it ended up containing a lot of island lore and Thompson ruminations on immortality. It was a series of bits in need of connection, and Thompson couldn't connect the dots.

Thompson and Laila Nabulsi rented a condo near Fairhope, and for a period, the two men met daily at Julwin's Family Restaurant and spread the pages over the table, hoping that some sense of order would appear. Despite the herculean effort, it never really did. After two years of wrestling with the unruly story, Thompson got his book published in 1983.

In Fairhope, Corcoran was still in the McGuane and Buffett orbit, as both had family there: the Buffett parents, J.D. and Peets. Jimmy Buffett had fled Key West but was still struggling to deal with some of the dangers of that paradise.

Relations had become strained between Tom and Judy Corcoran.

"The marriage was in trouble," he said. Like many freelancers with numerous sources of income, Corcoran usually filed an extension on his tax returns each year. On a humid summer afternoon in 1985, finally gathering his paperwork, he realized that he needed canceled checks for office supplies that Judy had bought for him the previous year. He went to the sunroom, which Judy used as a sewing room and office, and which contained her financial records.

"I went into the filing cabinet looking for check stubs," Corcoran said, "and at the back of one drawer there was a bottle of Liebfraumilch, hidden."

Startled, he looked through more of her canceled checks and discovered that she was buying wine and liquor secretly. "It made no sense. We always had beer in the fridge, wine and rum in the house."

When she came home, he confronted her with the evidence.

"Judy, what's the deal?"

"I think I have a problem," she said quietly.

He asked her to try to stop. They had a new life now and their son needed both parents in place.

Corcoran reached out to some friends, who suggested that Judy get into Alcoholics Anonymous. She agreed to attend meetings and seemed to be doing well in the program. So, months later, when Corcoran needed to travel, he felt that he could leave her and Sebastian for several weeks.

A friend wanted Corcoran to run a tropical-themed restaurant in Gulf Shores, Alabama, a job he needed. His freelance photography business had thrived in the early eighties in Mobile, but the sour economy was forcing ad agencies out of business. His income was thinning out.

To get ready for the Gulf Shores gig, Corcoran asked a Key West friend if he could watch him run his office at Louie's Backyard, which had grown into the most popular restaurant and bar on the island. With more knowledge of payroll and purchasing, Corcoran thought perhaps he could work similar magic in Gulf Shores. While he was in Key West for this temporary visit, Corcoran was asked to cover some shifts as the bartender on the Afterdeck at Louie's.

"I got called in as a pinch hitter," Corcoran said, "and I made a fortune. I couldn't believe the tips."

The new Key West was attracting rich tourists with lots of money to throw around.

After a couple of weeks, the apologetic owner said, "I'm sorry. I know you need to get back home. I'll find somebody new."

"Take your fucking time," Corcoran said. He was living cheaply and sending the money home to pay long-overdue bills.

Corcoran was still working there a month later when his wife called. "You need to come home because your son is acting like an idiot," she told him.

He returned to Fairhope and found there was nothing wrong with his son. The problem was with Judy.

"She had been fired from her job and was in real trouble with the alcohol," Corcoran said.

He told her that his being in Key West for those few weeks had eased his mind, had taken a weight off his shoulders and strain off their bank account.

"You really should go down there for a short time and relax, spend time with old friends, and concentrate on getting healthy," he said. "Chill out with a change of scenery."

He made a few calls and found that Buffett's partner, Sunshine Smith, would give Judy an office job at the Margaritaville Store. Judy agreed to give it a try.

Seven or eight of her friends were at the airport to greet her the afternoon she arrived, but she staggered getting off the airplane, already drunk. She also told them that her husband had thrown her out and she was there because she had nowhere else to go.

She got the job at Margaritaville, but soon Smith discovered that Judy was drinking lunch. Jimmy Buffett was concerned enough to send her to a rehabilitation center and pay for her stay.

"Nobody told me any of this," Corcoran said, "because I was supposedly 'the guy who threw her out.' "

A few weeks later, out of the treatment center, she called.

"Can I come home?" she asked.

"Of course," he replied. "It's your home."

She spent a long, good weekend with her husband and son, then decided she wanted to come home for good. She returned to Key West to close out her affairs.

A few nights before she was to return to Alabama, after drinks at Louie's, she went boating with four friends. It was a blustery night, and no one belonged on the water. For some reason, the boat captain stopped and jumped in for a swim. Judy and another woman jumped in, too. Too late they realized that the wind was blowing the boat one direction and the current was taking the swimmers the other way.

"So they all got separated from the boat," Corcoran recalled, "and the two still in the boat had no idea how to start the engine. Finally, the boat owner got back aboard. Within ten minutes they found one of the women. But they never found Judy."

The police ruled it a drowning. Judy Corcoran's body was never found.

"It was horrible for Sebastian," Corcoran said. "He was only fifteen. Judy's father and brother came down to Key West." They chartered airplanes and searched all of the surrounding island beaches. "But I just knew. I knew they wouldn't find anything."

Corcoran's prime concern was his son. He tried his best to avoid the human practice of play-by-play, trying to figure out what he should have done or what wrong turn they had made.

"I thought, 'This can weigh me down for the rest of my life or I can get on with things.' " Corcoran said.

And so he chose to go on.

The gatherings grew less frequent over the years. McGuane was firmly ensconced in Montana. He first moved near Livingston, near Becky and Peter Fonda. But he began to fear that the same sort of culture he had left behind in Key West would follow him, so he moved across the Crazy Mountains, settling into the peace of Sweet Grass County. There, he and Laurie raised their new daughter and the children from their blended family.

Valdene continued playing occasional host in Florida and there were regular fishing trips—if not to Key West, then to the Gulf of Mexico or the Upper Keys. With his Palm Beach and North Florida homes, Valdene could accommodate whatever The Boys had in mind. But The Boys, often as not, begged off on a Florida trip.

Without making a conscious decision to stay away from Key West, McGuane and Harrison and Chatham, with silent agreement, closed the books on that place and that time. Key West was a different place when they left it, and when they did visit, they saw that much had changed. The charming town was now a tourist destination. Honeymooners came. Gay couples visited, free in a way that they could not be anywhere else. Great wealth arrived. The tenor of the town changed. The Pier House became an upscale resort, and its funky little bar, the Chart Room, lost some of its earthy charm.

But, in the end, Key West is still Key West. Young writers still come down Highway 1, looking for the ghost of Hemingway and the inspiration that fed that earlier generation. The wild boys of the seventies are distinguished gray now.

Still they come, the young writers and artists. Some find what they want, and some don't. But each generation gets its time in the sun. It also rises; it also sets.

EPILOGUE

Don't Stop the Carnival

Well, I'm still here. I didn't have to go to rehab,
and I'm not broke.
—JIMMY BUFFETT

Every night in Key West, hundreds of tourists come to Mallory Square to watch sunset. Here *sunset* is as much a place as an event. Crowds gather in the square to view the magnificent end of the day, in the company of jugglers, mimes, and strolling guitar players. Someone's always got a drum circle going. Used to be, people would drop a line off the edge of the pier and catch mutton snapper or grouper. But these days, the sunset crowds don't leave much room for fishing.

No longer a working pier, Mallory is today intended primarily for viewing the nightly spectacle. Creosote and concrete have been replaced with pavers, and now there are booths and licenses required for vendors. Despite the institutionalization of the ritual, occasionally the old man on his bicycle still shows up, selling his homemade conch salad.

Look at the crowd: mostly tourists, prosperous from the looks of the clothing. College kids, young couples holding hands, gaggles of coworkers here to shrug off 9-to-5 life, to get drunk, and to find a partner for the nightly Bone Island mambo.

It's the first time to Key West for a lot of these people. They're seeing it all with fresh eyes and virgin sensibilities. The town changes and the people change, but no one gets tired of paradise.

You'll also see some locals at the square, because sunset is still sunset. They're the power structure of the town now, the shopkeepers, the business owners, the people who keep the city's lights on.

Some made their fortunes by selling marijuana a few decades back. Most everything is aboveboard now and legitimate, but it was that foundation of piracy that allowed many of them to stay here, to buy property before the market went insane, and to prosper in this playground of the rich.

The town's demographic has gone through a staggering change since the days of McGuane, Harrison, Chatham, and Valdene. Today, residents of Key West fall into one of two groups: millionaires or homeless, with hardly any in-between. The service workers who keep the town running and feed and water the tourist multitudes can't afford to live there anymore. They drive in from Big Pine or Sugarloaf, day laborers in paradise.

It's a warm February evening, and Tom Corcoran strides down Duval Street. He hasn't lived in Key West full-time since the end of the seventies, but he's back so much, it's like he never left.

Corcoran walks with purpose through the margarita gentry crowding the streets. Tourists stop in the middle of the sidewalk to debate their evening plans. *Sloppy Joe's? How about Hog's Breath? That dude with the piano on wheels, he's playing there tonight.*

Corcoran doesn't drink much, perhaps the reason he managed to survive so well and so long in Keys culture. No longer the young and hirsute Taco Tom, he's white-haired, but still tall and ramrod straight. Even though he's into his Social Security years, he walks with the urgency of an undergraduate, wearing a different uniform now: a pocket T-shirt under an open and flowing tropical raiment, cargo shorts, and a ball cap, this one advertising "Habana Club."

Key West has changed furiously since his arrival. The quaintness and weirdness that Corcoran found when he stepped off the plane in 1968 has largely been institutionalized. The little town that he first knew—not far removed from the town that Hemingway loved—has in some ways been embalmed as an alcoholic theme park. In the last third of the twentieth century, the state of Florida excelled in killing off that which was authentic and re-creating it as something sterile and animatronic. Where once the state had genuine wildness, Disney backhoes tore up the work of nature and replaced it with an easily controlled facsimile. And so with Key West. The new construction mimics the old: *This isn't a genuine Conch house, but is instead an incredible simulation!*

But in other ways, the town remains what it always has been: the little village at the end of the road.

A slow, methodical squeak behind him alerts Corcoran to the approach of a geriatric bicycle. By the pace, he knows it's a local, in no hurry to be anywhere. Some of the locals drive through town in their Conch Cruisers, rusting sloops of cars—maybe an old Bonneville or a Deuce-and-a-Quarter—and see how close they can come to scaring the bejeezus out of Duval crowds. "Tourist bowling," they call it, when a drunk staggers in front of their hurtling piece of machinery.

These drinkers are rank amateurs, Corcoran thinks, looking at the wobbly crowd on the streets. None of them could have kept up with Captain Berserko and the other babbling crazies in Club Mandible. They spent the seventies living, working, drinking, drugging, and fucking their way through Key West, for their *art*.

Tourists come to Duval wearing the uniform, but the clothes don't fit, in more ways than one. These three rubberneckers on Duval this evening are built like stevedores, straining the weird neon blooms on their flowered shirts. This guy blocking the intersection looks like a disheveled teamster, and the old, weathered woman on the bike nearly wipes out, as she swerves to avoid the suddenly inert tourist. Such inconvenience is part of resort-town life.

Finally, Corcoran arrives at his destination. Margaritaville was first a song, then a state of mind, and finally a franchise. This location was the first of the national chain of Key West–themed bars, and also the prototype for a series of restaurants called Cheeseburger in Paradise. The whole enterprise—and the beer company and the record company and the clothing company—all sprang from the mind of Jimmy Buffett, who arrived here in 1971, an official failure in the music business.

That was a long time ago, when that gang of writers and singers and painters moved to Key West and found their artistic identities. And now they were all gone, off to Arizona or Montana or Hollywood. Now and then they return, Corcoran more often than the others.

So here he stands at the bar, watching his new songwriting partner perform for the Margaritaville crowd. The visitors from Ohio and Ontario and Oregon all wear flowered shirts—and if they don't have one, they're available in the adjoining Margaritaville Store. At the bar, one of the beer drinkers asks the bartender, "Say . . . *Jimmy*: does he ever, like, come in here?" And the bartender assures his customer that yes indeed, Jimmy Buffett does "come through" whenever he's in town.

Corcoran smiles, standing at the bar with his arms crossed, listening to John Frinzi and Sunny Jim. They do all original songs, no Buffett material, and the crowd whoops and rebel-yells all through their set.

To Corcoran, it's all a little surreal. Here he is, in a restaurant based on a song his old friend wrote, in an old Navy town that was home to some of the most brilliant and creative writers, artists, and musicians in the country's history. It's not the same town, but *damn*.

He looks down at his shoes. Below them is the foundation left from Margaritaville's earlier incarnation as the S.H. Kress Five & Dime. And below that, the sand and coral and bone. It's hard to walk around Key West and not feel the history rumbling beneath your feet.

Ernest Hemingway's home in Key West was designated a literary landmark by the American Library Association in 2010. The recognition came as the fiftieth anniversary of his suicide approached.

Each tour guide at the Hemingway House has a separate schtick. They tell stories of the six-toed cats that dominate the grounds, claiming that all of them are descendants of Hemingway's many cats that also had six toes. Hemingway had but one cat, and reliable sources report it had the conventional number of toes.

The City of Key West began celebrating Hemingway Days in 1980. It's a weeklong festival of Hemingway that includes a look-alike contest. Imagine a convention of Elvis Presley imitators, only with white beards and safari jackets. The contestants seem to travel in a flock, flying from one bar to another, though they stay close to Sloppy Joe's because of the greater number of photo opportunities.

"Ernest would roll over in his grave," his niece, Hilary Hemingway, said of the spectacle.

Ernest Hemingway's novels and short-story collections continue to sell thousands of copies yearly.

Tennessee Williams died in 1983, at age seventy-one. He suffocated while trying to remove a cap from a pill bottle with his teeth. The cap popped off and lodged in his throat, cutting off air to his lungs.

As his friend TRUMAN CAPOTE wrote, "It was a strange end for a man obsessed with a rather poetic concept of death." All of his life, Williams had imagined his death would occur in the next moment or the next day. He had written of life's brutality with a keen understanding of the whole catastrophe of human endeavor, yet had died in a totally bizarre circumstance that would have been considered too strange for any of his dramas.

But by some accounts, Capote's among them, Williams had been dead for two decades by the time he died. Frank Merlo, the longtime companion of the great playwright, had died in 1962. "Tennessee died a little, too," Capote wrote in *Playboy*.

Rather than dwell on the sad decline in Williams's life after the death of his devoted lover, Capote used as centerpiece of his eulogy a story of the good times in Key West. He recalled a time in the late seventies when he and Tennessee went out to dinner at a crowded restaurant. Capote figured there were three hundred people in the establishment, "both gays and straights."

While Capote and Williams were dining, they noticed a rather drunk husband and wife at a nearby table. The woman, dressed provocatively in a halter-top and painted-on slacks, eyed them and eventually stood up, swayed toward them, and stood at their table. She produced an eyebrow pencil and asked Capote to sign his name around her navel.

"Oh, no," Capote laughed, "leave me alone."

Williams thought Capote was being too abrupt. "How can you be so cruel?" he asked his companion. He took the eyebrow pencil and wrote Capote's name in a circle around the woman's belly button.

Back at her table, her husband was visibly angry at the way his wife had been treated by Capote. He grabbed the pencil from his wife, marched over to the Capote-Williams table, unzipped his pants, and withdrew his penis.

"Since you're autographing everything today," he slurred, "would you mind autographing *mine*?"

The restaurant was dead quiet by this time.

Then Williams took the eyebrow pencil from the man and said, "I don't know if there's room for Truman to autograph it, but I'll initial it." Williams winked at Capote.

Phil Clark, the bartender who was the inspiration for Jimmy Buffett's great song "A Pirate Looks at Forty," disappeared. Nobody knows for sure what happened to him, though there are many theories.

Whether he was a drug smuggler or a bullshit artist, Clark charmed all who knew him.

The primary story was that he left the Keys just ahead of the law and ended up in Sausalito, California, where he fell overboard and drowned. That end seemed unlikely for a shrimper turned smuggler, but much about Clark was unlikely. Ashes purported to be his were stored in an urn above the bar at the Full Moon Saloon in Key West. Toasts were regularly offered in the direction of the urn, and on at least one occasion, friends at the bar claimed to have snorted his remains.

Some, including MURPHY, the young hippie girl who grew up to be one of Phil Clark's six wives, don't think he's really dead. A cadre of loyal friends believe he is still out there, living underground, like the pirate he claimed to be.

Becky McGuane had ridden off into the Montana sunset with her besotted movie-star husband, PETER FONDA. They lived near Tom McGuane and shared the parenting duties for THOMAS MCGUANE IV. The younger Tom grew up to be Hunter S. Thompson's bodyguard (for a brief stint) and a maker of fine knives. He trained with master knife makers in Japan, and his work is highly regarded and sought after.

Together, Becky and Peter Fonda helped raise Fonda's children, JUSTIN and BRIDGET FONDA. The daughter continued the notable acting legacy of the family, which included grandfather HENRY FONDA and aunt JANE FONDA. Peter Fonda's career never again achieved the commercial success it had with *Easy Rider* or the critical respect of his quiet western, *The Hired Hand*. But he did earn an Academy Award nomination for his lead performance in the independent film *Ulee's Gold*. As he aged, he became a more-frequent supporting player, in such films as *Ghost Rider* and *3:10 to Yuma*.

Becky Fonda kept the home fires burning and was a popular and vital part of the Livingston, Montana, community.

To the surprise of most everyone in the town—and to Becky Fonda—Peter Fonda announced in 2008, after thirty-three years of marriage, that he was separating from his wife.

Margot Kidder had her greatest commercial success after leaving McGuane, portraying Lois Lane in the *Superman* films. This led to other high-profile roles in *The Amityville Horror, Willie & Phil*, and *Trenchcoat*. She married again (twice), but neither marriage lasted as long as her union with McGuane.

She had a run of bad luck: A serious automobile accident sidelined her for two years. She went bankrupt. By the mid-nineties, she was back in *People* magazine, but for all the wrong reasons. She had suffered a mental breakdown and was discovered wandering, homeless, through Los Angeles, and was eventually found living under a family's porch.

She had suffered from bipolar disorder, but after treatment, she recovered and resumed her career, though not at *Superman* levels. She did series television, plays, and the occasional theatrical film. By the time her career was in recovery mode, her daughter, Maggie, was nineteen and about to marry novelist Walter Kirn, thirty-two. Maggie announced that she was moving with her husband to Montana, and so Kidder followed the couple to Livingston, to watch her grandchildren, Masie and Charlie, grow up.

Kidder became a favorite in Livingston, a good citizen, a welcome neighbor, and a political activist. The move also drew her back into Tom McGuane's life. They were bound by another generation.

"He is a wonderful grandparent," she said. "Maggie had us together for Thanksgiving, and Tom was bouncing the kids on his belly. Sometimes, when I'm with the grandchildren, I'll tell them about 'Captain Berserko,' and they'll look at me all puzzled and say, 'You mean *Grandpa*?'"

Kidder is comfortable with herself and her life, happy to have her network of Livingston friends, with her daughter and grandchildren nearby. Still, she wishes the relationship with her former husband was better. "I would love for there to be a friendship," she said. "He will not be my friend. I say harsh things about Tom, but I will love him until the day I die. He was the love of my life." After a pause, she laughed, and added, "Well, *one* of them, at least."

Jimmy Buffett, the man who figured out how to take the magic and mystery of Key West and condense it into a three-minute song, became one of the largest concert draws in America. His summer tours became quasi-religious rituals for his legions of fans, known as Parrotheads, and ensured his place as one of the most profitable acts in the music business.

He was willing to test his boundaries and try something not expected in the rock-star playbook. He took Herman Wouk's novel *Don't Stop the Carnival* and, at great financial risk, mounted a large-scale Broadway musical, with much of his own capital invested. It was not a commercial success, though critics were kind to it and no one could doubt Buffett's enthusiasm for Wouk's tale of the tropics.

Buffett always had literary ambitions, and his celebrity allowed him to publish his first collection of stories—some fact, some fiction—called *Tales from Margaritaville*. Unlike a lot of celebrity books intended to cash in on the fleeting notoriety of their "authors," Buffett's book had legs. He could write. Soon he published his first novel, *Where Is Joe Merchant?* He followed with a best-selling memoir, *A Pirate Looks at Fifty*, and other hugely successful books, such as *A Salty Piece of Land* and *Swine Not?* He routinely outsold his more literary friends, Tom McGuane and Jim Harrison.

Beyond his work as a musician and a writer, Buffett became a model musical entrepreneur. Years ago, a friend noted that parking-lot vendors made thousands of dollars at each one of his shows hawking T-shirts and ball caps. She suggested he do the same. With a hand-shake, he sealed a deal with that friend, Sunshine Smith, and made her a partner in the first Margaritaville in Key West. The combination bar–restaurant–souvenir shop was a success, and soon there were other Margaritavilles rimming the Gulf Coast. The concept later expanded to the family-restaurant chain Cheeseburger in Paradise. Buffett sold that enterprise to a Florida-based restaurant group in exchange for a partnership, and launched himself into multimillionaire territory.

Buffett has also used his money for a number of good causes, most of which are environmental.

Backstage at one of his concerts celebrating his fortieth year as a performer, Buffett was approached by an old friend from Key West, Vaughn Cochran. He'd been part of Buffett's original trio as the washboard player. Now a successful artist and fishing guide, he showed up to say hello after the show.

The two chatted and laughed for several minutes, then they hugged to say good-bye. Cochran started to walk away, but felt a hand on his shoulder.

"Damn, Vaughn," Buffett said, grinning at his friend. "Can you believe I'm still getting away with this?"

Jim Harrison finally found financial success from his writing after years of hand-to-mouth existence.

Through Tom McGuane and others, Harrison was introduced to actor Jack Nicholson. Nicholson loved the company of great writers and artists and soon forged a friendship with Harrison. He became aware of the difficulties Harrison had with money, and the fact that he lived in an isolated, primitive cabin in the Upper Peninsula of Michigan. He wanted to help.

When Nicholson called, Harrison had just started work on a novella that drew from the stories of his wife's family.

"We were dead broke," Harrison recalled. "Jack invited me to come down to Mexico for a couple of weeks." Harrison could not figure out the purpose of his visit to Nicholson's movie set other than to hang out and entertain his host with good stories over dinner. Finally, the actor made his intentions clear.

"The last day I was there, he said to me, 'How much do you owe in the world?' 'Fifteen grand,' I said. He asked, 'How much do you need to live for a year?' 'Fifteen grand,' I said again. By the time I got home, he had already FedExed the check for thirty grand."

The novella Harrison was writing became *Legends of the Fall*, which was featured on the cover of *Esquire* and illustrated by Russell Chatham. With Nicholson as its champion, it was sold to a motion picture studio, as was another Harrison novella, *Revenge*.

The sudden success vaulted Harrison into a new bracket of book sales. He wrote screenplays and began earning serious money. His older novels—*Wolf, Farmer, A Good Day to Die*—all had commercial rebirth. His 1986 novel, *Dalva*, told the story of a woman looking for the child she had given up for adoption when she was a teenager three decades before. So beautifully written was it that Nicholson asked the author, "When did you grow tits?" Critics often cite it as the best modern example of a novel written by a man from a woman's point of view.

Harrison and his wife, Linda, have been married for more than half a century.

In addition to the Michigan cabin, Harrison kept a winter residence on the Arizona border with Mexico. He gave up Michigan some years back and moved to Livingston, Montana, for the summers, not necessarily to be close to McGuane and Chatham but because one of his daughters had settled there after years of summer visits with her parents.

But Harrison rarely makes it back to Florida. "I can no longer bear to go to Key West," he said. "It was much better when most of the streets smelled like garbage and fish guts."

Content now, Harrison said that if he had only five minutes left to live, he would light up a cigarette and pet his dog.

Through Harrison and McGuane, Jack Nicholson became familiar with RUSSELL CHATHAM's artwork.

Harrison showed Nicholson some of Chatham's canvases. Nicholson asked, "What's his phone number?"

When word got out that the king of Hollywood loved Chatham's work, it brought the artist's paintings more attention, and a larger audience. His paintings appeared routinely on Harrison's book jackets and in other high-profile venues.

Like his friend Harrison, Chatham had endured years of living hand to mouth. When he began selling his art to the clerisy of Hollywood and having gallery openings that blocked traffic in New York, it all came as a sudden, sweet shock.

"I was never probably very aware of anything 'taking off,' " he said. "In the late eighties and early nineties, Montana was a big deal and I think they liked me because they saw me as somebody deliberately putting a boot to the establishment and doing okay. I was constantly being filmed and written up and so my income went up commensurately."

As fine a painter as he is, Chatham is also gifted as a storyteller and writer. A serious sportsman, he has published in a number of magazines and wrote a fishing memoir, *The Angler's Coast*.

He maintains Chatham Fine Art, his gallery in Livingston.

Long after the Key West years, Chatham entered into a sustained and deeply satisfying relationship with a woman in Livingston. She knew about the Key West trips and often asked him to take her. For their sixteen years together, she'd ask and he'd refuse.

"I loved her," he explained. That was the reason he couldn't take her to Key West. There would be too many temptations, too many opportunities to be unfaithful. "Why else would you want to go to Key West, except to get laid?"

Thomas McGuane rarely returns to Key West. When he heads south to fish, it's usually to his in-laws, the Buffetts, in Alabama, or to Boca Grande, Florida. He holds forth on his ranch, near a speck of a town called McLeod, Montana, best known for its one eatery, the Roadkill Café.

If you wonder why this distinguished man of letters makes his home at such a remote location, at the end of a road so rough it allows for a top speed of only four miles per hour, then you obviously have not made the drive. In a state already known for spectacular vistas, McGuane's ranch is beauty gently ladled on top of beauty.

Looking back on the days in Key West, GUY DE LA VALDENE recalls the role McGuane played in gathering friendships that have lasted a lifetime. "Tom brought that whole group together," Valdene recalled, "and then he brought that whole group together one more time in Livingston, Montana. Jim [Harrison] didn't live in Montana then, but he does now. But Chatham followed Tom to Livingston, and Richard Brautigan followed him there, and my wife and I, or just I, would go out there at least once or twice a year. That was just our little nucleus, our particular group. Tom was a magnet to a lot of other people as well."

McGuane agreed. "I ran around being a little bit of a pied piper," he said. "I had people following me wherever I went, including Livingston, Key West, and so on. That's one of the reasons I moved over here twenty-five years ago. Livingston had started to become like Key West."

These days, McGuane, the former king of excess, does only two things to excess: fishing and ranching.

In the study of his Montana home on a magnificent summer morning, he was asked about regret. He shrugged, noting that he had the "original regret" that he didn't save his parents from their dark course. He also said he couldn't get over his inability to save his sister from self-destruction.

"I have a mixed bag of regret about failing in marriage," he said. "I say mixed bag because I adore the children who came from my failures. And now I have an unbelievably good marriage and I'm in the third decade of this jubilant marriage. I might be a more important writer if I weren't so in love with the world, if I stayed home more. I would have written more, maybe written better, I don't know. I have never figured out if you're supposed to live it up or work on your legacy. In any case, I'm not particularly regret-ridden, that's for sure."

Aside from writing and ranching, fishing remains a prime concern. "I fish all the time when I'm at home," he famously said, "so when I get a chance to go on a vacation, I make sure to get in plenty of fishing." Around the time McGuane was inducted into the Academy of Arts and Letters, he was named Angler of the Year by *Fly Rod and Reel* magazine. He smiles when he is asked which honor means the most. "I should be more proud of my writing awards," he said, "but . . ."

Even now a strong and athletic outdoorsman, McGuane estimates he rides about 250 days of the year, on average two or three different horses a day. Despite his success in cutting-horse competitions, he does not consider himself at the level of his neighbors. "You can't be a writer-rancher, a dentist-rancher, a lawyer-rancher," he says. "It's too much work." What his life and his ranch give him is freedom. "If I want to get up in the morning, write for a few hours, go fish, ride a horse—I can do that."

"When you get rickety," he says, "you can still write, and fly fishing is not too demanding."

He seems miles away from the days when his life fed *People* magazine and the other gossip publications. His former lover, Elizabeth Ashley, wrote a memoir in which she wrote graphically of their affair. "I haven't read that," he laughs. He's content to live in flyover country, and feels distant from the American literary establishment.

And he is. There are few more beautiful spots in the world than this place right here, where McGuane straddles a chair in his writing cabin, stroking the head of his Labrador, at the junction of two babbling brooks. It's a happy ending too neatly tied up for a writer of McGuane's immense talent, but it is the hand he's been dealt and only a madman would refuse such a gift.

As he watches the two streams joining on his idyllic Montana ranch, McGuane talks about a recent visit from his brother-in-law, Jimmy Buffett. "Every time we get together, we're reminded of what a moment in time it was," McGuane says. "It's not like we haven't had other lives or haven't loved the rest of our lives, but that *was* unbelievably special. We all feel that way about it. We don't really know why. We were in a sympathetic culture to be an artist. That was really unique. It was a real chance to find out a lot in a short time in a small space."

Hunter S. Thompson got over his writer's block and signed on as a columnist, first for the *San Francisco Examiner* and then years later for the cable sports network ESPN.

He learned to better accommodate cocaine in his drug diet and again became a prolific writer. He recycled some of his older work in his collections of letters, and these books (*The Proud Highway* and *Fear and Loathing in America*) are considered some of his best. They form a personal history of the country from the fifties and into the twenty-first century and are the closest he came to writing an autobiography.

He wrote columns about Key West, but little else. He considered that place and that time as private.

He returned to the Keys in the eighties with filmmaker Wayne Ewing. The idea was to make a pilot for a television show featuring Thompson. For one sequence, Ewing filmed Thompson as he guided the Mako he'd bought years before with Dink Bruce. As Thompson gunned the motor and Ewing's camera rolled, a school of dolphins surfaced and began swimming alongside Thompson's boat.

"I'm back, Boys!" he screamed to the dolphins.

Thompson spent decades hoping to find a person who could be both muse and mother to him, as his wife Sandy had been. A parade of young women followed his divorce. He hired them as assistants, and then they became companions.

Finally, near the end, Thompson married Anita Bejmuk, the last of his assistants.

Thompson maintained his position as one of the most famous writers in the world. Even people who did not read books knew who he was because of his place in popular culture and his crushing celebrity. In addition to the portrayal by Bill Murray in *Where the Buffalo Roam*, Thompson was played by Johnny Depp twice, in film versions of the supposedly unfilmable *Fear and Loathing in Las Vegas* and *The Rum Diary*.

Though he had been a heavy drinker and smoker since his adolescence and a serious drug abuser all of his adult life, Thompson rarely showed the effects of his massive intake. Well into his sixties, he remained a vigorous, active, physical man. But eventually things began to catch up with him; his body slowed and did not function as he wished it would.

On February 20, 2005, Thompson was at his home outside of Aspen, Colorado. He was on the phone to his wife. His adult son, his daughter-in-law, and his grandson were elsewhere in the house. Thompson put his 45-caliber automatic into his mouth and pulled the trigger.

His suicide devastated his family, his friends, and his enormous network of young admirers. Though he had talked about suicide in his writing for many years, even his closest friends were shocked and reeled with grief and anger.

"I had just talked to him," McGuane recalled. "I had a very pleasant conversation with him. It was the Hemingway story. Hunter had acquired a public role and he had sycophants around him to encourage him. He had become a kind of a parody of himself. He was a wonderful writer and he loved being a celebrity but, once again, that comes and goes. Literature is always there and writing is always there. They don't come and go. If you get addicted to being popular, you're hosed."

Soon after the suicide, friends held a wake for Thompson in Aspen. But Thompson had been very public about what he wanted for his send-off: he wanted his remains shot from a huge tower to be built on his Colorado farm, while Bob Dylan sang "Mr. Tambourine Man."

Actor Johnny Depp funded the memorial, which cost by some estimates $4 million. The huge tower was erected near Thompson's cabin, with his symbol, a double-thumbed fist clutching a peyote button, throbbing with light in the middle of a giant dagger.

Bob Dylan was not available, so his recording of "Mr. Tambourine Man" was played instead.

A viewing pavilion was constructed near the tower to house the couple of hundred invited guests for the event. It was furnished with fully stocked bars and artifacts of Thompson's life. As a decoration, Tom Corcoran had provided a huge blown-up picture of Thompson from his Key West days. In the photograph, Thompson was shirtless, intent as a pro quarterback, about to pass a football to young Sebastian Corcoran in the front yard of their home in Key West.

Tom and Sebastian Corcoran were among guests gathered for a series of eulogies in the pavilion. Childhood friends and the reigning kings and queens of Hollywood and Washington were present to talk about their dear, departed friend. But it was a local who stole the show.

For the last thirty years of Thompson's life, his closest friend had been the Pitkin County, Colorado, sheriff, Bob Braudis. A tall, commanding man with a mop of unruly gray hair, Braudis spoke movingly of his great friend, praising Thompson as an artist and citizen of the world. Then Braudis turned to look at Corcoran's huge portrait of Thompson throwing the football. Braudis paused, slowly shook his head, and then shouted at the picture, "You motherfucker!"

Tom Corcoran now owns two houses, side by side, in a central Florida town at the outer reaches of Orlando's sprawl. His adult son, Sebastian, lives in one, presiding over Corcoran's huge, moody Russell Chatham lithographs and some of the artifacts from his father's life and career. Corcoran lives a few steps away in the house he reserves for his other possessions—a marvelous collection of books, more lithographs, more of his beautiful photographs of a golden age of Key West.

Corcoran sleeps here.

It's hard to find a seat. The place is more warehouse than home. It is also where Corcoran works. There are no couches, no tables, no barstools. The dining room holds most of the inventory for his small publishing business, The Ketch & Yawl Press. More books and boxes of Jimmy Buffett calendars, another Corcoran enterprise, fill the living room.

There are two chairs in the largest of the three rooms devoted to his library. One is a remnant from Buffett's Waddell Street apartment. Corcoran could put a plaque on it and sell it to the Hard Rock Café: "Jimmy Buffett Sat Here." It could also say, "Tom McGuane Sat Here" or "Hunter S. Thompson Sat Here."

In the office, where Corcoran writes his novels, there is a desk chair and a small chair for visitors, usually covered in piles of manuscript pages.

Tom Corcoran was long ago priced out of Key West, and after several years in Fairhope, Alabama, he found work writing about automobiles and became editor of a magazine about the cult surrounding the Ford Mustang. That job brought him back to Florida, and he settled smack-dab in the middle of the state. He published three books about cars, but he knew it was time for him to realize that long-dormant ambition to be a novelist. His muse, of course, was Key West.

He couldn't afford to live there, but when he left the magazine job, he moved to Cudjoe Key in the nineties and finally began writing the novels he'd always planned to write. They were mysteries set in Key West, built around a photographer who knew the island and all of its history. The character, Alex Rutledge, gets pulled into solving crimes.

In his fiction, he's dealt—tangentially, mostly—with a lot of the real mysteries of Key West, including the disappearance of Bum Farto. He has not written, and will not write, about the disappearance of Judy Corcoran. That would cause a raft of pain.

When his first novel, *The Mango Opera*, was published, his friends Tom McGuane, Hunter Thompson, Jim Harrison, and Jimmy Buffett lined up to praise it with dust-jacket blurbs that would be the envy of any American writer. He became one of the best mystery writers in America. Though he does not sell books by the truckload, he earns the praise of masters of the craft. Best-selling author Michael Connelly called one of Corcoran's books "the reading highlight of my year."

He gave up the Cudjoe Key house some years back and now shares the twin houses with Sebastian. He goes to the Keys a half-dozen times a year, usually staying with DINK BRUCE. He still collects a handsome royalty each year for a few minutes of collaboration with Jimmy Buffett three decades ago.

Out at dinner, he is kind and solicitous to his young waitress. The talk turns to music, and Corcoran's dinner companion tells her, "This dude wrote songs with Jimmy Buffett."

"Really?" she asks.

"Not only that," the companion says. "He once wrote a movie with Hunter Thompson. *And* he's a big-time mystery writer."

"Really?"

It's dark in the restaurant, so it's not clear if Corcoran is blushing, but the smart money is on it.

He tells her a few stories about Buffett and Thompson in the old days in Key West. She's smiling, ignoring all of her other tables.

"I've never been," she says. "Key West, I mean. I've lived in Florida my whole life, but I've never been."

"You should go." Corcoran's matter of fact, serious even. "It's not what it was in my day, but you should still go."

She smiles.

"I can't finish this," he says, nodding toward his plate. "Could you bring me something to pack it up in?"

"Yes, sir."

Back at his house, he's getting out of his car when he hears a *hello* as a bicycle speeds past in the dark. It's Sebastian, home from an evening with friends. Corcoran walks over to his other front yard.

"Hello, Son," he says. "I couldn't eat all my dinner. Would you like it?"

"That'd be great," Sebastian says. "I haven't gotten around to eating yet."

"It's Italian. It's good. I just wasn't that hungry."

"Thanks, Dad."

Corcoran turns back toward his other house. "Good night, Son."

"Good night, Dad."

But Corcoran isn't ready for bed just yet. If he didn't have a visitor, he might be at work on his next Alex Rutledge novel. Instead, he looks through his files of photographs of Key West. He's published one limited-edition art book of black and whites. Now he's contemplating a companion book in color.

The photographs are sharp and vivid, not faded and blurred with time. Corcoran examines each one carefully, seeing occasional flaws, remembering the instant each photograph was taken.

He treats everything with surgical care: photographic prints are in plastic slipcases; valuable books have Mylar covers. He has a whole bookcase devoted to his Key West collection, many of them rare, precious, and beautiful.

You should turn this into a museum, the guest says.

He nods. "Perhaps I will."

It's well after midnight when he finally puts away the pictures and announces he's ready for bed.

He locks the front door, turns out the lights, crosses the hall to his bedroom, and gets between the covers.

Thinking about Key West again invigorates him, but he's tired, so he falls asleep quickly, slipping into a dream. Soon, he can see the blue water.

AUTHOR'S NOTE

Tom Corcoran found me while I was working on *Outlaw Journalist*, my biography of Hunter S. Thompson.

I awoke one morning to an e-mail message from Corcoran that said, "I put 'Hunter S. Thompson' and 'Bob Dylan' into a search engine and your name came up. Why?" So I wrote back and told him I'd written books on both Dylan and Thompson and was at the moment working on my second book on Thompson. My first came out in 1991, when Thompson was very much a work in progress. *Outlaw Journalist* would be postmortem.

Corcoran wrote back to say that he'd been friends with Thompson. I asked for an interview, found out he was a mystery novelist, and ordered a few of his books. They were terrific stories about a photographer in Key West pulled into police work. I read two of them in the week before our scheduled meeting and interview.

Visiting Corcoran was like two middle-aged men having a play date. He has so much stuff—books, art prints, and mementos—that he has two side-by-side houses to hold it all. I also discovered that in addition to a rich archive—this dude saves everything—he has a steel-trap mind. While everyone around him had been snorting coke and getting drunk, Corcoran had managed to remain relatively clean and sober.

There's no doubt that meeting Corcoran enriched my book.

Douglas Brinkley, the great writer and historian, served as Hunter S. Thompson's literary executor. After Thompson's suicide, there had been a lot of books devoted to the iconoclastic writer. But Brinkley said my book stood out, in part because I was the only one to deal with the "missing years" of Thompson's life in Key West.

All credit, of course, to Corcoran.

I was nearly finished with that book when Corcoran began telling me that I needed to write a book about Key West in the seventies. He even showed me a message from Thompson, dated less than two months before the suicide, suggesting that such a book needed to be done.

"Why don't you write it?" I asked.

He was too close to it, he said. It needed to be written by someone on the outside. It needed to be me, he said.

It didn't take a lot of convincing. I'd married a beautiful woman from Key West and both sides of her family went back several generations on the Rock. I had always wondered what a life hatched there would be like. Yet my wife spoke of "getting out" of Key West, as if it was something bad, a place to be avoided. It was paradise, but also dangerous.

As I thought about that era and considered the writers working and playing in Key West, I began to see it as a parallel to Paris in the twenties, when Ernest Hemingway, F. Scott Fitzgerald, Gertrude Stein, and the others redefined the landscape of American literature. Key West in the seventies even had Thomas McGuane, the writer so often called the "new Hemingway" that he probably flinched at the mention of the name.

As a teenager, even before I'd read a book by McGuane, I knew who he was. Like Thompson, he was a writer so famous in his era that even people who didn't read books knew who he was. He was the drug-crazed new Hemingway getting married every twenty minutes or so down there in Key West.

That had been the public portrayal at least. I'd seen what being a celebrity writer had done to Thompson. Yet I knew McGuane and his friends not only survived but prospered.

Whether that press portrayal was accurate or not, it intrigued me enough to want to know how McGuane, Jim Harrison, Russell Chatham, and the others lived their lives. I'd gone on to read their books and I viewed writing this book as an opportunity, among other things, to revel in their work.

I saw the potential of the story that Corcoran had told me. After generously giving me the idea, he stepped back. I think he had no interest in being the central character, the focal point, of the book. That part was my idea.

This book could not have been written without Corcoran's monumental help, cooperation, and steadfast kindness. I also thank Beef Torrey, who not only helped me meet and interview the central characters of the book but also was generous with ideas, obscure publications, and advice.

As I traveled the country working on this book, I met so many people who deserve thanks. Some names, I'm afraid, I've forgotten. But I'll never forget the generosity of Paul Toppino and Dink Bruce, who hosted me in Key West and Livingston.

Above all, I thank my family. I'm in a cabin near Pine Creek, Montana, now. I've been working through the night on this book as deadline looms. It's been nearly two weeks since I've seen my wife and children, but I'm going home tomorrow. It reminds me that this book ultimately is the story of trying to find a home. In that sense, this is a book with a happy ending.

William McKeen

Key West / Gainesville / Denver / Livingston / Boston

March 2009–May 2011

ACKNOWLEDGMENTS

For expertise and enthusiasm: Jane Dystel, Miriam Goderich, and Lauren Abramo of Dystel and Goderich Literary Management. At Crown, I am indebted to executive editor John Glusman, who in addition to being a wise and talented editor was a big fan of Key West. He was so enthusiastic during our first phone conversation that I had to hold the receiver three feet away from my head. I am also grateful for the care and precision of associate editor Domenica Alioto, who kept chanting, "Keep your eyes on the prize." I also want to recognize production editorial director Mark McCauslin, copy editor Nancy Stabile, text designer Song Hee Kim, jacket designer Laura Duffy, and production supervisor Kevin Garcia.

For help above and beyond: Tom Corcoran and Beef Torrey.

For hospitality: Dink Bruce, Paul Toppino, and the Pine Creek Lodge near Livingston, Montana.

For research assistance: David Cumming, Alexandra Hamilton, Savannah McKeen, Steve Miller, Alex Orlando, Dominick Tao.

For conversation and correspondence: Ellis Amburn, Dink Bruce, Suzie Byrd, Russell Chatham, Danilo Cisneros, Nicole Cisneros, Vaughn Cochran, Sebastian Corcoran, Tom Corcoran, Kelly Castellanos, Mingo Castellanos, Montgomery Chitty, "Barry Cuda" (Kent Smith), Scott DeWolfe, Bill Dixon, Wayne Ewing, John Frinzi, Nancy Harris, Jim Harrison, Richard Hatch, Carl Hiaasen, Marian

Hjorstberg, Nelson Jamardo, Don Jordan, Margot Kidder, Toni Kokenzie, Dan Mallard, Thomas McGuane, Kerri McLean, "Murphy," Laila Nabulsi, "Norma Jean," David Potter, Rudy Prazen, Chris Robinson, Victoria Solodare, Andy Thurber, Cassandra Toppino, Edward Toppino Sr., Edward Toppino Jr., Paul Toppino, Beef Torrey, Guy de la Valdene, Richard S. Wheeler.

For general advice and counsel: Tom Fiedler, Mike Foley, Jon Roosenraad, Ted Spiker.

For serving as tribal council: Andrea Billups, Wayne Garcia, John Marvel, Stephen Orlando.

For being my reasons for living: Sarah, Graham, Mary, Savannah, Jack, Travis, and Charley.

For inspiration: Charles and Martha McKeen.

For saintliness: Nicole Cisneros McKeen.

NOTES

1: The Taco Man

2 "If there was a war in the jungle": Tom Corcoran interview, July 2, 2008.

2 "What?": Ibid.

7 "Suddenly I was living in Key West": Corcoran interview, December 20, 2005.

7 "I lived off-base": Corcoran interview, June 5, 2006.

8 "I had a pocketful of those things": Corcoran interview, 2008.

8 "Maurice looked like": Ibid.

9 "By the time we got there": Ibid.

9 "Key West was peaceful": Ibid.

9 "Where you from?": Ibid.

12 "I want your job": Ibid.

12 "It's all yours": Ibid.

2: Island of Bones

General sources: Richard Bache, *The Young Wrecker on the Florida Reef* (Marathon, Fla.: Ketch & Yawl Press, 2007; orig. pub. 1869); Jefferson B. Browne, *Key West: The Old and the New* (St. Augustine, Fla.: Record Company, 1912); J. Wills Burke, *The Streets of Key West: A History Through Street Names* (Sarasota, Fla.: Pineapple Press, 2004); Stetson Kennedy, *Grits and Grunts: Folkloric Key West* (Sarasota, Fla.: Pineapple Press, 2008); Stuart McIver, *Touched by the Sun: The Florida Chronicles* (Sarasota, Fla.: Pineapple Press, 2001); Maureen Ogle, *Key West: History of an Island of Dreams* (Gainesville, Fla.: University

Press of Florida, 2006); Pat Parks, *The Railroad That Died at Sea: The Florida East Coast's Key West Extension* (Marathon, Fla.: Ketch & Yawl Press, 1968); Dorothy Raymer, *Key West Collection* (Key West, Fla.: Ketch & Yawl Press, 1999); and Stan Windhorn and Wright Langley, *Yesterday's Key West* (Miami: E.A. Seamann Publishing, 1973).

3: The Template

28 "If you are lucky enough": Ernest Hemingway, *A Moveable Feast: The Restored Edition* (New York: Simon & Schuster, 2009), p. xii.

36 "Christ, this is a fine country": Ernest Hemingway, *Selected Letters, 1917–1961*, ed. by Carlos Baker (New York: Charles Scribner's Sons, 1981), p. 292.

37 "People don't stare at me": *The Syracuse* (New York) *Herald-American*, February 22, 1997, p. 148.

37 "as grand a group of men": Stuart McIver, *Hemingway's Key West* (Sarasota, Fla.: Pineapple Press, 2002), p. 12.

General sources: Ernest Hemingway, *Selected Letters, 1917–1961*, ed. by Carlos Baker (New York: Charles Scribner's Sons, 1981); James McLendon, *Papa: Hemingway in Key West* (Marathon, Fla.: Ketch & Yawl Press, 2008, rev. ed.); and Stuart McIver, *Hemingway's Key West*, 2nd ed. (Sarasota, Fla.: Pineapple Press, 2000).

4: A Different Society

41 "The bike had a bright aluminum box": Tom Corcoran interview, July 2, 2008.

41 "Things were slow in 1970": Ibid.

42 "His tongue seems coated": Rex Reed, "Tennessee Williams Turns Sixty," *Esquire*, September 1971, p. 105.

43 "He had an entourage": Corcoran interview, December 20, 2005.

43 "I took to solitary amusements": Lynn Mitsuko Kaufelt, *Key West Writers and Their Houses* (Sarasota, Fla.: Pineapple Press, 1986), p. 55.

44 "I was a manual laborer": Ibid.

44 "It's better than being called Mississippi": "Tennessee Williams," Oracle ThinkQuest, thinkquest.org.

45 "Key West was the southernmost": Tennessee Williams, *Memoirs* (New York: Doubleday, 1975), p. 64.

45 "It was the center": Kaufelt, p. 57.

46 "In New York": Louise Davis, "That 'Baby Doll' Man, Part 1," *The Tennessean Magazine*, March 3, 1957, p. 12.

46 "The one I set for myself": Joanne Stang, "Williams: Twenty Years After 'Glass Menagerie,' " *New York Times*, March 28, 1965, sec. 2, p. 1.

46 "I can't stand": Stang, p. 1.

47 "She was as unconventional": Williams, p. 162.

48 "It was a little weird": Danilo Cisneros interview, December 26, 2008.

49 "I hope you enjoyed yourself": Cassandra Toppino interview, February 6, 2010.

5: McGuane

51 "Hey, what're you doing?": Tom Corcoran interview, July 2, 2008.

52 "Hey Tom!": Ibid.

54 "I thought writers were": Leonard Michaels, "The Novelist in Hollywood: A Conversation with Thomas McGuane," *Threepenny Review 1*, no. 4 (Winter 1981), pp. 4–5.

54 "His writing leads": Christine June, "A Passion for Ranching, Fishing, and Writing," *Bloomsbury Review* 20, no. 4 (June/August 2000), p. 13.

54 "I like images": Hank Nuwer, "The Man Whose Soul Is Not for Sale: Jim Harrison," *Rendezvous with Eight Contemporary Writers: A Special Issue of Rendezvous, Idaho State University Journal of Arts and Letters* (Fall 1985), p. 26.

55 "It's a pyramid scheme": Ibid.

55 "I told a rather snotty younger novelist": Nuwer, p. 28.

56 "He came up hard": Beef Torrey, "A Dialogue with Tom McGuane," in Beef Torrey, *Conversations with Thomas McGuane* (Jackson: University Press of Mississippi, 2007), p. 203.

57 "a crappy little parochial": Toby Thompson, *The '60s Report* (New York: Rawson, Wade, 1979), p. 216.

58 "I grew up in a household": June, p. 13.

58 "as I tended to do": Albert Howard Carter, "Thomas McGuane: An Interview," *Fiction International* 4/5 (1975), p. 50.

58 "I conducted a mixed-bag": Thomas McGuane, *The Longest Silence: A Life in Fishing* (Knopf, 1999), p. 4.

59 "My mother had": Carter, p. 52.

59 "was a very, very": Torrey, p. 203.

59 "My father hated people": Sinda Gregory and Larry McCaffery, "The Art of Fiction LXXXIX: Thomas McGuane," *Paris Review* 27, no. 97 (Fall 1985), p. 35.

60 "I remember when I was twelve": Dexter Westrum, *Thomas McGuane* (Boston: Twayne Publishers, 1991), p. 2.

60 "We had good times together": McGuane, *The Longest Silence*, p. 272.

60 "I was not very good": Michaels, p. 5.

61 "He was so intense": Torrey, p. 202.

62 "It turned out that the people": Jim Harrison interview, August 8, 2010.

62 "He wrote me a letter": Ibid.

64 "Whenever we are around each other": Westrum, p. 5.

64 "We talk about literature": Harrison interview.

66 "I first came to Key West": Jim Harrison, "A Chat with a Novelist," *Sumac* IV (Fall 1971), p. 121.

66 " 'What the hell is everyone' ": Steve Chapple and David Talbot, *Burning Desires: Sex in America* (New York: Doubleday, 1989), p. 103.

66 "When I decided to come back": Harrison, p. 123.

67 "It was a great place": Thomas McGuane interview, August 10, 2010.

6: The Boys

69 "I like the fecund smell": Liz Lear, "A Conversation with Thomas McGuane," *Shenandoah* 36/2 (1986), p. 12.

70 "I wrote *Wolf*": Jim Harrison, interview, August 8, 2010.

71 "He would never go out": Russell Chatham interview, August 9, 2010.

71 "I was kind of the rich sporting friend": Guy de la Valdene interview, August 15, 2010.

72 "Guy would pull a skiff": Thomas McGuane interview, August 10, 2010.

72 "It was just kind of unwritten": Chatham interview.

72 "We were portrayed as these three fellows": Valdene interview.

72 "What I really wanted to do": Tom Corcoran interview, December 20, 2005.

73 "People slept in their cars": Tom Corcoran, *Jimmy Buffett: The Key West Years* (Marathon, Fla.: Ketch & Yawl Press, 2006), p. 15.

73 "Dogs would sleep": Dink Bruce interview, August 9, 2010.

74 "Corcoran," he said, "why'n't you": Tom Corcoran interview, June 2, 2010.

75 "Jim and Tom had gone": Chatham interview.

75 "obsession with the sporting life": Jim Harrison, "An Appreciation," in *Russell Chatham* (Livingston, Mont.: Clark City Press, 1987), p. 61.

76 "By the way": Valdene interview.

77 "In those days": Russell Chatham interview, July 26, 2006.

77 "He's perhaps the greatest": Hank Nuwer, "The Man Whose Soul Is Not for Sale: Jim Harrison," *Rendezvous with Eight Contemporary Writers: A Special Issue of Rendezvous, Idaho State University Journal of Arts and Letters* (Fall 1985), p. 28.

77 "Because Harrison was more": Tom Corcoran correspondence with author, May 28, 2010.

78 "Within two years' time": Corcoran interview, 2005.

78 "The Chart Room was a trip": "Murphy" interview, June 12, 2010.

7: Nowhere to Hide

82 "When my father drank": Jim Fergus, "After the Storm," *Rocky Mountain Magazine* (December 1981), p. 46.

82 "I'll tell you what I am": "Conversations: Guy de la Valdene," *MidCurrents*, 2009.

83 "At least three prominent homosexuals": Maureen Ogle, *Key West: History of an Island of Dreams* (Gainesville, Fla.: University Press of Florida, 2006), p. 229.

84 "It was a redneck town from before": Tom Corcoran interview, June 5, 2010.

85 "just a good-natured hippie": Corcoran interview, July 8, 2010.

85 "Bill Huckel put a lot": "Murphy" interview, June 10, 2010.

85 "I hear you're": Corcoran interview, July 8, 2010.

89 "Jim bullshitted *Sports Illustrated*": Russell Chatham interview, August 9, 2010.

89 "You could fly to Key West," Ibid.

89 "Well, Dink": Dink Bruce interview, August 9, 2010.

90 "I just tell women": Ibid.

90 "The locale suggests promiscuity": Chatham interview, 2010.

90 "one of the greatest": Chatham interview, July 26, 2006.

91 "Sam was a straight guy": Chatham interview, 2010.

91 "We went over to Buffett's house": Ibid.

8: The Failure

94 "I loved it": "Murphy" interview, June 12, 2010.

95 "People who live on islands": Dink Bruce interview, August 7, 2010.

95 "an artist's colony, homosexual colony, hippie colony": Steve Eng, *Jimmy Buffett: The Man from Margaritaville Revealed* (New York: St. Martin's Press, 1996), p. 135.

96 "He had just recorded": Murphy interview.

98 "I started out wanting": Jimmy Buffett, *A Pirate Looks at Fifty* (New York: Random House, 1998), p. 11.

98 "The only reason I went to Nashville": Jimmy Buffett interview with *High Times* magazine, 1976.

100 "It was a bad time": Gordon Chaplin, "Jimmy Buffett's Escape Helped Launch His Career," *Winnipeg* (Manitoba) *Free Press*, March 24, 1977, p. 26.

101 "I was flat broke": Buffett, *A Pirate Looks at Fifty*, p. 234.

102 "I was sitting under": Ibid., p. 235.

103 "This was Kerouac stuff": Ibid., p. 241.

103 "tropical Fellini movie": Ibid.

9: This Republic of Ours

106 "Jerry Jeff and Murphy": Jimmy Buffett, *A Pirate Looks at Fifty* (New York: Random House, 1998), p. 11.

106 "The most important thing": Gordon Chaplin, "Jimmy Buffett's Escape Helped Launch His Career," *Winnipeg* (Manitoba) *Free Press*, March 24, 1977, p. 26.

108 "Hi, Jimmy": Paul Toppino, interview, February 8, 2010.

108 "Strangely enough": Jimmy Buffett promotional interview with MCA Records, 1985.

109 "There was much more of a literary presence": Ibid.

109 "That's where we met Buffett": Russell Chatham interview, August 9, 2010.

110 "You could go swimming naked at noon": Steve Eng, *Jimmy Buffett:*

The Man from Margaritaville Revealed (New York: St. Martin's Press, 1996). p. 135.

111 "a passion for the manly world": Jonathan Yardley, "The Bushwhacked Piano" [review], *New York Times Book Review*, March 14, 1971, p. 6.

111 "the work of a writer": Ibid.

111 "joyous inventions": L.E. Sissman, "Inventions," *New Yorker*, September 11, 1971, p. 124.

112 "It was a horrid movie": Jim Harrison interview, August 8, 2010.

114 "It took two years to write": Leonard Michaels, "The Novelist in Hollywood: A Conversation with Thomas McGuane," *Threepenny Review* 1, no. 4 (Winter 1981) pp. 4–5.

114 "Anyone can learn the technical end": Albert Howard Carter, "Thomas McGuane: An Interview," *Fictional International* 4/5 (1975), p. 50.

115 "When fame hit": Tom Corcoran interview, June 13, 2010.

115 "She was small, blonde, cheerful": Toby Thompson, *The '60s Report* (New York: Rawson, Wade, 1979), p. 199.

116 "I took the clay": Vaughn Cochran interview, July 12, 2010.

118 *Why not*: Jim Fergus, "The Sporting Club," *Outside*, March 1989, p. 43.

118 "Tom went crazy": Chatham interview.

118 "Tom was a big, strong": Guy de la Valdene interview, August 15, 2010.

118 "We'd been there": Chatham interview.

120 "What is most emphatic": Thomas McGuane, *The Longest Silence* (New York: Knopf, 1999), p. 121.

120 "You never see a painting": Christian Odasso and Guy de la Valdene, directors, *Tarpon* (UYA Films, 1974).

121 "absolutely pure fishing": Ibid.

121 "Places that are heightened": Jean W. Ross, "*Contemporary Authors* Interview," *Contemporary Authors: A Bio-Bibliographical Guide to Current Writers in Fiction*, vol. 24 (Detroit: Gale Group, 1988), p. 310.

121 "American writers love exotic": Liz Lear, "A Conversation with Thomas McGuane," *Shenandoah* 36/2 (1986), p. 12.

121 "You're at the end of America": Odasso and Valdene, *Tarpon*.

122 "I felt as if I had": Mark Harris, "*Publishers Weekly* Interviews Tom McGuane," *Publishers Weekly*, September 29, 1989, p. 50.

122 "As I wrote": Dexter Westrum, *Thomas McGuane* (Boston: Twayne Publishers, 1991), p. 41.

123 "his metallic extremist view": Jim Fergus, "The Sporting Club," *Outside*, March 1989, p. 43.

124 "fished quietly and seriously": Ibid.

124 "We just wore": Cochran interview.

125 "It led to a whole": Tom Corcoran correspondence with author, February 20, 2010.

125 "I kept thinking I had died": Westrum, p. 10.

10: Square Grouper

127 "an open town of smugglers": Jimmy Buffett interview with *High Times* magazine, 1976.

128 "If capture is unavoidable": Tom Corcoran, "Wasting Away in Marijuanaville," *Crawdaddy*, December 1977, p. 29.

128 "To live on an island this small": Stuart McIver, "Where Is Bum Farto?" (South Florida) *Sun-Sentinel*, October 6, 1996.

129 "We will not begin": Associated Press, "Governor Raps Users of Drugs," *Key West Citizen*, January 20, 1970, p. 2.

130 "We were the Robin Hoods": Paul Swider, "The High Life," *St. Petersburg Times*, April 23, 2006, p. D-1.

131 "Mostly it was marijuana": Mark Humphrey with Harris Lewine. *The Jimmy Buffett Scrapbook*, 3rd ed. (New York: Citadel Press, 2000), p. 90.

132 "By then he'd had about": "Murphy" interview, June 12, 2010.

132 "Phil would stand at the bar": Humphrey with Lewine, *Scrapbook*, p. 90.

132 "He would always get the tourists": Steve Eng, *Jimmy Buffett: The Man from Margaritaville Revealed* (New York: St. Martin's Press, 1996), p. 124.

132 "He was a real pirate": Ibid.

133 "I guess everybody would": Buffett, *High Times* interview, July 1976.

134 "The town was not": Cochran interview, July 12, 2010.

11: A Year of Living Dangerously

137 "We fished and filmed": "Interview: Guy de la Valdene," *MidCurrent*, May 15, 2007.

137 "There were hundreds and hundreds": Guy de la Valdene interview with author, August 15, 2010.

138 "Nobody had ever done anything": Vaughn Cochran interview, July 12, 2010.

138 "I had the problem": Thomas McGuane interview, August 10, 2010.

138 "This is going to be a hard film": Ibid.

140 "I had to give every man": Elizabeth Ashley with Ross Firestone, *Actress: Postcards from the Road* (New York: M. Evans, 1978), p. 141.

140 "funny and off the wall": Ibid., p. 142.

141 "Let's fuck": Ibid., p. 146.

142 "Thomas told me all about last night": Ibid., p. 148.

143 "Everythin' you are doing": Ibid., p. 154.

143 "I imagine that sex": Ibid., p. 155.

144 "Bullshit.": Susan Compo, *Warren Oates: A Wild Life* (Lexington: University Press of Kentucky, 2009), p. 322.

144 "I hope you enjoyed": Ashley, p. 176.

145 "Any asshole can direct": McGuane interview.

147 "I was upset I didn't get": Compo, p. 305.

148 "Fonda was really very hard to direct": McGuane interview.

148 "Warren, myself, and at least": Compo, p. 320.

148 "I do remember when": Margot Kidder interview, November 2, 2010.

149 "I think you're a genius": Ashley, p. 179.

149 "great, zippy one-liners": Kidder interview.

149 "I was a sixties girl": Ibid.

150 "Shooting was chaos": Ibid.

150 "There was a century between": Ibid.

150 "Key West was a rather forced": Ibid.

151 "I was involved in all": Cochran interview.

152 "I don't think I partied": McGuane interview.

152 "I have some pretty good friends": Jim Fergus, "After the Storm," *Rocky Mountain Magazine*, December 1981, p. 46.

152 "It was a wonderful time": Kidder, quoted on Internet Movie Database.

153 "I knew all about": Ashley, p. 161.

154 "Elizabeth, this whole thing": Ibid., p. 184.

154 "In the confrontation": Tom Corcoran correspondence with author, July 23, 2009.

155 "A genuine fictional talent": Jean W. Ross, "*Contemporary Authors* In-

terview," *Contemporary Authors: A Bio-Bibliographical Guide to Current Writers in Fiction*, vol. 24 (Detroit: Gale Group, 1988), p. 310.

155 "It became clear": Sinda Gregory and Larry McCaffery, "The Art of Fiction LXXXIX: Thomas McGuane," *Paris Review* 27, no. 97 (Fall 1985), p. 35.

155 "Cinema has enormously to do": Albert Howard Carter, "Thomas McGuane: An Interview," *Fiction International* 4/5 (1975), p. 50.

155 "Flyer, you know that Becky and Tom": Compo, p. 329.

155 "It was love for eternity": Kidder interview.

12: Margaritaville

156 "I fed him": Tom Corcoran interview, December 20, 2005.

157 "People get by and people get high": Jimmy Buffett and Tom Corcoran, "Cuban Crime of Passion," *A White Sport Coat and a Pink Crustacean* (Los Angeles: ABC Dunhill Records, 1973).

157 "Just look for me on Duval Street": Steve Eng, *Jimmy Buffett: The Man from Margaritaville Revealed* (New York: St. Martin's Press, 1996), p. 138.

158 The folk orientation: Tom McGuane, liner notes, *A White Sport Coat and a Pink Crustacean* (Los Angeles: ABC Dunhill Records, 1973).

159 "I was hearing a lot of": Jimmy Buffett, *The Parrothead Handbook* (Los Angeles: MCA Records, 1993), p. 54.

160 "Jimmy was able to personify": Vaughn Cochran interview, July 12, 2010.

161 "In the end": Ibid.

162 "We went at it": Buffett, *A Pirate Looks at Fifty* (New York: Random House, 1998), p. 11.

165 "I heard it on the radio": Jimmy Buffett, *The Parrothead Handbook*, p. 56.

169 "The answer is no": Buffett, *The Parrothead Handbook* in *Boats, Beaches, Bars and Ballads*, (Los Angeles: MCA Records, 1993), p. 50.

13: The King of Gonzo

171 "That place in Key West": Chris Robinson interview, June 7, 2006.

173 "Maybe he thought": George Plimpton, *Shadow Box* (New York: G.P. Putnam's Sons, 1977), p. 251.

175 "I was angry": Wayne Ewing correspondence with author, July 9, 2010.

176 "Here comes this guy in a suit": Robinson interview.

176 "He kept the dog": Dan Mallard interview, April 24, 2007.

176 "We lived right next door": Robinson interview.

176 "Hunter would rant and rave": Ibid.

179 "There was this guy lying": Laila Nabulsi interview, October 10, 2006.

179 "more fun in twenty minutes": *Rolling Stone*, April 29, 1982.

179 "'Suddenly,' she said": Nabulsi interview.

180 "I had never met anyone": Ibid.

180 "The way he was talking": Ibid.

182 "probably the worst-edited": David Felton, "Hunter S. Thompson Has Cashed His Check," *Rolling Stone College Papers*, Spring 1980, p. 47.

182 "I thought it would": Ibid.

183 "the same admiration": William F. Buckley Jr., "Gonzo's Great Shark Hunt," *New York Times Book Review*, August 5, 1979, p. 1.

183 "I have already lived": Hunter S. Thompson, *The Great Shark Hunt* (New York: Summit Books, 1979), p. 17.

184 "It's a decadent place": Ewing correspondence.

184 "Hunter, are we going to go?": Dink Bruce interview, August 9, 2010.

185 "'Hunter!' Bruce yelled": Ibid.

186 "You fucking pigs!": Bruce interview, August 14, 2010.

186 "Judy: Miami Herald, bank, Visa": List, from the Tom Corcoran Archive.

186 "'Sebastian!' he would announce": Sebastian Corcoran interview, June 5, 2006.

187 "Hunter was always 'Doc'": Tom Corcoran interview, June 5, 2006.

187 "So this family came over": Robinson interview.

187 "In private life": Nabulsi interview.

187 "He didn't care if people": Robinson interview.

189 "I don't know how much": Postcard, Corcoran Archive.

189 "What lame instinct prompts you": Letter, Corcoran Archive.

189 "I don't know why people": Felton, p. 51.

190 "Writing the screenplay is easy": Corcoran interview, December 20, 2005.

191 "Hunter, just keep the wheel straight": Robinson interview.

191 "It went airborne": Ibid.

192 "We made up the characters": Corcoran interview, 2005.

193 "What Hunter dreamed up": Ibid.

194 "Hunter was too naïve in those days": Ibid.

194 "In those days": Russell Chatham interview, July 26, 2006.

194 "Fucking Hunter couldn't even make": Ibid.

195 "Notorious most of his life": Montgomery Chitty correspondence with author, January 25, 2006.

195 "He was a much deeper": Chatham interview.

196 "Hunter S. Thompson was one of the sexiest": From an unpublished memoir by "Norma Jean."

199 "People I don't know expect me": Nigel Finch, director, *Fear and Loathing on the Road to Hollywood* (London: British Broadcasting Corporation, 1978).

14: Bum Farto and Ping-Ping

201 " 'Jesus,' Papa Hemingway supposedly said": Dink Bruce interview, August 9, 2010.

205 "Bum was not an exemplary": Tom Corcoran correspondence with author, August 8, 2010.

206 "The Keys were the Keys": Nelson Jamardo interview, February 5, 2010.

206 "Developers started developing": Ibid.

207 "The Conchs now are priced out": Ibid.

207 "The Bubba system was simple": Ibid.

207 "At one time in the seventies": Ibid.

208 "It came from Colombia": Ibid.

208 "We'd maybe unload it up the Keys": Ibid.

208 "There were sellers that would come": Ibid.

208 "In them days": Ibid.

209 "Cocaine's when it got worse": Ibid.

209 "If you took in three–four bales": Ibid.

210 "observed two large truckloads": United States District Court Case No. 80-549-Cr-JLK, "Memorandum in Support of Government's Sentencing Recommendations," p. 2.

210 "speedy, shallow-water boats": Michael Capuzzo, " 'Big Pine 29' Trial Features Evidence Argument Today," *Miami Herald*, February 4, 1981, p. 1.

211 "Amazingly, a dizzying array": Ibid.

211 "conspiracy to knowingly": Wendy Tucker, "Pot Trial Begins in Federal Court," *Key West Citizen*, February 2, 1981, p. 1.

211 "Where the hell am I": "Lawmen Catch 30 at Big Pine Site," Sheila Quickstad, *Key West Citizen*, November 16, 1980, p. 1.

211 "The Lower Keys home": Mike Capuzzo, "Drug Smugglers Led the Good Life; Prosecutor Describes Their Lavish Purchases," *Miami Herald*, TK

211 "Rivas was reportedly waiting": Ibid.

212 "Jail wasn't too good": Jamardo interview.

212 "After three or four months": Ibid.

212 "I'd had enough": Ibid.

212 "I bought a house": Ibid.

212 "I spent it": Ibid.

213 "He knew a lot of people": Ibid.

15: Redemption

217 "By the time he had": Author uncredited, "Tom (McGuane) & Margot (Kidder) & Peter (Fonda) & Becky (McGuane) & Whoops," *People* magazine, February 9, 1976, p. 31.

217 "is finishing up his next": Ibid.

218 "bagged an antelope": Ibid., p. 33.

218 "Like Papa": Ibid.

218 "the folks a mile down": Ibid., p. 31.

218 "It was a film": Margot Kidder interview, November 2, 2010.

219 "We're kind of starved for news": Thomas McGuane, *The Missouri Breaks* (New York: Ballantine Books, 1976).

221 "This will sound like": McGuane interview, August 10, 2010.

221 "I fell in love with": Nathan Rabin, "Random Roles: Margot Kidder," *Onion (A.V. Club)*, March 3, 2009.

221 "After we got married": Tara Walton, "The Red Carpet Still Beckons for Margot Kidder," *Toronto Star*, August 15, 2010, p. C-1.

221 "I was totally unsuited": Kidder interview.

221 "We did make": Ibid.

222 "he looked at me": Ibid.

222 "I was so addicted": Ibid.

222 "I just didn't feel anything": Jim Fergus, "After the Storm," *Rocky Mountain Magazine*, December 1981, p. 46.

222 "My mother was a very troubled person": McGuane interview.

223 "Something would tweak in his head": Guy de la Valdene interview, August 19, 2010.

224 "She's got big eyes": McGuane interview.

224 "We're stretched out": Ibid.

225 "Hunter was so imprisoned": Ibid.

226 "It was a disaster": Ibid.

226 "He was out of control": Russell Chatham interview, August 9, 2010.

226 "I had a very close relationship": McGuane interview.

226–227 "I went from being": Ibid.

227 "He thinks he was far worse": Kidder interview.

227 "I really loved": McGuane interview.

228 "We were at the house": Ibid.

228 "It had become kind of": Ibid.

228 "I'm thrilled it happened": Ibid.

229 "I think we were able": Ibid.

16: Evacuation

230 "We just looked at each other": Guy de la Valdene interview, August 19, 2010.

231 "I hopped on my motorbike": Tom Corcoran interview, December 20, 2006.

232 "I've come to die in a free land": Keith Graham interview, August 4, 2010.

232 "The town is different": Ibid.

233 "Tennessee?": Ibid.

235 "If I hadn't had": Corcoran interview, August 27, 2010.

235 "He was ten": Ibid.

235 "It was just part": Ibid.

236 "The immediate impact": Ibid.

236 "Judy and I felt": Ibid.

237 "I'm a property": Ibid.

238 "The marriage was": Ibid.

238 "I went into the filing": Ibid.

239 "I got called in": Ibid.

240 "She had been fired": Ibid.

240 "Nobody told me": Ibid.

241 "So they all got separated": Ibid.

241 "It was horrible": Ibid.

Epilogue: Don't Stop the Carnival

247 "Ernest would roll over": Associated Press, "Festival Insult to Heming-way," Elyria, Ohio, *Chronicle Telegram*, July 24, 1983, p. F-2.

247 "It was a strange end": Truman Capote, *Portraits and Observations* (New York: Random House, 2007), p. 500.

248 "Tennessee died a little": Ibid, p. 501.

248 "Oh no": Ibid., pp. 502–503.

251 "He is a wonderful grandparent": Margot Kidder interview, November 2, 2010.

251 "I would love for there to be": Ibid.

251 "He was the love of my life": Ibid.

253 "Damn, Vaughn": Vaughn Cochran interview, July 12, 2010.

253 "We were dead broke": Jim Harrison interview, August 8, 2010.

253 "The last day I was there": Ibid.

254 "I can no longer bear": Jim Harrison correspondence with author, July 12, 2010.

255 "I was never probably": Russell Chatham interview, August 9, 2010.

255 "I loved her": Chatham interview.

256 "Tom brought that whole group": "Conversations: Guy de la Valdene," *MidCurrents*, May 15, 2007.

256 "I ran around being": Thomas McGuane interview, August 10, 2010.

256 "I have a mixed bag of regret": Beef Torrey, "A Dialogue with Tom McGuane," in Beef Torrey, *Conversations with Thomas McGuane* (Jackson, Mississippi: University Press of Mississippi, 2007), p. 204.

256 "I fish all the time when I'm at home": Thomas McGuane, *The Longest Silence: A Life of Fishing* (Knopf, 1999), p. 89.

257 "You can't be a writer-rancher": Patrick Cross, "Literary Laurels," *The Big Timber* (Montana) *Pioneer*, June 24, 2010, p. 1.

257 "If I want to get up": McGuane interview.

257 "When you get rickety": Cross, p. 12.

257 "I haven't read that": McGuane interview.

257 "Every time we get together": Ibid.

258 "I'm back, Boys!" Wayne Ewing, *The Gonzo Pilot* (Carbondale, Colo.: Ewing Films, 2009).

259 "I had just talked to him": Torrey, p. 200.

260 "You motherfucker!": Tom Corcoran interview, June 12, 2010.

262 "This dude wrote songs": Ibid.

BIBLIOGRAPHY

Ashley, Elizabeth, with Ross Firestone. *Actress: Postcards from the Road.* New York: M. Evans, 1978.

Bache, Richard Meade. *The Young Wrecker of the Florida Reef.* Marathon, Fla.: Ketch & Yawl Press, 2007. (Orig. pub. 1869.)

Bonetti, Kay, et al., eds. *Conversations with American Novelists.* Columbia: University of Missouri Press, 1997.

Browne, Jefferson B. *Key West: The Old and the New.* St. Augustine, Fla.: Record Company, 1912.

Buffett, Jimmy. *Tales from Margaritaville.* New York: Harcourt Brace Jovanovich, 1989.

———. *Where Is Joe Merchant?* New York: Harcourt Brace Jovanovich, 1993.

———. *A Pirate Looks at Fifty.* New York: Random House, 1998.

———. *A Salty Piece of Land.* New York: Little, Brown, 2004.

———. *Swine Not?* New York: Little, Brown, 2008.

Buffett, Jimmy, and Savannah Jane Buffett. *Jolly Mon.* New York: Harcourt Children's Books, 1988.

———. *Trouble Dolls.* Boston: Harcourt Children's Books, 1991.

Burke, J. Wills. *The Streets of Key West: A History Through Street Names.* Sarasota, Fla.: Pineapple Press, 2004.

Chapple, Steve, and David Talbot. *Burning Desires: Sex in America.* New York: Doubleday, 1989.

Chatham, Russell. *The Angler's Coast.* Rev. ed. Livingston, Mont.: Clark City Press, 2001.

Compo, Susan. *Warren Oates: A Wild Life.* Lexington: University Press of Kentucky, 2009.

Corcoran, Tom. *The Mango Opera.* New York: St. Martin's Press, 1998.

———. *Gumbo Limbo.* New York: St. Martin's Press, 1999.

———. *Bone Island Mambo.* New York: St. Martin's Press, 2001.

———. *Octopus Alibi.* New York: St. Martin's Press, 2003.

———. *Air Dance Iguana.* New York: St. Martin's Press, 2005.

———. *Jimmy Buffett: The Key West Years.* Marathon, Fla.: Ketch & Yawl Press, 2006.

———. *Key West in Black and White.* Marathon, Fla.: Ketch & Yawl Press, 2007.

———. *Hawk Channel Chase.* Marathon, Fla.: Ketch & Yawl Press, 2009.

———. Cox, Christopher. *A Key West Companion.* New York: St. Martin's Press, 1983.

Curnutt, Kirk, and Gail D. Sinclair, eds. *Key West Hemingway.* Gainesville, Fla.: University Press of Florida, 2009.

DeMott, Robert, ed. *Conversations with Jim Harrison.* Jackson: University Press of Mississippi, 2002.

Devlin, Albert J., ed. *Conversations with Tennessee Williams.* Jackson: University Press of Mississippi, 1986.

Eng, Steve. *Jimmy Buffett: The Man from Margaritaville Revealed.* New York: St. Martin's Press, 1996.

Flippo, Chet. *Everybody Was Kung-Fu Dancing.* New York: St. Martin's Press, 1991.

Griffin, Peter. *Along with Youth: Hemingway, the Early Years.* New York: Oxford University Press, 1985.

Gutelius, Scott, et al. *True Secrets of Key West Revealed.* Key West, Fla.: Eden Entertainment, 2003.

Harrison, Ben. *Undying Love: The True Story of a Passion That Defied Death.* Marathon, Fla.: Ketch & Yawl Press, 2009.

Harrison, Jim. *Plain Song.* New York: W.W. Norton, 1965.

———. *Walking.* Cambridge, Mass.: Pym Randall Press, 1967.

———. *Locations.* New York: W.W. Norton, 1968.

———. *Outlyer and Ghazals.* New York: Simon & Schuster, 1971.

———. *Wolf: A False Memoir.* New York: Simon & Schuster, 1971.

————. *A Good Day to Die.* New York: Simon & Schuster, 1973.

————. *Letters to Yesenin.* Fremont, Mich.: Sumac Press, 1973.

————. *Farmer.* New York: Viking, 1976.

————. *Returning to Earth: Poems.* Berkeley, Calif.: Ithaca House, 1977.

————. *Legends of the Fall.* New York: Delacorte Press/Seymour Lawrence, 1979.

————. *Warlock.* New York: Delacorte Press/Seymour Lawrence, 1981.

————. *Natural World: A Bestiary.* Berrytown, N.Y.: Open Book, 1981.

————. *Selected and New Poems, 1961–1981.* New York: Delacorte Press/ Seymour Lawrence, 1981.

————. *Sundog.* (New York: E.P. Dutton/Seymour Lawrence, 1984.

————. *The Theory and Practice of Rivers.* Seattle, Wash.: Winn Books, 1986.

————. *Dalva.* New York: E.P. Dutton/Seymour Lawrence, 1988.

————. *Book for Sensei.* Pacifica, Calif.: Big Bridge Press, 1990.

————. *The Woman Lit by Fireflies.* New York: Houghton Mifflin, 1990.

————. *Just Before Dark: Collected Nonfiction.* Livingston, Mont.: Clark City Press, 1991.

————. *Julip.* New York: Houghton Mifflin/Seymour Lawrence, 1994.

————. *After Ikkyu and Other Poems.* Boston: Shambhala Press, 1996.

————. *The Road Home.* New York: Atlantic Monthly Press, 1998.

————. *The Shape of the Journey: New and Collected Poems.* Port Townsend, Wash.: Copper Canyon Press, 1998.

————. *The Beast God Forgot to Invent.* New York: Atlantic Monthly Press, 2000.

————. *The Boy Who Ran to the Woods.* New York: Atlantic Monthly Press, 2000.

————. *The Raw and the Cooked: Adventures of a Roving Gourmand.* New York: Atlantic Monthly Press, 2001.

————. *Off to the Side: A Memoir.* New York: Atlantic Monthly Press, 2002.

————. *True North.* New York: Atlantic Monthly Press, 2004.

————. *The Summer He Didn't Die.* New York: Atlantic Monthly Press, 2005.

————. *Saving Daylight.* Port Townsend, Wash.: Copper Canyon Press, 2006.

———. *Returning to Earth: A Novel.* New York: Atlantic Monthly Press, 2007.

———. *The English Major.* New York: Atlantic Monthly Press, 2008.

———. *The Farmer's Daughter.* New York: Atlantic Monthly Press, 2009.

———. *In Search of Small Gods.* Port Townsend, Wash.: Copper Canyon Press, 2009.

———, et al. *Stony Brook Holographs.* Stony Brook, N.Y.: Stony Brook Poetics Foundation, 1968.

———, et al. *Five Blind Men.* Fremont, Mich.: Sumac Press, 1969.

Harrison, Jim, and Ted Kooser. *Braided Creek: A Conversation in Poetry.* Port Townsend, Wash.: Copper Canyon Press, 2003.

Hemingway, Ernest. *A Farewell to Arms.* New York: Charles Scribner's Sons, 1929.

———. *To Have and Have Not.* New York: Charles Scribner's Sons, 1937.

———. *For Whom the Bell Tolls.* New York: Charles Scribner's Sons, 1940.

———. *The Old Man and the Sea.* New York: Charles Scribner's Sons, 1952.

———. *A Moveable Feast.* New York: Charles Scribner's Sons, 1964.

———. *By-Line: Selected Articles and Dispatches.* Edited by William White. New York: Charles Scribner's Sons, 1967.

———. *Islands in the Stream.* New York: Charles Scribner's Sons, 1970.

———. *Selected Letters, 1917–1961.* Edited by Carlos Baker. New York: Charles Scribner's Sons, 1981.

———. *The Complete Short Stories of Ernest Hemingway: The Finca Vigia Edition.* New York: Charles Scribner's Sons, 1987.

Hersey, John. *Key West Tales.* New York: Knopf, 1993.

Hiaasen, Carl. *Kick Ass: Selected Columns.* Edited by Diane Stevenson. Gainesville, Fla.: University Press of Florida, 1999.

Humphrey, Mark, with Harris Lewine. *The Jimmy Buffett Scrapbook.* 3rd ed. New York: Citadel Press, 2000.

Kaufelt, Lynn Mitsuko. *Key West Writers and Their Houses.* Sarasota, Fla.: Pineapple Press, 1986.

Kennedy, Stetson. *Grits and Grunts: Folkloric Key West.* Sarasota, Fla.: Pineapple Press, 2008.

Langley, Wright, and Joan Langley. *Key West and the Spanish-American War.* Key West, Fla.: Langley Press, 1998.

Leen, Jeff, and Guy Gugliotta. *Kings of Cocaine.* New York: HarperCollins, 1990.

Maltz, Alan S. *Key West Color.* Key West, Fla.: Light Flight Publications, 1994.

McGuane, Thomas. *The Sporting Club.* New York: Simon & Schuster, 1969.

———. *The Bushwhacked Piano.* New York: Simon & Schuster, 1971.

———. *Ninety-Two in the Shade.* New York: Farrar, Straus and Giroux, 1973.

———. *The Missouri Breaks.* New York: Ballantine Books, 1976.

———. *Panama.* New York: Farrar, Straus and Giroux, 1978.

———. *An Outside Chance: Essays on Sport.* New York: Farrar, Straus and Giroux, 1980.

———. *Nobody's Angel.* New York: Random House, 1982.

———. *Something to Be Desired.* New York: Random House, 1984.

———. *In the Crazies: Book and Portfolio.* Seattle, Wash.: Winn Books, 1985.

———. *Keep the Change.* Boston: Houghton Mifflin/Seymour Lawrence, 1986.

———. *To Skin a Cat.* New York: E.P. Dutton/Seymour Lawrence, 1986.

———. *Nothing but Blue Skies.* Boston: Houghton Mifflin/Seymour Lawrence, 1992.

———. *Sons.* Northridge, Calif.: Lord John Press, 1993.

———. *Live Water.* Stone Harbor, N.J.: Meadow Run Press, 1996.

———. *The Longest Silence: A Life in Fishing.* New York: Knopf, 1999.

———. *Some Horses: Essays.* New York: Lyons Press, 1999.

———. *Upstream: Fly Fishing in the American West.* New York: Aperture Foundation, 2000.

———. *The Cadence of Grass.* New York: Knopf, 2002.

———. *Gallatin Canyon: Stories.* New York: Knopf, 2006.

———. *Driving on the Rim.* New York: Knopf, 2010.

McIver, Stuart. *Hemingway's Key West.* 2nd ed. Sarasota, Fla.: Pineapple Press, 2000.

———. *Touched by the Sun: The Florida Chronicles.* Sarasota, Fla.: Pineapple Press, 2001.

McKeen, William. *Outlaw Journalist: The Life and Times of Hunter S. Thompson.* New York: W.W. Norton, 2008.

Ogle, Maureen. *Key West: History of an Island of Dreams.* Gainesville, Fla.: University Press of Florida, 2006.

Parks, Pat. *The Railroad That Died at Sea: The Florida East Coast's Key West Extension.* Marathon, Fla.: Ketch & Yawl Press, 1968.

Raymer, Dorothy. *Key West Collection.* Key West, Fla.: Ketch & Yawl Press, 1999.

Reed, Rex. *Do You Sleep in the Nude?* New York: New American Library, 1968.

Reilly, Edward C. *Jim Harrison.* Boston: Twayne Publishers, 1996.

Reynolds, Michael. *Hemingway: The 1930s.* New York: W.W. Norton, 1997.

Sabbag, Robert. *Snowblind: A Brief Career in the Cocaine Trade.* Indianapolis: Bobbs-Merrill Company, 1977.

Shultz, Christopher, and David Sloan. *Key West 101: Discovering Paradise.* Key West, Fla.: Phantom Press, 2005.

Smith, Jedwin. *Fatal Treasure: Greed and Death, Emeralds and Gold, and the Obsessive Search for the Legendary Ghost Galleon* Atocha. Hoboken, N.J.: John Wiley & Sons, 2005.

Thompson, Hunter S. *The Great Shark Hunt: Strange Tales from a Strange Time.* New York: Summit Books, 1979.

———. *The Curse of Lono.* New York: Bantam Books, 1983.

———. *The Proud Highway: The Saga of a Desperate Southern Gentleman.* New York: Villard Books, 1997.

———. *Fear and Loathing in America: The Brutal Odyssey of an Outlaw Journalist.* New York: Simon & Schuster, 2000.

Thompson, Toby. *The '60s Report.* New York: Rawson, Wade 1979.

Torgoff, Martin. *Can't Find My Way Home: America in the Great Stoned Age, 1945–2000.* New York: Simon & Schuster, 2004.

Torrey, Beef, ed. *Conversations with Thomas McGuane.* Jackson: University Press of Mississippi, 2006.

Viele, John. *The Florida Keys: A History of the Pioneers.* Sarasota, Fla.: Pineapple Press, 1996.

Westrum, Dexter. *Thomas McGuane.* Boston: Twayne Publishers, 1991.

Windhorn, Stan, and Wright Langley. *Yesterday's Key West.* Miami: E.A. Seamann Publishing, 1973.

INDEX